W.O. BENTLEY

The Man Behind The Marque

W.O. BENTLEY

The Man Behind The Marque

MALCOLM BOBBITT

breedon **books**
PUBLISHING

First published in Great Britain in 2003 by
The Breedon Books Publishing Company Limited
Breedon House, 3 The Parker Centre,
Derby, DE21 4SZ.

ISBN 1 85983 352 7

Printed and bound by Butler & Tanner,
Frome, Somerset, England.

Cover printing by Lawrence-Allen Colour Printers,
Weston-super-Mare, Somerset, England.

Contents

Acknowledgements

THIS book has been produced with the kind help of many people, and in particular I would like to thank the following individuals. Andrew Minney for his considerable number of visits to the Public Record Office and Family Research Centre on my behalf, and for searching through countless files, and Sarah Minney for her researches as a genealogist into the Bentley family ancestry. Without Andrew's determination in seeking out the answers to all my questions the book would be all the poorer. Martin Bourne and Richard Mann I thank for their many helpful comments on my manuscript and the many hours they spent reading through it making pertinent suggestions. Tom Gover, Secretary of the Old Cliftonian Society, gave permission for reproducing photographs and supplied details of W.O.'s schooling. I also thank Malcolm Thorne, Malcolm Parsons and Jonathan Day at the National Motor Museum, Tim Wright for providing me with some of Bentley racing history, and his namesake at LAT Photographic for making available those photographs that originally appeared in *The Autocar* and *Motor Sport*. Sir Roger Hurn and Peter Mason, late of Smiths Industries, and Graham Nangreave of Severn Valley Railway Society, as well as Philip Hall of the Sir Henry Royce Memorial Foundation, allowed me to use specific photographs. Thanks also to the library staff at the London Borough of Camden and the British Newspaper Library at Colindale, Jolyon Broad for access to his photographic collection and Bentley Motors for use of archive images. Last but not least, I thank those Bentley enthusiasts, particularly J.G. Stamper, who gave up their time to talk to me and allowed me to photograph their cars. Finally, my appreciation to my wife Jean for her forbearance in having for so long to sustain all matters Bentley.

Introduction

THE Bentley insignia that graces some of the finest and most revered sports cars in the world is a symbol of all that is best about Britain's rich motoring history. Whatever the Bentley, whether it be an open tourer travelling along leafy lanes with its unmistakable exhaust note burbling excitedly, or a racing machine surging towards victory at Le Mans, it is sure to stir one's emotions. Without Bentley's significant contribution, motorsport would be all the poorer.

Bentley cars, vintage or modern, have acquired a distinct and deep-rooted reputation for quality and performance. They are, and have always been, among the most expensive of motor cars; they represent a certain individualism which has resulted in a unique charisma that surrounds the marque.

Concealed within the Bentley image and far removed from any grandiose perceptions that might exist, is the hallmark of the car's founder, Walter Owen Bentley – W.O. as he became known. W.O. was remarkably modest and shied away from publicity, often choosing to slip into the background whenever there was a camera around. Those who knew him speak of a man quiet in temperament, charming and quite unassuming.

W.O. came from a large family, ample even by Victorian standards, and he followed his brothers through the rigours of boarding school before enduring all the hardships that public school afforded. Born in 1888, he was shy as a child and lacked the more sociable nature of some of his siblings; being the youngest of nine surviving children he was accustomed to spending long hours on his own. More interested in science and physics than the classics, W.O. was at a disadvantage from the very beginning. That he'd far rather take a mechanical object to pieces and rebuild it than struggle with history or Latin was a progression from his childhood, when his world consisted of playing with a model steam engine or being taken for a walk to watch the express trains on their way north from Euston to Scotland.

W.O. failed to achieve much at school. He was nevertheless a talented scholar, trapped in a quest to understand the reason for everything, just like any distinguished engineer. It was W.O.'s ambition to be a locomotive designer, to follow in the footsteps of Henry Ivatt, Sir Nigel Gresley and William Stanier, but ultimately bicycles, motorcycles and motor cars dominated his life.

Without his introduction to the motor car, through a career with the National Cab Company followed by acquiring the franchise to sell the French DFP car, W.O. might not have been prepared to develop the use of aluminium pistons in aero engines. However, he was awarded an MBE for his work on aero engine technology during World War One and his significant contribution to the war effort, and his name became synonymous with motor cars. At the end of World War One he believed there to be a market for a quality sports car that was exquisitely engineered, and one which, in his own words, could be described as 'A fast car, a good car, the best in its class'.

W.O. established Bentley Motors in 1919. Soon it was evident that the Bentley had huge potential and character. Mention of Brooklands and Le Mans is all that is required to evoke an image of stamina, reliability and determination.

The man behind the Bentley marque was beset by tragedy and misfortune. Léonie, his first wife, died suddenly in 1919 after contracting influenza; his second marriage to Audrey Hutchinson was a disaster. Bentley Motors, undercapitalised from the outset, was besieged by financial problems and in 1926 W.O. lost control of the business to Woolf Barnato, the millionaire racing driver. Then in 1931 Bentley Motors was plunged into receivership and acquired in a controversial manner by Rolls-Royce. When W.O. went to work for Lagonda that relationship with Rolls-Royce continued to dog him, and a bitter court case eventually caused Lagonda to go into liquidation as well.

However, there were better times too. Throughout the struggles to keep his business afloat he enjoyed the utmost loyalty from his workforce. When Margaret Hutton became his third wife it was a lasting and loving marriage.

His greatest success was the motor car bearing his name. That a good proportion of the 3,061 cars that were built before the firm's collapse in 1931 have survived is testament to W.O.'s dedication.

Today Bentley continues to command a particular place in the world car market, thanks to W.O.

Malcolm Bobbitt
Cumbria, 2003

CHAPTER 1

Clockwork Trains and Steam Engines

REGENTS Park and St John's Wood were very respectable in the final years of the 19th century. In addition to being desirably fashionable, the houses were large and architecturally fine; many had servants' quarters, and were occupied by a society that was definitely upper middle class. Avenue Road had a gracious air about it – it was a wide boulevard extending from Prince Albert Road, which ran parallel to the Grand Union Canal and formed the north-western boundary with Regents Park – and it led northwards almost to Swiss Cottage. Its residents were comfortably 'well-to-do', and it was some time in 1884 that No.78, also known as Burbank House, became the second marital home of Alfred and Emily Bentley. It was here that Emily gave birth to her tenth and final child, Walter Owen, who was to become known simply as 'W.O.'

The Bentleys were of solid Yorkshire stock on both sides of the family, the paternal side tracing its ancestry to William Bentley of Helmsley, who signed a royalist petition in 1645. Burbank House was named after Alfred's grandmother Mary Burbank, who was born in Whitby in 1739. His grandfather was Peter Bentley, and their only child, Robert, was born on 31 October 1799. Robert met and married Martha Holt (who was born 9 May 1903) in 1827 and by 1840 had moved south, dealing in silks and woollens from 136 Cheapside, London, but living at 6 St John's Wood Park. Their son, Alfred, was born on 21 October 1841 and joined his father in the family business as soon as he was old enough. By 1860 the business had moved to 46 Gutter Lane, London EC2, and on his father's retirement Alfred took over. Robert died on 29 February 1884, Martha having predeceased him by three years.

Emily's father, Thomas Greaves Waterhouse, had left his native Conisborough in Yorkshire, a few miles south of Doncaster, in the late 1830s to emigrate to Australia, settling in South Australia where Colonel William Light had established the first port on an inlet of St Vincent's Gulf. Thomas made good of his life, setting up a successful grocery business before experimenting with copper mining. An enterprising young man, his success in the mining business introduced him to the banking profession, and this was the field in which he was to make a fortune. Choosing not to remain in Australia he eventually returned to England with his wife and daughter Emily to enjoy an early and comfortable retirement, not in Yorkshire, but at 'Willenhall', in New Barnet in Hertfordshire, and then at 'Sunnyfield', West Heath, Hampstead.

Thomas Waterhouse was by now a man of considerable means, his profession being recorded as that of 'Gentleman'. He was married to Eliza, originally from Swinefleet in Yorkshire and 14 years his junior. The couple employed seven servants, a gardener, kitchenmaid, cook, two housemaids, a parlourmaid and a lady's maid. According to Mrs Beeton's *Household Management*, the lady's maid's duties were particularly onerous as she was required to be acquainted with millinery, dressmaking and hairdressing, as well as possessing 'some chemical knowledge of the cosmetics with which the toilet-table is supplied, in order to use them with safety and effect.' The household also included two temporary nursemaids, presumably to care for the Bentley grandchildren! Waterhouse died on 6 October 1885 during a visit to Leamington, and probate records show his will to have been a lengthy and complicated affair extending to some 10 pages. The estate amounted to a little over £27,520 by limitation, itself a very considerable sum, but with the collection of assets, the total estate became worth in excess of £60,000, in today's terms more than £6.5 million. In spite of his wealth Thomas Waterhouse was a kind and sensitive man, having a keen regard for his fellow men, and he became a noted philanthropist. As we shall see, W.O. inherited much of his maternal grandfather's character and personality.

Alfred Bentley was 33 years of age when he married Emily Waterhouse, then aged 20, at the New Wesleyan Chapel at Wandsworth on 10 December 1874. Alfred is described on his marriage certificate as a warehouseman still living at his parents' address of 6 St John's Wood Park. Emily's address appears as Wood Lea, Balham, and quite why this should be the case is not known. According to the 1881 census, the Bentley's first marital home was 35 St John's Wood Park, which adjoins Avenue Road at the junction with Adelaide Road.

Alfred and Emily Bentley were blessed with 10 children, all of whom survived except the fourth, Emily Maud, who died when aged only six months. The exact point at which it was decided that 35 St John's Wood Park was inadequate for the growing family is not known, but in around 1884 the move was made 'around the corner' to Burbank House at 78 Avenue Road. Here was room enough for both the growing family and a complement of servants and housekeepers, and to give some indication of the size and nature of the new Bentley home, the children were still young enough to share a nursery but each had a bedroom of their own. It is obvious from W.O.'s own childhood recollections that his parents were devoted to each other and to every one of their children.

The first child was Clara, born on 30 October 1875, followed by William Waterhouse Bentley (W.W.) on 4 September 1877 and Alfred Hardy (A.H.) exactly one year later on 5 September 1878. Emily Maud was born on 4 October 1879 but died six months later on 11 February 1880. She was followed by Edith on 21 March 1881, and Hilda on 27 April 1882. Leonard Holt (L.H.) was born on 2 July 1883, and Arthur Waterhouse (A.W.) on 3 August 1884, followed by Horace Milner (H.M.) on 15 December 1885. Finally Walter Owen Bentley (W.O.) was born in the early hours of 16 September 1888. In his later years it amused W.O. (he disliked being called Walter) to think that his arrival at what he termed 'A most disagreeable hour' was the cause of much commotion within the household.

The 1881 census records the existence of two live-in servants, cook Agnes Phillips and housemaid Fanny Jacobs. Also recorded as a visitor was Hephzibah Coxall, a monthly nurse, no doubt engaged to look after the infant Edith who was one month old at the time. The fact that Clara, William and Alfred Hardy had been temporarily deposited with grandparents Thomas and Eliza Waterhouse at their home at New

Barnet indicates the family was already outgrowing 35 St John's Wood Park.

Of the Bentley children Clara and Hilda remained unmarried at the time of the 1911 census. Edith had married Archibald Harry Montgomery John Ward in January 1907 and had two daughters, Elizabeth and Virginia. William Waterhouse married Winifred Morgan in September 1903 and lived at Pinner in north-west London; they, too, had two daughters, Marjorie and Kathleen. A lieutenant in the Royal Army Service Corps (RASC) in World War One, William died in 1927.

Alfred Hardy (he was usually referred to as Hardy) married Ethel Johnston in July 1907 and they had two sons, John Hardy and James Sydney. A competent sportsman, Alfred won his cap for rugby and played in the 1st XI team at Clifton College. Having qualified as a solicitor, A.H. reached the rank of captain in World War One, and was later much involved with H.M. and W.O. in their business ventures. Leonard Holt also became a lieutenant in the RASC but died in the Mediterranean in 1918. Arthur Waterhouse died in December 1913 from the effects of a severe throat infection at the age of 29; he was unmarried. Horace Milner qualified as an accountant, and for much of his working life was involved with the motor industry one way or another; he married Rose Whittingham in 1916.

The youngest child, W.O. earned the nickname 'The Bun' on account of his shape and the fact that he had dark eyes. One family portrait shows W.O. aged about four, seated very sedately in a finely carved wooden chair with leather seat, posing for the camera. Even then it is clear to see the child had acquired a placid disposition, although he was evidently in control of the situation. His sailor suit, shorts and long socks are typical of the era, when it was the fashion to dress boys in such attire. The occasion of the photograph is not recorded, but having to endure the gaze of the camera was the lot of every well-represented young boy. In another photograph the young W.O., now aged six or seven, has joined his brothers for a formal study. All are turned out in exemplary fashion and are wearing top hats, except W.O., who is wearing a boater and is seated instead of standing. With an obvious look of delight on his face, W.O. appears to be enjoying the event immensely. In later life W.O. recalled that his brothers and sisters loomed over him in almost overwhelming profusion.

Such evidence of family harmony suggests that W.O.'s childhood was happy and without serious event. Certainly life in Avenue Road, at the house with its abundance of rooms rambling over four storeys including the basement, the stables area and outhouses, was a source of contentment and security. The 1901 census shows Eliza having moved to 78 Avenue Road to live with her daughter at the Bentley family home. By then the Bentleys employed 10 servants.

Alfred Bentley was of a sensitive and quiet disposition. W.O. recalls his father being terribly shy and seemingly very retiring, almost to the point of being unsociable with those outside the family and a few close friends. What Alfred lacked in outgoing nature, Emily made up for. She was confident and bright, had a warm heart and yet was determined, always being certain of what she wanted from life. Emily was the backbone of the household and her husband's strength came from her; her personality was one of kindly forthrightness to the point that she never failed to make a good impression on everyone she was acquainted with. In recalling childhood memories, and those of his brothers and sisters, W.O. was aware, from an early age, of the extent of his mother's influence.

Alfred was the perfect father nevertheless; there is evidence that he was just and fair with his children and never anything but good humoured. Of religious nature and upbringing, Alfred adopted a simple philosophy of life: he viewed and accepted success just as he experienced failure or misfortune. To say that Alfred did not have a great influence on his children would be wrong. W.O. inherited his calmness and humble nature, and later in life this had a profound effect on the many difficult decisions that he would have to make.

There can be little doubt that the Bentleys had independent means. Alfred Bentley, according to W.O. in later life, lacked business acumen; this, more than likely, was owing to his inherent shyness, and he retired early.

Like most young children W.O. was fascinated by toys, which were a luxury in those days, and it can be supposed that some of those that his brothers had were handed down. Even at an early age the young W.O. had a penchant for taking the few toys he had to pieces, and he would then spend hours quietly amusing himself putting them back together again. Being the youngest child it was inevitable that he would experience some isolation, which was something that he did not find particularly daunting.

Given their social standing, it was not unusual that the Bentley family employed a governess. Her role was to attend to her charge's daily routine and exercise, and she obviously had a considerable influence on W.O.'s formative education. It can be supposed, too, that the baby of the family had an influence of his own on the governess, and there is little doubt that the two got on well together. The governess was also likely to have been responsible for allowing W.O. to develop his association with all things mechanical, and may have unconsciously stimulated his interest in the railways. Her nephew was in fact apprenticed to the railway industry at Doncaster on the Great Northern Railway. This was the age of steam and the arrival of the internal combustion engine was imminent: the meaning of *horse power* was about to change.

The final decade of the 19th century and the opening years of the 20th were exciting times. This was the heyday of steam travel, and the sight of trains heading from London on their long runs to the north of England evoked adventure. The expresses destined for Scotland were particularly romantic and engrossing for any young boy.

W.O. was certainly fascinated by steam, and he successfully cajoled his governess to choose a route for their walks that crossed the main line from Euston where it emerged from Primrose Hill tunnel near Loudoun Road. From here he would insist on watching the crack west coast main line expresses of the London North Western Railway (LNWR), hauled by Mr Francis Webb's Crewe-built compounds, the Teutonics, the Jubilees and the Dreadnoughts. The highlight of the day, possibly eagerly awaited by the young W.O., would have been the *Corridor*, the regular 2pm Euston to Glasgow express, hauled almost exclusively between 1891 and 1899 by the immortal Teutonic *Jeanie Deans*. The sense of power that a locomotive with a full head of steam getting into its stride for an all-out attack on the eastern Chilterns up to Tring can evoke has to be seen to be fully appreciated. It seems likely that hours spent watching steam engines were responsible for W.O.'s determination to embark on a career in the railway industry.

As a boy W.O. was given a stationary steam engine by an uncle, as well as a clockwork train set. The mechanics of these were probably another factor in influencing his choice of future career. Although the steam engine was doubtless well-built and reliable, it was presumably dismantled and rebuilt several times.

In time, therefore, railways came to dominate W.O.'s life. Neighbours of the Bentleys at 80 Avenue Road were the Thornhills, another relatively large family by contemporary standards, the three boys and four girls being of comparative ages to the Bentley children. W.O. was friendly with Geoffrey, and together they shared a common interest in railways. Because Edward Thornhill, head of the family, was chief engineer in a civil capacity with the LNWR, Geoffrey was understandably loyal to that company. Edward's two elder sons also worked for the LNWR, Henry as a solicitor and Frederic in the drawing office. W.O.'s loyalties, however, despite his frequent visits to Loudoun Road to watch the expresses thunder past, were firmly with the Great Northern. As might be expected from two young boys, the rivalry between them was fierce yet good natured.

Both boys' rooms were filled with railway ephemera, from books to journals, the latter including *The Railway Magazine*, that bastion of the railway industry. There were pictures too, and maps. Other forms of transport seemed to interest W.O. little, except for the bicycle; cycling offered some independence, although initially this served as a tool to travel to those locations that afforded the best views of passing steam locomotives.

It is pertinent to mention at this point that papers lodged regarding H.M. and W.O.'s business affairs show their address as 80 Avenue Road. Over the years this disparity has been the cause of much confusion but the explanation is straightforward. The even-numbered houses were renumbered by the local authority in around 1910. Sadly the house was destroyed in the Blitz of World War Two.

The advent of the motor vehicle was hardly appreciated by W.O., who was uninterested in the potential it offered commercially and for independent travel. W.O. once recorded that, as a boy, he viewed motor vehicles as slow, inefficient and draughty. 'Motor cars', he said, 'splashed people with mud, frightened horses, irritated dogs and were a frightful nuisance to everybody.' Indeed, W.O. reached the age of 16 before he experienced any type of motor vehicle travel. This initial acquaintance was not an ideal one; while staying on a farm in Scotland where his brother Leonard was studying agriculture, he travelled to Inverness in an already aged Daimler omnibus with tube ignition. Considering W.O.'s lack of interest in motor transport, the fact that he even recalled that the omnibus was a Daimler is remarkable, even if the journey wasn't so. In his opinion the journey aboard the vehicle was a wretched ordeal, made worse by the solid tyres and elementary suspension, not to mention the wooden slatted seats that were dreadfully uncomfortable.

The arrival of the motor car, mainly French types at first before the British motor industry was allowed to fully develop, had little effect on W.O.'s formative years. Nor did the arrival of the motor bus, apart from the aforementioned experience with a Daimler. Horse-drawn trams had arrived in London during the 1870s, and it was not until 1901, by which time W.O. had reached the age of 13, that electric trams became a familiar sight in London. The motor car was really reserved for an affluent and select clientele, and remained so until after World War One.

W.O. was enrolled at Lambrook School near Ascot to complete his preparatory education. The choice of Lambrook was, for W.O.'s parents, specific – the school's headmaster was a strict disciplinarian. E.D. Mansfield was an old boy of Clifton College at Bristol. Clifton was the public school attended by all the Bentley sons.

For many boys of 10 the experience of leaving home for the first time is traumatic, but the young W.O. appears not to have been unduly worried. This was probably because he had seen his brothers Horace and Arthur leave home, and knew that such a fate awaited him. Although the prospect of starting school might not have concerned him, W.O. did, nevertheless, suffer some apprehension at being put on a train, along with his immediate baggage, to Ascot, especially as it was occupied by Lambrook pupils, all of whom appeared to know each other well and did not make any particular effort to get to know the shy newcomer in their midst.

Elsewhere, W.O. has been described as a stoic. He was, in fact, far from being without emotion, and there are several clues from his early life which support that belief. Certainly the shyness that he inherited from his father gave him an air of independence, which could have been interpreted by some as aloofness. In fact he was not at all aloof, but his manner did reflect the fact that he was not particularly academically minded. There is no inference that W.O. lagged behind any of his contemporaries, but he found the majority of subjects rather dull and had to put a lot of effort into finding some facet that interested him. Not only that, the same inquisitiveness that had led him to take his toys apart as a young boy meant that he continually questioned the whys and the wherefores of his classroom studies. It is not surprising that his favourite subjects were physics and chemistry.

W.O. admitted that he did not excel at lessons. However, in those subjects that he found stimulating his quest to understand natural law and the principles of science led to a desire for further knowledge. Here in fact was a fertile mind that was not satisfied until every question and answer had been fully explained and understood, a trait which tended to impede his academic progress. It is for this reason that he received his fair share of Mansfield's cane. W.O. said of his academic performance at Lambrook, 'I didn't like doing the things I didn't like and that was that.'

When it came to the sports field W.O. suffered again. Social points were won or lost at games – boys who were good at rugby and cricket immediately became popular. Rugby was not W.O.'s favourite sporting event; he found it difficult, and to excel in the game in any way at all was hard work. Cricket was a different matter, however. Even as a youngster playing with his brothers and Geoffrey, his neighbourly friend, he had enjoyed the game, and as might be expected, Yorkshire was his favoured county. So it remained throughout his life. Every boy who has a passion for cricket has a hero, and W.O.'s was Wilfred Rhodes. The first cricket match that W.O. attended was at Lords in 1897 when Yorkshire were playing the MCC. For no reason other than that it was Rhodes's first season with Yorkshire, (aside from the fact that he was a first-rate player, that is) W.O. placed him at the top of his list of cricketing giants.

W.O.'s first couple of terms at Lambrook were arduous. Not only was there the task of making friends, which he found difficult, but he also had to get used to boarding school life. The fact that Lambrook had an excellent gymnasium gave W.O. some comfort, since he enjoyed his pursuits there, even though games were an uphill struggle. This helped him to acclimatise to his new surroundings. Some 60 pupils attended Lambrook, which along with its severe discipline had an unusually tough regime. W.O. missed his hobbies and having his favourite mechanical possessions around him, and he pined for the long walks that he had previously enjoyed. More than anything else though, it was his bicycle that was his real loss, for without it he felt that he had given up his independence.

W.O.'s introduction to cycling had occurred at the age of seven when he rode a machine with solid tyres. There is every indication that the bicycle was one that he shared with his brothers, and immediately he began saving every penny from his pocket money to afford a machine of his own. Cycling then was entirely safe as long as one avoided the horse-drawn traffic, which in St John's Wood was relatively scattered. The independence that W.O. gained from cycling meant that he could travel at will, usually towards some railway line or other. At the age of nine he acquired a much more modern second-hand machine, the frantically saved pocket money not quite amounting to the asking price. Mother came to the rescue and contributed the remaining money.

The bicycle, in true W.O. fashion, was systematically taken apart, and it was not unusual for his mother to find her youngest son sitting patiently on the floor surrounded by gears, bearings, nuts and bolts. Mother was naturally not impressed at the sight of the hard-earned bicycle in so many pieces. The chain and wheels, along with the frame, were all laid out in precise order. She was nevertheless gratified to see that her son carefully and deliberately pieced everything back together in working order. The bicycle served W.O. for a number of years. One of the longest and most adventurous trips that he undertook was when he was 14; with his brother H.M. he cycled from London to Wroxham in Norfolk in a day, a distance of 130 miles, to be with the rest of the family who were holidaying on the Broads. Cycling such a distance, even for someone so young, would have been achievable given the advances in bicycle design. W.O.'s feat was obviously an accomplishment, and considering the quality of the roads at the time he would have arrived at Wroxham in a state of exhaustion.

There were restrictions at Lambrook: W.O. and his fellow pupils were allowed out only on organised walks, and he resented not being able to wander at will. Visits away from school were seldom, apart from going to church on Sundays, which meant having to dress accordingly and wear a top hat. There was, however, sufficient spare time, and although he might have wanted more, W.O. spent many an hour tending his own plot in the school's gardens.

Gardening might have developed into a hobby had it not been for his love of anything mechanical. Indeed, gardening at Lambrook took second place when W.O., at the age of 12, acquired a five-shilling Brownie box camera. Gadgets fascinated the young Bentley, and the most appealing of them all at that time was this camera. His early attempts at photography left much to be desired, but like everything he tried it had to be done to the best of his ability. Improvements were soon apparent after much experimenting, and as well as taking snapshots,

W.O. discovered how to develop and print his own pictures, which gave him a great deal of satisfaction. The camera was also instrumental in bringing him greater happiness at Lambrook. The teacher that W.O. had found to be the most severe, and whose cane he had so felt, was a keen photographer, and this shared interest helped to foster a better understanding between them.

When W.O. acquired his camera the Brownie was a relatively recent introduction, the first models having been made available by Eastman between 1888 and 1889. Marketed as the Kodak, the camera had been developed by Frank Brownell and became a favourite among amateur photographers for many years.

As an interest it was photography that most shaped the young W.O.'s developing personality and character. The hours that he spent taking pictures and then developing them produced distinct pleasure when the results were good. When the results were less than he would have wished, that pleasure turned to acute depression. Being shown the most appropriate techniques of developing and printing his negatives not only gave him encouragement, but also the thrill of achievement.

In terms of sport W.O. excelled at cricket. Possibly it was thoughts of Wilfred Rhodes and that other great England batsman, Gilbert Jessop, that spurred him on. His love of the game was sufficient for W.O. to try his hardest when playing on the school cricket pitch, and he had the satisfaction of being picked for the school eleven. Nothing gave him more pleasure than being invited to open the innings for Lambrook against a school in Reading. W.O. might have drawn inspiration from the determination of Jessop when he saved the final test match against the Australians at the Oval in 1902, for at Reading he put in one of his finest performances and scored 79 not out. On that occasion his opening partner was S.S. Bonham-Carter, who was destined to become a distinguished admiral.

W.O.'s placid nature made him an ideal candidate for boarding school. Nothing overly worried him, and he coped well with the daily routine, although he looked forward to the end of term and being able to escape from the constraints of Lambrook to Avenue Road and home comforts. Family holidays were a delight, the Bentley household sometimes taking over country houses or a vicarage for the duration of their stay. Of the places that W.O. recalled most affectionately, Bridling-ton in Yorkshire was a favourite, as was the aforementioned Wroxham on the Norfolk Broads, where the family had access to a boat. Sailing invited new adventures, and the younger Bentleys loved sleeping on the craft overnight. When it came to sailing the vessel, W.O. might well have had the urge to take the tiller but he had to wait his turn. Being the youngest, and the most inexperienced, there were few opportunities for him to take charge.

His placid nature was seldom ruffled, but when it was, the change in W.O.'s behaviour was very marked. Even at such a young age any form of bullying, whether physical or emotional, was abhorrent to him, and this continued throughout his life. The sight of anybody being bullied stirred fire in W.O.'s heart and he would do everything in his power to stop the abuse from happening. It was at Lambrook that this was first noticed, and W.O. earned a reputation for going to the defence of the victim. Not generally thought of as having a fiery nature, it was remarkable to see the boy enter the fray with fists swinging and with little regard for his own safety or protection.

In 1902, when W.O. was 14, it was time for him to leave Lambrook. That he did not achieve outstanding success in his academic studies was no detriment to him, although others might have considered differently. An interest in science and its related subjects nevertheless meant that he was well positioned to continue with a public-school education. Each of W.O.'s brothers had attended Clifton College, and H.M. was in his final terms there, so it was almost a matter of course that the youngest brother would also endure the rigours of life at this well-respected establishment. In later life W.O. often wondered that he was admitted to Clifton in the first place, given his seeming unwillingness to make an effort with his studies.

Clifton College, with its fine architecture and mellow Cotswold stone, enjoyed an enviable position amid delightful grounds and well-appointed playing fields. The school also had a reputation for having a tough regime that varied in severity according to the particular house to which one was appointed. The daily routine was arduous, with pupils having to be ready for morning prayers with the house tutor at seven o'clock. Woe betide any boy who was late or not immaculately groomed! Following prayers there was an hour's prep, after which breakfast was taken. Boys were then required to be in the school chapel for nine o'clock, lessons continuing thereafter until six in the evening. The exception to the agenda was when, two afternoons a week, games were compulsory. All this left little time for other pursuits, although it is recorded elsewhere that boys frequented the college baths, the pool being indoors, which was then quite a luxury.

On his arrival at Clifton W.O. entered Tait's House, where his brother H.M. held a position of seniority. Tait's House was situated at 26 College Road in Clifton, an imposing property that was once a large private residence. The house took its name from its Scottish housemaster, Charles W.A. Tait, a bachelor. As with most public schools Clifton had a system of fagging, which as far as Tait's House was concerned was relatively sophisticated. The intention was to introduce pupils to accepting authority from their seniors, and in turn to administer discipline, albeit in a just manner. Each house was different in the manner in which it was administered. Tait's House was regarded as particularly civilised and had facilities, including its own squash court, which were envied by other pupils at Clifton. Tait's House took the name Rintoul's House in 1905 but eventually reverted to Oakley's House, its original name. Tradition was that each house adopted the name of its current housemaster, and in subsequent years this caused much confusion. In time the decision was made for each house to revert to its first title. Today Clifton is a mixed school and Oakley's House is now occupied by girls.

W.O. left few clues about the customs at Clifton. During his time there he would have experienced the senior boys running the house; prefects ruled and imposed a severe regime that would frequently lead to beatings. The housemasters often, perhaps wisely, chose to keep a discreet distance. As to the conditions, these would have been basic in the extreme. Other pupils remember that the washing facilities were primitive: in each dormitory cold water was provided in a row of tin basins adjacent to a window, and beside each bowl was placed a flat tin containing whitening powder for teeth cleaning. Boys were awakened each morning by the senior housemaid, who supervised the daily ablutions. It is recorded by a Cliftonian that some 20 years later conditions had barely improved, and were so harsh that new boys would take to their beds on their first night at the school and weep themselves to sleep. Silently, of course, to avoid courting trouble and attracting beatings.

Despite being brothers, H.M. and W.O. had little to do with each other, apart from H.M.'s helpful advice to his sibling regarding

Clifton's tradition of dining-hall boxing. This event was a huge entertainment for established pupils, who avidly watched the painful and energetic boxing contest between new boys. Just as with games at Lambrook, credibility and popularity rested on winning one's initial bout. H.M.'s advice to his brother was to practise and give the match his best effort. When the day of the boxing duel arrived, W.O. did not feel unduly worried, such was the determined effort he had put into preparing for it. His opponent was a boy called Murray who, in W.O.'s eyes, seemed very formidable. But from the very moment the bout started, W.O. uncharacteristically went into the attack with arms and legs flying in all directions. Finesse hardly mattered when one's reputation was at stake, and he fought – to use his own words – 'like a demented monkey'. W.O. was pleased with his efforts, as he won his bout and created for himself an instant charisma. Boxing, being a sport that was part of Clifton's sporting curriculum, meant that W.O. went on to meet Murray in the ring again from time to time. Whether or not it was because Murray had never forgiven W.O. for beating him on that day, W.O. never managed to beat him again.

Cross-country running and cricket were more to W.O.'s liking. Like most things in his life, W.O. excelled at those activities that he could manage. Sprinting was something that he disliked, but a cross-country run meant that he could develop his own programme and manage his performance accordingly. He didn't particularly enjoy rugby, but he did break his collar-bone and both wrists in his quest to excel at the game.

Cricket at Clifton, as at Lambrook, was of immense importance and it was here that W.O. really excelled. In his second year at the college he was invited to join the house team, where he discovered that his talent was for fielding in the slips. Batting and bowling held little attraction for him, until, that is, he was included in the house team the following season. By this time W.O. had got into his stride; he was opening bat, and as well as scoring the highest number of runs, he took more catches than any other player. His bowling became noted too, and he took several wickets during the season.

Although he probably would not have admitted it, W.O. did get some satisfaction from being at Clifton. He enjoyed the lessons no more than he had done at Lambrook, but at least the discipline, while strict, was less severe. He found the masters more approachable, or was he merely getting used to the public school system? Unlike his time at Lambrook, where he made few friends and was content with his independence, at Clifton he formed a number of friendships.

At least two of the friendships that he established while at Tait's House were to endure throughout his later life, and both of them would have a major impact on his working life. One was Roy Fedden (later Sir), who between the wars was thought one of the finest engineers in the world. A designer of aero engines – his name is synonymous with the Bristol company – Fedden actually began his career in the early years of the 20th century by recognising the motor car's huge potential. Such was his belief that he designed his own vehicle, the details of which he submitted to John P. Brazil of Brazil Straker. Known as the Shamrock, the car was produced in time for the 1907 Motor Show in London. An accomplished driver and motor sportsman, Fedden was soon acquainted with drivers F.C. Clement and R.S. Witchell, both of whom were destined to play a significant role in W.O.'s life. Witchell was W.O.'s other friend at Clifton: he joined the Royal Flying Corps (RFC) as a pilot and after the war worked on aero engines for Fedden before becoming Bentley's works manager at Cricklewood. Fedden, incidentally, was encouraged by the government to develop a radical car during the later stages of World War Two, but it failed to achieve the success it deserved.

As we have seen, W.O. was not particularly noted for his academic achievement. He found his studies difficult, often because he had to examine every aspect of the subject in question and understand it fully before he allowed himself to progress to the next phase. In later life, of course, this close attention to the most minute of detail would be used to good advantage. But at Clifton the emphasis was on the classics, and it was unfortunate for W.O. that he could not explore his interests in more practical subjects.

So he remained frustrated during his three years at Clifton. Intellectually, he was brilliant, but his approach to study held him back in the school environment. On his arrival at the college he had been assigned to the third year, and such was his tardy progress that he never advanced beyond that level to the fourth or fifth forms, which led to his departure from Clifton after only three years.

His father, probably exasperated by his youngest son's apparent lack of impetus when it came to his academic education, was sufficiently understanding to accede to the boy's wish to embark on a career in the railway industry. Considering his own path in life, Alfred would have had some sympathy with his son's attitudes to academic study. W.O.'s outlook on life, combined with his relaxed personality, at least allowed him to view his educational progress, or lack of it, with some equanimity. There was also the financial factor to consider, since Clifton's fees were expensive. So in July 1905, at the age of 16, W.O. left to begin a course of engineering theory at King's College in London. He found this dry and monotonous, mainly because it lacked any practical element. However, the course was merely an interlude of a few months as a precursor to joining the Great Northern Railway at Doncaster as a premium apprentice.

W.O.'s objective was not only to work within the railway industry, but to become a locomotive designer. To do this meant enduring five years' slog as an apprentice, gaining experience in all the departments. He had to undertake many menial and fundamental tasks before moving on to assignments of greater complexity requiring great skill. His passion for anything mechanical made W.O. the ideal candidate for a career in the railway industry. His obsession with railways, the engineering and performance of steam locomotives in particular, increased his commitment to his chosen career path. He fully understood that an apprenticeship was never going to be easy. The regime at Doncaster was severe, and that he was able to survive the daily discipline had much to do with his independent nature as a child, and his experiences at Lambrook and Clifton.

There were two grades of apprenticeship with the Great Northern Railway. A trade apprentice was one that had a father or close relative in the railway industry. The other was premium apprenticeship, which W.O. had secured. Trade apprentices were paid the sum of five shillings (25p) a week, but the parents of premium apprentices were required to buy into the industry and pay a fee of £75, which over the term of five years was paid to the apprentice as wages.

Premium and trade apprentices tended to come from very different social backgrounds. Those who had followed their forebears into the railway industry were well used to the gritty and grimy daily life that was part of working in a harsh environment. Most of the trade apprentices at Doncaster were from the local area, and for them the Great Northern was more than just a way of life. The railway was the lifeblood of Doncaster. With their public school backgrounds and southern accents, and having bought their way into the industry, premium apprentices were usually thought to be soft snobs. W.O. was no exception to this, despite his Yorkshire roots.

W.O., however, was a fighter who did not let the situation in which he found himself deter him from his chosen path. Even by Clifton standards the routine at Doncaster was grim, and run along military lines with fierce discipline. The working week comprised something approaching 60 hours over five and a half days, which meant getting out of bed at a quarter past five in the morning, including on Saturdays, to get to the plant, as the works were known, in time to start work at six.

During summer the journey to work by bicycle was not too unpleasant, but in winter it was a very different story. Having risen from his slumbers, W.O. would grope his way downstairs afraid of waking the household. In the kitchen he would still be half asleep as he started the day with a steaming mug of Bovril. Lighting the lamp on his bicycle before wheeling it outside, he would pedal furiously down Netherhall Road, where he lodged, to avoid arriving late at the plant, for to do so was an offence, even by 30 seconds. Numb with cold, and with his eyes streaming water, W.O. was fully awake by the time he arrived.

W.O.'s lodgings in Netherhall Road were a mile and a half from the plant on the opposite side of the town. His home throughout his apprenticeship was with the two Creaser sisters, a delightful couple as W.O. recalled, who regarded him as a young brother. Lodging there was idyllic and the memory of cycling back there in the evening after the working day had finished at 5.30pm to be greeted by a steaming bath, a change of clothes and a massive and delicious high tea remained with him throughout his life. With a constant throughput of apprentices there was always a requirement for lodgings within the town. Before W.O.'s arrival at Doncaster, the question of his living quarters was settled as part of the premium apprentice scheme. That W.O. was assigned to the Creaser sisters was his good fortune.

Doncaster was established as the headquarters of the Great Northern Railway in 1853. The company's first chairman was Edward Denison, and the town was his birthplace. The arrival of the railway works therefore heralded Doncaster's expansion and its ensuing wealth. Perhaps his family's Yorkshire connections, as well as the town's position as the centre of locomotive design and construction, meant that W.O. felt thoroughly at home there. Although he thought the town was not a particularly pretty place, he nevertheless liked it and enjoyed venturing into the surrounding countryside on his bicycle during summer evenings and weekends when he did not go home to Hampstead. Central to Doncaster was the River Don, with its coal barges that served the South Yorkshire coalfields, and overlooking the Don, the town's parish church with its tall pinnacled tower dominated the skyline.

In his autobiography, W.O. provided a charming cameo of life with the Creaser sisters. They were obviously delighted to have him living with them, and set a table each night with 'Great spreads of chicken or pork pies or thick steaks, a man's food for a ravenous young man.' It was while he was at Doncaster that W.O. succumbed to the charms of the gramophone. In town one day he was looking in the window of Clark's music shop when he saw one of the latest Pathé models, the type which had a sapphire needle. This development in gramophone technology eliminated the tiresome chore of regularly changing the needles. Having decided he could afford the machine, it gave him many hours of pleasure listening to records during the evenings. From his room at Netherhall Road could often be heard the delights of Tchaikovsky, Chopin, Rachmaninov and Grieg, as well as some more popular pieces. Music remained a passion throughout W.O.'s life and was as important to him as his beloved cricket.

W.O. was 17 when he arrived at Doncaster, a raw recruit among others who quickly learnt that being tough was the only way to survive. Possibly it was the GNR's aim to intimidate its apprentices, and if it were so, then the ploy succeeded. W.O.'s arrival at Doncaster on his first morning when he joined the new intake of apprentices was a bewildering experience. Little expression of welcome was given, just a few curt words from an uninspiring man with a drooping moustache who, as quickly and unfeelingly as he could, outlined what the newcomers could expect. It was left to the first foreman, whose name W.O. remembered as Treece, to describe the strict routine in detail. His chilly words and lack of any hint of compassion were designed to instil fear into any new recruit: 'being at the plant at six o'clock *means* six o'clock.' The plant's gates were closed on the dot of six, and to be shut out meant a disciplinary warning. Just as intimidating was the under-foreman, a man by the name of Growcock, whom W.O. regarded as equivalent to a sergeant-major. The apprentices, including those in their second and third years, lived in fear of his presence.

Allowing the apprentices to 'sink or swim' was the only practical way of assessing their stamina and qualities, and those who were capable of surviving the course were soon identified. With a background of being able to stand up for himself, it was very soon apparent to those responsible for the apprentices that W.O. had much to offer the GNR. The first few weeks were particularly difficult but his personality ensured that he always took a pragmatic view of every situation, and his understanding of his fellow apprentices allowed him to make friends easily. The social barriers that existed among the two tiers of apprentices did not affect W.O. and he was always able to get along with people from all walks of life.

As in his school days, W.O. had to understand every aspect of each project in hand, and without doing so he was unable to progress to the next phase. Fortunately his contemporaries accepted this, seeing it as an asset rather than a failure, and would help him out. In turn he would assist them.

Those early days were hard work: the first session continued until 8.15am, by which time the 45-minute break for breakfast was very welcome. At nine it was back to the grindstone for four hours until one o'clock when there was an hour's relief for lunch. The afternoon began at 2pm precisely, ending at 5.30pm. There was precious little time for any social life, but what there was often centred around the railway works. After having high tea at his Netherhall Road lodgings W.O. would sometimes meet a friend or two who were fellow apprentices. More often than not they would end up on one of the platforms at Doncaster station, where they would watch the arrivals and departures of trains and talk shop with the drivers and firemen before returning to their digs.

Premium apprentices were assured of hard work, which in W.O.'s case was highly satisfying. In addition to the more mundane work there was always the opportunity to see at close quarters the engines that he had admired for so long. For months though this was the nearest W.O. got to real engineering: he pined to be allowed to work on a locomotive and jealously watched as the older apprentices learnt how to light a fire and stoke it to achieve the best results.

For W.O., Saturdays came around too slowly. Most weeks he took advantage of the privilege tickets available to apprentices and returned home to Avenue Road. Leaving the plant at midday he would dash back to Netherhall Road, where he washed and changed at breakneck speed, before racing to the station to catch the 1.03pm London train, which invariably he did but with only seconds to spare. His comrade on those journeys to London was often G.C. Gowland, who was on a course at the plant on behalf of the army at Woolwich. Gowland shared W.O.'s enthusiasm for sport, and as well as playing rugby for the army he had also been included in the Scottish and London Scottish teams. Each man would go his own way on arrival at Kings Cross, but they would meet up again on the 8.45 back to Doncaster on Sunday evenings. Arriving back at his lodgings after midnight, and having an early start the next morning, was the penalty W.O. paid for enjoying home life.

Despite liking Doncaster, W.O. relished going home as often as he could. Returning to the bosom of family life was idyllic, for he could meet up with his brothers when they were at home and go into town to see a show. Life in the capital was glamorous and sparkling compared to the grimy atmosphere of Doncaster.

Another particular friend of W.O.'s at the time was Arthur Peppercorn, a fellow premium apprentice. Peppercorn worked under Sir Nigel Gresley until the latter's untimely death in 1941. Working with Gresley's successor, Edward Thompson, he produced some outstanding work in the drawing office and designed what emerged as the A1 and A2 Pacifics. On Thompson's retirement Peppercorn was appointed chief of the locomotive department.

During W.O.'s time at Doncaster, the head of the locomotive department was that highly respected engineer H.A. Ivatt. Known to be rather austere and cautious, it was a surprise to see as his deputy the younger and more confident Nigel Gresley, who was at the time carriage and wagon superintendent. When Gresley was appointed locomotive engineer in 1911 he was 35 years old; 12 years later, at the time of the grouping of the railways in 1923, he was appointed chief mechanical engineer of the LNER. There is little doubt that W.O. adopted Gresley as a role model.

W.O.'s first real disappointment at Doncaster came in the autumn of 1906, during his first year as an apprentice. Until then premium apprentices had been allowed on the footplates of locomotives to gain experience of the fireman's duties. It was not usual for an apprentice to take the duties of the first fireman, and it was with excited anticipation that W.O. awaited his turn. In the event, owing to a change in policy following a disastrous accident, he had to wait a further three years to get onto the footplate.

The accident affected W.O. personally. A fellow apprentice by the name of Talbot had been assigned to fire the train in question as far as York. No doubt W.O. would have liked to have taken his place on the footplate as he watched the train pull out of Doncaster. Under the watchful eye of driver Fleetwood, Talbot then had the opportunity to fire the York to Peterborough train. Arriving at their destination the pair were assigned to the semi-fast service mail train from Kings Cross to Edinburgh, which would bring them back to Doncaster. The locomotive pulling the train was one of the then newly-introduced Ivatt 4–4–0 Atlantics, one of the most successful engines to run on the Great Northern. The train had been scheduled to stop at Grantham but instead thundered through the station, ignoring both the distant signal, which was set at caution, and the home signal that was showing danger. The train hit the junction north of the station with points set against it. The engine derailed, tore up the tracks and caused the coaches behind it to be mangled into smouldering wreckage. The engine itself was virtually destroyed. Fleetwood and Talbot were killed along with 10 passengers. The cause of the accident and the circumstances surrounding it were never fully accounted for by the Board of Trade inquiry, and to this day the incident remains something of an enigma. Conflicting evidence about what was happening on the footplate was given; one report said that the two crew members were struggling with one another. Another suggested all was well, with both driver and fireman looking straight ahead from the cab.

At Doncaster the accident led to a depressing atmosphere that remained for weeks, and the friends of the driver and the apprentice were devastated. In later life W.O. recalled the incident with deep sadness. The outcome of the tragedy for the premium apprentices was that they were restricted from serving on the footplate except as second firemen. However, W.O. was still able to admire from a distance some of those engineers, particularly Henry Ivatt, Nigel Gresley and O.V. Bullied, whose engines were to become a most significant part of railway heritage.

It was with some relief that W.O. was at last appointed to the engine-erecting shop. Until then he had endured all sorts of tedious duties, including many hours spent polishing wheel connecting rods. When fitted to a steam locomotive the rods, otherwise known as coupling rods, transmitted the motive power derived from steam to the wheels, providing propulsion. The rods, which could be several feet in length, were rough forged and it was an apprentice's job to polish them until smooth. In the horizontal plane a freshly forged connecting rod has the appearance of a letter 'H' and the apprentices were required to achieve a radius on each of the edges along the rod's length. To achieve the radii meant that the eight corners of a rod's H-section had to be chipped painstakingly away by hand, using special chisels to maintain an even cut of a quarter of an inch. The work was demanding, noisy and exhausting, but W.O. nevertheless found it satisfying, although it was comparatively unskilled. Being confined to the workshop day after day did at least have one compensation, as from where W.O. worked he could see through an adjacent window the main line below and watch the passing locomotives. The majority of the engines were Atlantics but occasionally there was the nostalgia of spotting one of the few surviving Stirling Singles that he used to be so happy to watch as a boy at Loudoun Road.

After weeks of polishing connecting rods W.O. was transferred to the foundry with its immense heat and noise. It was extremely dangerous for inexperienced workers, and it took time to get used to the many complicated and highly skilled operations. Not that premium apprentices were allowed anywhere near the cascading molten metal, for to work in that environment called for the most delicate handling. Here locomotive cylinders were cast, a process which always fascinated W.O. Apprentices, however, were set to work on relatively straightforward tasks, such as producing brackets for carriage luggage racks and humdrum but nevertheless essential items such as maximum weight tablets for goods wagons. Apart from going back to his lodgings at the end of the day in a weary and grimy state, life for W.O. was getting better. At this stage in his apprenticeship he had found the measure of his tutors, and they of him.

At last, W.O. was able to work on the magnificent engines that he had admired for so long. W.O. found the work initially exhausting, both mentally and physically, and he would return to his lodgings tired and extremely dirty. The work he had previously undertaken at Doncaster seemed to have little bearing on what he experienced in the erecting shop, although he did recognise some of the many parts that he had spent weeks painstakingly preparing. All of his earlier experience was finally coming together.

The engine shop was a place of grease and filth. W.O. spent hours smothered in congealed grease, and feeling among the quagmire attached to a locomotive's running gear for essential nuts and bolts called for some deft skills. To most people such an experience would have been purgatory, but W.O. resigned himself to the task. To him, clawing away for several minutes just to expose one set of bolts was not the most romantic work on a steam engine, but it was necessary. He accepted that the worst jobs on engines that had been brought in for repair or overhaul had to be done, and that included the awful task of having to remove the flange on an engine's blast pipe. Having pounds of soot smother one's face every time a hammer and chisel was taken to a corroded bolt, and there were many of them, proved horribly uncomfortable. He survived the ordeal but not without a great deal of determination.

By sheer resolve he endured working on a locomotive's firebox. There was never sufficient time to allow it to entirely lose its heat before climbing inside; it was a case of getting on with the job in hand. Working 10 hours a day meant that at the end of the shift he would wearily trudge home to the Creaser sisters and sink thankfully into a hot bath before devouring a huge and excellent meal. Despite the hardship W.O.'s tenure in the engine-erecting shop was a happy one. He enjoyed the finer aspects of work, including the fitting of slide bars and connecting rods, and work that called for sheer brute strength as well as a feel and an eye for accuracy.

It was during the second year of his apprenticeship that W.O.'s comrades began to influence him with their talk of motorcycles. Other than his trusty bicycle W.O. had considered no other form of transport, apart from the railway. There was always a copy or two of *The Motor Cycle* magazine left around the rest quarters, and W.O.'s curiosity finally got the better of him. He took a copy back to his lodgings at Netherhall Road.

W.O. was obviously intrigued, and began to read *The Motor Cycle* from cover to cover. He soon realised that the simple addition of an engine to a bicycle would enable it to carry its rider up hills and over long distances with no physical effort whatever. W.O. was hooked. He read with fascination about all the different machines that were available, and scanned the classified advertisements to ascertain prices. A 2hp Minerva could be purchased for £27 and a further £5 would buy the altogether more superior 3½hp model. The Light Rex cost 50 guineas, while the Ariel models started at £37 5s, rising to £52 10s for the most powerful type. His enthusiasm soon got the better of him and one weekend in London he went along to E.T. Morris's cycle and motorcycle shop in the Finchley Road.

For W.O. it was like going into Aladdin's Cave, for there were many machines, both new and second-hand. In typical W.O. fashion he refrained from taking the plunge there and then but sought advice from his brothers and, no doubt, from his parents. Exactly how much his budget extended to is unknown, but W.O. did return to Morris's shop to purchase a used Quadrant 3hp machine. W.O. recalled later that the Quadrant had seen a good amount of service and was at least third or fourth-hand. The registration number of the machine has been recorded, and A4667 was first issued between January 1904 and May 1905.

That one simple purchase of a motorcycle was ultimately to change W.O.'s life. Moreover it was the first self-propelled vehicle in the Bentley family. Not long after he had purchased the Quadrant W.O. made the acquaintance of S.C.H. (Sammy) Davis who lived near the Bentley home. Sharing a love of motorcycles and all things mechanical, the two young men got on well. Their meeting, although neither knew it at the time, was to have huge consequences for them both in later years.

On returning to Doncaster W.O. took the Quadrant on the train with him. Even by contemporary standards the Quadrant was a very basic affair with a single-speed transmission, belt drive, and a surface carburettor. The carburettor was the subject of some controversy among motorcyclists because in use it could be troublesome. Like most things, getting the best out of it was achieved by trial and error, and W.O. succeeded in operating it as efficiently as was possible. More than anything else the machine was noted for its economy, which suited W.O. But above all, his journeys to work now became a pleasure, especially the effortless ascent of the steep incline of Netherhall Road!

At weekends W.O. continued to dash for the 1.03pm London train, leaving his Quadrant in the care of his landladies. That is, until he decided to forsake the train and ride the 166 miles to London. At the beginning of the 1900s the Great North Road was not noted for its smooth surface, and leaving Doncaster at lunchtime he would arrive at Avenue Road at around nine in the evening in a very dishevelled state.

With a top speed of 35mph, the journey was a long one, and was worse in bad weather. W.O.'s courage is admirable, especially given that he had to return to Doncaster in time to start work early on Monday mornings.

It was with a great deal of sadness that W.O. left Doncaster in 1909 in order to complete his apprenticeship in London. By then he was one of Henry Ivatt's pupils, and as such enjoyed a number of privileges that accompanied the promotion. It would appear that he was even able to take additional time off, which was useful especially as by then he was becoming more involved in motorcycling and competitive racing events. Henry Ivatt, in adopting W.O. as one of his pupils, had recognised the young man's abilities and his careful attention to engineering. Throughout his apprenticeship W.O. had worked extremely diligently, and his efforts had paid dividends.

The accident at Grantham had changed the policy of footplate training, and it was decided that W.O.'s experience would be better undertaken at Kings Cross. No doubt Ivatt had considered his pupil's circumstances and concluded that London offered greater opportunities in the long term, or was it simply because W.O. was finding it difficult to combine his motorcycle interests with travelling to and from the capital?

It was with more than a touch of sorrow that W.O. said farewell to the Creaser sisters, and no doubt the separation was just as painful for them. The town and the plant had been his home for so long, and he felt happy in Yorkshire, especially with its family connections. There were, however, great opportunities to look forward to, especially as he had so wanted to feel the footplate of a moving engine under his feet. There was also the satisfaction of living at home. Packing his belongings he set off for London, taking his Quadrant motorcycle with him.

After the gritty atmosphere of Doncaster, London with its lively social scene was a delight. W.O. loved to attend the Promenade Concerts which at that time were held at the Queen's Hall, and in lighter mood would frequent the many theatre shows.

His first footplate duty was as second fireman on local goods trains. No matter, he was firing a locomotive, and it probably wouldn't have mattered if he were on menial shunting duties. This was followed by work as second fireman on local passenger trains, and before too long an opportunity arose to fire a Leeds-bound express.

Although he would have quite happily have continued with local and passenger duties, W.O. did find firing express passenger trains absolutely exhilarating. He became quite accustomed to the constant shovelling and maintaining the fire until the engine, with its heavy chain of carriages, had pounded up the incline out of Kings Cross all the way to Potters Bar. The engine's sudden surge of speed when the line levelled out never failed to excite him and was well worth the several hundred-weight of coal that had to be fed to the fire during this demanding stretch of the journey.

It was not always such fun. Driver and firemen forged a bond so that one knew exactly the other's preferred way of doing things. Someone new on the footplate always ran the risk of upsetting the equilibrium. The dreaded rise immediately outside Kings Cross station was always a battle, and to make matters worse it was in a tunnel. More than once an engine's wheels slipped on the incline and the weight of the train meant that there was a danger of losing all forward momentum. An engine had even been known to slip so severely that it actually rolled backwards, the rear carriages emerging from the tunnel mouth.

One such incident happened to W.O. when, in the smoke-filled blackness of the tunnel, he had no idea whether the engine was moving forwards or backwards. Only by leaning from the cab and feeling the tunnel wall could he determine the engine's direction.

The longest run W.O. experienced was to Leeds and back in a day, which meant covering some 400 miles and shovelling in excess of seven tons of coal. The footplate experience, he found, could sometimes produce a hypnotic effect, especially at night when the open firebox provided the only means of illumination. Because of the speeds the train was travelling, station lights were a mere flash and relief from the long periods of darkness. There was also an eerie glow from towns as they passed in the night.

All too soon W.O.'s final year as an apprentice was over. The difficult part of his railway career nevertheless lay ahead of him, and first he faced the prospect of finding a suitable position with the Great Northern that both interested him and paid him a realistic salary. Appreciating that to become a locomotive designer entailed undertaking relatively menial tasks for many years before being promoted to more responsible positions, there is little wonder that at this point he began to question whether the railway industry offered him the challenge he was seeking. Then there was the matter of the salary, which promised no more than £250 per annum. Certainly locomotive designers and senior engineers were well paid, and commanded salaries of around £3,500, but the wait for such opportunities was usually endless. W.O. faced something of a dilemma.

One cannot help but wonder that had it not been for finding that copy of *The Motor Cycle*, buying the Quadrant and experiencing the thrill of speed on two wheels, W.O. might well have been content to endure the wait for promotion.

CHAPTER 2

The French Connection

AS SOON as he acquired his Quadrant motorcycle W.O., understandably, took great pleasure in stripping the machine down to see exactly how it worked. He then painstakingly examined and cleaned every part before reassembling it to his satisfaction in prime working order. The experience gained from taking his machine to pieces he put to good use. The Quadrant was of much interest to his brothers H.M. and A.W., and so infectious was W.O.'s enthusiasm that, before long, they too succumbed to the pleasures and excitement that motorcycling offered.

Happy were the days that W.O. spent with the Quadrant. It did not particularly matter to him that it was already obsolete, it had served its previous owners well, and the fact that it had been used to its full potential was certainly no problem. The important thing was that it provided much gratification, and its purchase was indicative of W.O.'s astute nature. Although he might not have realised it at the time, the speed and the independence the motorcycle brought slowly began to erode W.O.'s love of steam engines.

These were the pioneering days of motorcycling but already there existed names that had become firmly established, and remained thus for generations to come. Makes such as Ariel, BSA, Norton and Triumph had earned a distinct respect; and there were others that were deservedly highly regarded, including Excelsior, Humber and Rex.

W.O.'s escapades with his Quadrant were typical of a young man who valued his independence and enjoyed travelling and exploring the countryside at will. The fact that he chose to ride home to Hampstead from Doncaster at weekends is sufficient to illustrate his ambitious and adventurous nature. Not that he returned home every weekend; some he would spend exploring the Yorkshire countryside, often venturing into neighbouring counties. He liked nothing better than to study maps, to gauge the topography of a region and satisfy himself as to its general geography. Being a good map reader he could derive a mental picture of a route merely by studying contours and features, and the twisting and turning of a road. By the early 1900s Ordnance Survey maps had become highly sophisticated, the one-inch series having materialised shortly after 1863. By 1888 the series of four miles to an inch maps was complete and covered the entire country.

W.O.'s Quadrant proved to his brothers that motorcycling could indeed be regarded as a pleasure as well as a means of transport. It could, additionally, be a sporting activity. W.O. would have been aware that in 1903 Tom Silver completed the Glasgow to London trial non-stop with his Quadrant. In the same year an organised event was held at Nice in France along the Promenade des Anglais, where competitors produced some breathtaking speeds with the winning machine covering a mile from a standing start in a fraction under 77 seconds. During that year speeds of over 60mph were achieved at a similar trial in Paris, and Harry Martin, competing in London at Canning Town with his 350cc Excelsior, bettered the existing records for his class. Martin, incidentally, riding a Bayliss Thomas, became the first to beat the mile-a-minute barrier when he competed in Dublin. Whenever W.O. took his Quadrant home to Hampstead the machine always came in for some scrutiny by like-minded individuals. Whether the sound of motorcycles revving their engines was wholly appreciated by the other members of the Bentley household, or the neighbours for that matter, is open to conjecture.

The late Michael Frostick once described an occasion when W.O.'s father had his patience tested to the extreme by the constant sound of motorcycle engines outside the family home. Sammy Davis and W.O. had met on their machines at Avenue Road and had decided to use the street as a race track. The noise of the engines had annoyed Alfred to the point that he made his feelings known in no uncertain manner, and there is reference to him having hurled the family Bible at the two boys in order to quell the uproar. In fact Sammy refers to the incident in his autobiography (less the Bible-hurling) and recalls that the Bentley family was beginning to see W.O. and his motorcycle as rather a problem. Frostick refers to a time when W.O. had become so unpopular with his parents that they dispatched him to a cousin for a couple of weeks, hoping that the change of surroundings would do him good. Sammy, who was ordered not to go anywhere near the Bentley home for a while, also makes the point that W.O. was known to disappear on his motorcycle for hours at a time, in pursuit of some secret adventure. If the Bentleys had any misgivings, however, they were short lived, and they accepted that the age of the motorcycle had arrived. Moreover, the family was a close-knit unit, and a very loving one at that, and any thought of a family feud can be firmly discounted.

W.O.'s enthusiasm for his motorcycle ultimately spilled over to his brothers to the point that H.M. and A.W. also bought motorcycles. H.M. purchased a Quadrant similar to W.O.'s, but A.W., who was always more romantically inclined and enjoyed a carefree and relaxed lifestyle, decided that he should have a Triumph. Triumph produced its first motorcycle in 1902 and designed its machines to be as simple and reliable as possible. W.O. could not resist wanting to examine every aspect of his brothers' motorcycles, and while he understood the Quadrant from personal experience, he was attracted to the Triumph's technology. A.W.'s machine had a magneto rather than a hot tube ignition, and the engine was fitted with a mechanically operated inlet valve.

Whenever the three brothers were together they talked of little else but their motorcycles; they ventured off together on Saturday afternoons and took part in Sunday runs. Both H.M. and W.O. were technically minded, but not so A.W. Where H.M. and W.O. appeared to worry about the smallest detail, their brother was more inclined to push such matters to the back of his mind, and set about enjoying motorcycling for more social purposes. He did, nevertheless, possess a competitive spirit, and after some persuasion encouraged W.O. and H.M. to enter trials and other events.

All three brothers joined the two essential motorcycling clubs of the day, the Auto-Cycle Union and the Motor-Cycling Club, as well as their local society, the North West London Motorcycle Club. It wasn't long before A.W., to the concern of his brothers, announced that he would attempt the journey from Lands End to John O'Groats, known then as the 'End-to-End'. W.O., especially, was quite perturbed by this idea, but A.W. was convinced that under the right conditions he could actually take the record for completing the journey in the shortest time. Perhaps if A.W. had had more experience of motorcycling W.O. might have thought better of his brother's plan, but this, coupled with A.W.'s complete lack of mechanical knowledge, convinced him that the idea was entirely foolhardy.

A.W.'s mind was made up nevertheless, and he could not be persuaded otherwise. Even when W.O. told him he thought it absurd for anyone to consider such a journey, 'especially someone who hadn't the least idea whether a cylinder worked inside a piston or vice versa', he remained resolute. Against all advice A.W. therefore set off on his mission, with both W.O. and H.M. convinced that he would retire en route owing to fatigue or mechanical failure. The fact that A.W. did complete the run despite the primitive state of some of the roads, a complete absence of signposting in some areas, and the fact that his Triumph lacked any sophisticated lighting, was all the more remarkable because he actually succeeded in beating the existing record. Arriving at Lands End, A.W. was tired but in high spirits. His casual approach to life had seen him through a particularly tough ordeal.

Roads then were not as they are today; in fact road technology had scarcely advanced beyond the Roman era. In cities they were at least regularly swept and watered, but in rural areas they were potholed and covered with flints and horseshoe nails. Clouds of dust would be strewn into the air following the passage of a vehicle, and travelling in the wake of any wheeled machine or cart was very uncomfortable. Not only were motorcycles, and cars for that matter, still viewed with little enthusiasm by the majority of people, fuel was often difficult to obtain. While petrol was relatively inexpensive, it was substantially more volatile than it is now.

That the Bentley family had achieved recognition through A.W.'s record-breaking attempt prompted W.O. and H.M. to enter similar events. The year after his End-to-End success A.W. convinced W.O. that they should enter the 1907 London–Edinburgh trial, which was recognised as being one of the most difficult events in motorsport. This was not only aimed at amateur enthusiasts and it attracted professional riders, who entered with the support of a works' team or sponsor. As can be expected from such a competition the rivalry among the teams and participants was fierce, although there was a deep sense of camaraderie.

W.O. had deep reservations about entering the London–Edinburgh. There was his apprenticeship to consider, and arranging for time off to take part. Additionally there were preparations to make, and he was uneasy about competing without knowing that his motorcycle was in top condition. His misgivings about the escapade were all too apparent, and he confided in various people that he and A.W. must be mad to have even considered it. However, he eventually relented and allowed A.W. to enter them both in the event.

The trial was scheduled to be held in May 1907, this being the fourth year the event had been staged. From the very beginning it had attracted a popular response, and each year the competition became tougher. In addition to motorcycles there were now classes for both cars and tricars, and this alone gives an indication of the extent of the rally, which was a highly organised affair. All along the route, which followed the A1 via Biggleswade, Stevenage, Stamford, Newark, Doncaster, Wetherby, Newcastle and Berwick, there were checkpoints and controls, all of which were compulsory stopping places. The organisers ensured that the participants were cared for en route, with drinks and hot meals being available.

The starting point was near to the Gatehouse Hotel at Highgate, and the first entrants were dispatched soon after 10pm on the Friday night, overseen by chief timekeeper F.T. Bidlake, a respected cyclist and motorist. The rally had already attracted a lot of interest, and as a result a large gathering of spectators had formed to see the entrants depart on their way to Scotland. Motorcyclists were the first to be flagged away, ahead of tricars, and cars were the last to leave. Once out of London cars and tricars began overtaking the slower motorcyclists, and the dust that was generated from the faster vehicles would have been unpleasant to say the least for those entrants that followed. Riding his 3hp Triumph A.W. got away to a good start despite the weather, which was unusually cold for mid-spring, and he kept up the momentum through to the finish.

W.O., however, was not so lucky. Having initially achieved a good pace he began to lose the speed he had maintained, which after a time compromised his position in the field. With his optimism waning he must have wondered if his debut in motorsport was really worth the effort, and whether he might be better off doing something considerably less energetic and more profitable.

He did at least manage to keep to the schedule and check in at the control points, but only with the narrowest of margins to spare, which left him no time to stop for any refreshments. The lowly output of his Quadrant meant that he had to pedal up every hill to maintain the best speed possible. Luckily he had put sandwiches, apples and some chocolate in his jacket pockets as emergency rations, and these kept him going. The route to Doncaster he knew well enough, but it was at Morpeth in Northumberland that he faced his first real dilemma. Not only was he tired, cold and hungry, and somewhat despondent, the tyre on his rear wheel went flat. Had it not been for a fellow competitor (his name was Baddeley, one of two brothers from Newcastle who had entered on machines they had built themselves) coming to his aid he would have surely retired from the race.

The flat tyre repaired, W.O. was soon on his way again, his spirits having been sufficiently revived knowing that with some effort he could still reach Edinburgh within the allotted time. Disaster struck a second time when, almost within sight of Edinburgh, the Quadrant's engine died. The fault was a broken wire to the contact-breaker but repairing it was not an easy task because of its inaccessibility. Frustrated and annoyed at getting so far and yet being thwarted, W.O., tired and dishevelled, refused to give in. His insistence on taking his motorcycle to pieces on various occasions in the past was to be his salvation, and he was able to effect a temporary repair. Spurred on by the belief that he could make the final control in time, he covered the remaining miles at the fastest speed he dared.

W.O. could hardly believe his luck when he crossed the finish line with minutes to spare before the control closed, making him eligible for a gold medal awarded to competitors completing the course on schedule. The arduous route and difficult conditions, not to mention a lack of proper sustenance for many hours, may have been the cause of misgivings at times, but at that moment success overtook all other feelings. That gold medal meant everything to W.O., and winning it helped to change the course of his life.

The limitations of the Quadrant were obvious to W.O., and although he persevered with it for some time to come, even taking a motorcycling holiday in Scotland with A.W. and H.M., he had made the decision to purchase a new and more powerful machine as soon as was practical.

With one success under his belt, W.O. decided he should enter other events. A.W. tried to convince him to enter the London–Plymouth 24-hour trial that was scheduled for mid-July. Again this was a Friday night start, and as he was unsuccessful in arranging any time away from his apprenticeship he had to forego competing. He was, however, able to afford a new machine, and chose a 3½hp Bell-Quadrant, so named because it was designed and built by L.W. Bellinger, the Quadrant hill-climb specialist. A one-off machine, it sported a lighter frame and more powerful engine than would otherwise have been found. The perform-ance was a total revelation compared to his old machine, and W.O. leaves us with the impression that he was more than satisfied with it. Neverthe-less, the quest for speed and greater power continued, and it was not long before he was looking for a more sophisticated motorcycle again.

It was September 1907 before W.O. was able to compete in any other official event; this time it was the Motor-Cycling Club's hill climb tests at Sharpenhoe Hill in Bedfordshire. The Sharpenhoe trials comprised two separate hill climb attempts, one at the greatest possible speed, which demanded performance with ability, the other at the slowest speed, thus calling for some pretty skilful bike control. The object was to have the maximum time difference, and while W.O. did not win the event, he received a silver medal, which was the reward for a very credible effort.

When W.O. and A.W. entered for the May 1908 London-Edinburgh trial, which like the previous event was organised by the Motor Cycle Club, success for W.O. remained out of reach. For reasons that were not recorded at the time, A.W. failed to participate, and at the last moment his place was taken by H.M. riding his brother's 3½hp Triumph. Leaving Highgate at some time after 10pm on the Friday evening – the starting arrangements had differed from earlier years with motorcyclists segregated from cars and tricars so that the former took a position on the right-hand side of the road while the latter contestants were on the left – the going was fine until Grantham, despite some reported spills on the uneven road surface at Baldock. Both W.O. and H.M. reported in for breakfast, and the two checked in at the Wetherby control, but after that W.O. was forced to retire, leaving his brother to continue to Edinburgh and claim a gold medal having completed the journey within the stipulated 24 hours and having the least penalty points.

Having failed to complete the London to Edinburgh course, W.O. decided that he should attempt the London to Lands End event that was held the following August. He did not ride his Bell-Quadrant, but took a brand-new Rex 5hp twin instead, having been greatly impressed by these machines in competitive events. While they were no more reliable than Quadrants, the Rexes had a reputation for being considerably faster. Their frames were recognised as having a particularly good design, and the 5hp twin was renowned for being technically advanced. There was a downside, however: Rex motorcycles, which were designed and built at Coventry by the Willliamson brothers, were all hand-made and therefore individual quality was known to vary. Get a well-balanced machine and it would offer outstanding performance, but other machines were not always so fine, and there remained a risk that it might not meet expectations.

W.O. was fortunate; when his Rex was delivered it proved to be everything that he had hoped it would be. Before riding it in competition he took time to practise so that he could improve his handling skills as well as discovering how to squeeze every last ounce of power from the engine. W.O.'s penchant for all things mechanical quickly led him to attempt some subtle engine tuning, but London streets, which even then were congested, were hardly ideal for testing the results of his endeavours. Encouraged by his friend Jack Withers, whom W.O. had met during competitive events, he found it more suitable to make for north London, putting motorcycles through their paces in the dark along the straight roads between Barnet and Hatfield. Years later W.O. recalled those heady days – or rather nights – and admitted that his and Jack's actions could certainly have been classed as foolhardy. Withers, incidentally, was an exceptionally competent motorcyclist and became recognised as an equally good driver in subsequent years. Not only did Withers remain a friend during the Bentley Motors era, but in the shorter term their friendship was also to have an impact on events.

The London to Lands End race with its severe time restrictions was renowned as one of the most arduous of trials, made more so by its 4am start on a Monday morning. The start was at the Berkeley Arms Hotel at Cranford near Hounslow, and W.O. and A.W. made the decision to stay there the night before the start of the event. (The hotel remains to this day, although it is now surrounded by housing and industrial estates and is close to the perimeter of Heathrow Airport.) Had it not been for the fact that the brothers could not sleep because of the revelry outside, A.W., at least, might well have been prevented from taking his position in the event. In the early hours the brothers dressed in their riding gear and went for a walk, calling on their way back to check the condition of their motorcycles. Whether it was a case of sabotage or merely an unfortunate incident is unclear, but for some reason all the oil had drained from the engine of A.W.'s Triumph. It took until 10 minutes before the start of the race to clear out the remaining old oil and refill it with clean oil. Even then the performance of the machine was compromised, for when A.W. was flagged away from the start line he left behind him clouds of thick smoke, and it was some miles before the engine was running as it should.

This was not an entirely happy event for either of the brothers. They had decided at the outset that they would ride together, to give each other moral and technical support, and as a result they both lost out on valuable points and time. Notwithstanding A.W.'s problems, W.O.'s Rex began to falter, not through any engine malfunction but because W.O. had chosen, in the interests of economy, to fit a set of sparking plugs that were already well used. Once he had changed the plugs the going began to improve, and progress was maintained until after Basingstoke. The poor road surface was the cause of many problems: thick dust choked the filter on A.W.'s carburettor, while sharp flints were to play havoc with W.O.'s tyres. Once into Cornwall there were further problems with W.O. experiencing a loose tappet, which prevented the exhaust valve from closing fully, and a further series of punctures that resulted from running over a horseshoe laden with nails.

Having eventually arrived at the Lands End control with some unwanted penalty points, the brothers decided it was in their best interests to ride back to Cranford separately on the second stage of the event. Both W.O. and A.W. experienced problems on the return journey, with W.O. having to rectify an engine malfunction en route. As it happened both brothers made it to the finish within the stipulated time only to find themselves disqualified because of a misunderstanding regarding the rules.

The Bentley brothers were under the impression that it was necessary to keep to a time schedule between control points and that making up for lost time outside set speed limits was not allowed. As they left the final checkpoint at Basingstoke they were told by officials that time limits had been waived and that they could proceed to the finish without fear of contravening regulations. Arriving at Cranford having ridden at full speed they discovered to their cost that the information given at Basingstoke had been incorrect, that time limits remained in force and that being ahead of schedule disqualified them from receiving an award.

Not letting this set-back deter him, W.O. immediately entered for the 24-hour London–Plymouth–London event that was scheduled to start within a couple of days. This gave him sufficient time to prepare the Rex, taking care to avoid short cuts as far as maintenance was concerned. His efforts paid off because he was rewarded with a silver medal.

W.O.'s passion for speed had become entrenched. Even the 5hp Rex, which had served him so well, now lacked the performance he enthusiastically sought. After studying manufacturers' catalogues and advertisements as well as talking among his motorcycling friends he decided to buy a new machine to run alongside his plodding 5hp Rex, and he chose the speed that the single-cylinder 3½hp Speed King Model Rex promised. He was so pleased with his new machine that he was determined to enter motorcycle racing events in addition to endurance events. He entered several more competitions with the 5hp twin, including another London to Edinburgh, and used the Speed King at the 1909 Shrewsbury Centre Six Days' Trial.

His first race on a track was the Spring Motor Cycle Handicap at Brooklands on Easter Saturday, 10 April 1909. Brooklands had been open for almost two years and was the result of efforts by H.F. Locke King to provide Britain and the British motor industry with a motor track. Built on land that had been owned by the Locke King family for generations, work constructing the track had begun in the winter of 1906 and was complete by June 1907, at a cost in excess of £150,000. A month before W.O. entered his first race there, the famous test hill with its series of gradients ranging from 1 in 8 to 1 in 4, which happily survives to this day, was opened. Forty-one entrants roared away from the start line; racing was neck-and neck and although W.O. performed creditably, he was unplaced.

W.O. returned to Brooklands with his Speed King on 31 July when he competed in the 5½-mile Junior Motor Cycle Handicap for machines under 500cc. Having put up a desperately good fight he was pipped for third place by having to concede a five-second handicap. Despite his disappointment, W.O. had proved that even at this early stage he was a competent if not formidable challenger on the racing circuit. Competing at Brooklands on an Indian motorcycle at the same time was a young man, Guy Lee-Evans, who was to remain both a rival and staunch friend. Lee-Evans's Indian motorcycle, a machine that proved to be a great force in competition, so impressed W.O. that he determined that he should some day own one.

Of all the motorcycle trials of the period none surpassed the excitement and charisma of the Isle of Man Tourist Trophy, first staged in 1907. W.O.'s application to enter the 1909 event cost him five and a half guineas, which represented a considerable investment. He was accepted, and it was with much excitement, if not some trepidation, that he set off with his Rex to Douglas in September.

By competing in the TT, W.O. could battle against some of the most respected riders of the day, and no longer did he feel that he was an apprentice in motorsport. The Isle of Man course was one of the toughest in Europe, and therefore attracted works' teams and their most formidable riders. Whereas the French could easily close the long straight roads of France for speed events, and the Italians could shut off the punishing mountain passes, the Isle of Man was the only place in Britain that could stage a road-race event, it having been outlawed on the mainland.

In the weeks before leaving for Douglas, W.O. spent as much spare time as he could afford preparing his Speed King Rex. He would have liked even more speed and power than his motorcycle gave, and since he was unable to invest in another new machine, he devised as many permitted tuning modifications as he could. Spurred on by his mechanical knowledge and expertise, W.O. fathomed that by introducing a degree of upper cylinder lubrication he could gain greater rpm and reliability. A particular problem experienced by W.O. and some other Rex users was that the engine's piston had a tendency to seize when being subjected to sustained high speeds. A straightforward modification to the engine oil feed arrangements substantially reduced the risk of seizure. Moreover, when W.O. advised the makers of the Rex of the benefits of his modification they adopted it as standard throughout production.

W.O. arrived on the Isle of Man a week ahead of the TT start. His aim was to fully acquaint himself with the course and to practice in accordance with the regulations, which restricted the competitors from the circuit after 10am on weekdays and at all times at weekends in the interests of the island's resisdents, who were known to complain about the disruption caused by the build-up to the race. On the Monday morning, therefore, there was a rush by the TT entrants to try out their machines, but wet conditions the night before meant that some of them decided to wait until the following day, as the road surface was not at its best. Being impatient, W.O. was resolved to take to the road in any event, and as a result of the slippery surface suffered a nasty spill which, in addition to shaking him rather badly, damaged his machine. Happily other Rex riders came to his rescue, and between them they managed to repair the damage in time for the TT race.

All expectations of winning a place in the TT on his Speed King were dashed when W.O. crashed on the first lap of the race. Despite practice and having made a preliminary examination of the course as well as taking advice from more experienced riders, W.O. failed to anticipate a damp surface on a bend generated by moisture from overhanging trees. Halfway round the bend and travelling at 50mph, he felt his bike slide beneath him and knew there was absolutely nothing he could do but wait for the collision with a dry stone wall. With his pride dented he emerged from the experience winded, with no more than a few superficial scratches and minor bruising. More serious was the condition of his bike: the rear wheel was buckled and had fouled the forks of the frame so that it was unable to revolve. Unable to effect any repair W.O. had no choice but to admit defeat and retire from the race. The accident could have been far worse, and in true W.O. fashion he put the event behind him, becoming all the more determined to succeed next time around.

W.O. had become absolutely smitten by Indian motorcycles. There is little doubt that Guy Lee-Evans was largely responsible for this, W.O. having the highest respect for him, both as a rider and a technician. The two shared a penchant for tuning their bikes, and W.O. took Lee-Evans's lead as he recognised the extent of his expertise. Not only was the Indian technically advanced with its chain drive (almost everyone else used belts), it was superbly quiet but extremely powerful. Above all, it demonstrated terrific performance. While deciding whether or not he could afford an Indian, W.O. entered his Rex for two races at Brooklands early in October 1909. These were the last events that he competed with the machine, and the fact that he was unplaced in them confirmed his decision to buy a new motorcycle. The Rex, despite its fine service and the fact that it had convinced W.O. that he had a future in racing, no longer had the speed or power to compete with more modern bikes.

W.O. purchased his Indian at the end of 1909 with a view to entering competitive events during the early months of the following year. 1910, incidentally, happened to be the final year of his apprenticeship with the GNR. The machine in question was the very latest then available from the American manufacturer, and was specified with a 638cc 5hp V-twin engine. The price of the machine was £52, which at the time represented a considerable investment.

Designed by Carl Oscar Hedstrom and built in conjunction with George M. Hendee, Indian motorcycles were first made in 1901 and quickly acquired a fine reputation. After 1903 when Harley-Davidsons came on the scene there was much rivalry between the two makes. The model that W.O. purchased was fitted with mechanically operated inlet valves and detachable cylinder heads, along with side exhaust valves. Of robust nature, the frame was of the loop variety and sported a unique design of cradle spring front forks, trailing links being supported by a quarter-elliptic leaf spring. Modern features included twist-grip controls which eliminated having to remove hands from the handlebars, something that riders found extremely useful, especially when it came to racing.

'Astonishingly fast' was W.O.'s description of the Indian. He also found the machine to be delightful to ride. The performance compared to the Rex, and indeed the Quadrant, was outstanding, and W.O. considered this to be the most up-to-date and technically advanced bike available. He was in good company in this, as Guy Lee-Evans also acquired a similar machine. Among experienced riders Indians were understandably popular, and a good showing of the latest machines was present at the January meeting of the ACU Quarterly Trials. The course of the event was from Uxbridge, the starting point being the Chequers Hotel in the High Street, an old coaching inn that was demolished in around 1959, through to Banbury, the route following the A40 road for much of the way. Dashwood and Rectory hills en route provided observed hill climbs, both of which called for some pretty expert manoeuvring given the severe wintry conditions. W.O. did well at that meeting, scoring 190 out of a possible 200 points. Moreover he was one of the few riders not to experience a spill on the icy surfaces.

A couple of months later, in March, W.O. was racing at Brooklands with his Indian. Prince Francis of Teck, brother of Princess Mary, who within months was to become Queen Mary, attended the meeting. As patron of the Brooklands Motor Cycle Racing Club, Prince Francis's appearance was the first time that a member of the British royal family had attended a motorcycle event, and his presence brought huge support to the race track. Success was again on W.O.'s side, and his expertise qualified him into second place.

Second place was also his reward in the race that immediately followed, which was conducted complying with the regulations that had been set for the 1910 TT. The only diversion from earlier TT ruling was that the motorcycles were permitted to run with touring equipment removed, and the machines on the grid were therefore devoid of mudguards and lamps.

W.O.'s Indian was one of three entered for the race, Lee-Evans's and C.E. Bennett's being the others. After an exciting start W.O. was in third place at the end of the first lap, the remaining Indians taking first and second positions. When he saw an opportunity to roar into second place he did so, maintaining that position until the chequered flag. It was a promising win for Indian machines, which took the first three places, Lee-Evans in first place.

Easter was at the end of March and W.O. was able to enter the Brooklands Easter Monday race. He was competing against some very formidable and experienced riders, and that he managed seventh place was to his credit. Some three weeks later he attended the second BMCRC meeting at Brooklands, where he challenged old rivals Lee-Evans and H.H. Bowen. He would have liked to better his second placing of a few weeks earlier but had to be content at coming in third, a creditable result in view of the times that were achieved.

Three further meetings were scheduled before the TT event in May. W.O. won a gold medal at the Princes Risborough Hill Climb on 1 May, beating several professional riders. At the BARC meeting at Brooklands four days later he was disappointed at having to retire because of a rear tyre failure. Another meeting for BMCRC members in early May saw W.O. in action again, but as in the previous event he failed to finish.

Despite the two setbacks he was looking forward to the end of the month and the Isle of Man TT, scheduled for 26 May. His confidence was such that as an independent competitor he felt that, circumstances permitting, he could better the performance of professional riders and official works' teams.

When W.O. arrived on the Isle of Man he was instantly welcomed into the Indian works' team headquarters. It mattered little that he remained an independent, and as far as the works' team members were concerned, all that really mattered was that an Indian should win. W.O. was therefore offered the best hospitality along with the benefits of the expertise and facilities the team had at its disposal.

As it happened, preparations for the TT got off to a bad start as far as W.O. was concerned. At a practice session a scuffle broke out when a farmer caused chaos by insisting on using the assembly area for his own requirements. Just when the course officials thought they had brought the situation under control, the farmer's pony, which had become separated from its harness with the cart it was pulling, reared up on its rear legs, bringing its front feet down on W.O.'s machine and damaging the number plate.

It seems that some of the riders were paying more attention to other attractions the island had to offer than to practising on the course. When several competitors developed relationships with certain island girls the ensuing flirtations were the subject of some scandal, which the island newspaper was delighted to report. As for W.O., he was committed to producing the best result he could, and thought his Indian among the fastest machines present.

When at last the TT was under starter's orders, W.O. was fifth away. Determined to put in as good an effort as he dared, he was virtually flying along when he almost came to grief at Ballig Bridge. W.O. was going so fast that when he hit the humpback bridge his machine took off. Landing awkwardly he swerved and weaved along the road for some distance before regaining proper control.

Having completed lap one with no further worries, W.O. entered lap two with aggression. While roaring down Creg Willey's Hill the rear tyre on his bike burst. The situation could have been disastrous, especially as his machine, now out of control, hit a policeman and sent spectators tumbling. Fortunately neither the policeman nor the spectators were injured, and W.O. was able to bring his Indian under control and come to a halt. The tyre was so badly damaged with the inner tube and tyre caught around the rim that he had no alternative but to retire, frustrated and annoyed that the equipment had failed him.

What he did not know was that other Indian riders were also experiencing tyre problems. The vulcanising of the tubes was not up to standard, and one by one they ripped apart.

All was not lost though. W.O. stayed on the Isle of Man for a couple of days to relax, and with Guy Lee-Evans he played cricket, a TT Eleven against the local side. This he enjoyed immensely and took the opportunity to plan future competitive motorcycle events. The remainder of the racing season was, however, uneventful – W.O. had still failed to achieve what he had set out to do, win races.

There is every indication that the TT debacle, together with not performing as well as he had hoped in subsequent meetings, had led W.O. become somewhat disenchanted with the Indian. In notes that have survived him, W.O. was at one time full of praise for the machine, but this is contradicted elsewhere and he wrote of parting with it.

It was in the aftermath of the unlucky TT that W.O. considered his future. His apprenticeship was almost over, and he no longer felt as committed as he once had to the railway industry. There was not only the question of finding a suitable position with an adequate salary, something else was now preoccupying his mind: the internal combustion engine. His experience with motorcycles had given him an insight into motor engineering generally, and the motor car in particular.

The realisation that the railway industry offered little in the way of prosperity both in monetary and creative terms left W.O. in a state of some disquiet. It worried him little that he had accomplished an apprenticeship and had gained an excellent understanding of engineering that he could not put to immediate good use – his philosophy of life saw to that.

What constituted the best direction, he considered, was a position in the motor industry, in any area.

W.O.'s experience in competitive motorsport had given him many introductions and he used these to explore the possibility of suitable employment. Among his first contacts was a friend he had got to know through motorcycle racing events who was on the staff of *The Autocar*, E.M.P. Boileau, who offered to make a number of enquiries on W.O.'s behalf. W.O. had already gained a reputation for being as good an engineer as he was a motorcyclist, and he was regarded as having an astute nature. Boileau's efforts quickly bore fruit and he was able to put his friend in contact with the general manager of the National Motor

Cab Company, which was based at Hammersmith in west London, whose name was Greathead.

W.O. was 22 years of age when he was invited by Greathead to an interview. That he presented himself well there is no doubt, for he was appointed there and then to work under the direction of E.C. Esse, who was second-in-command and answered to the general manager. W.O.'s designation was somewhat vague but in effect was assistant to the works superintendent. Whereas Greathead controlled the company's finances and in name took overall charge, the day-to-day running of the firm's affairs fell to Esse. Esse, with his calm and efficient personality, took everything in his stride; even his tall stance, severe moustache and spectacles were the epitome of a business-like nature.

W.O. took to Esse immediately, and the feeling was mutual. Esse recognised W.O.'s abilities as an engineer and mechanic and saw that he had developed a particular skill in dealing with his fellow workers, something that was essential in the cab trade. The rapport between them was furthered when each discovered the other's interest in photography.

The cab trade was a complex arrangement and traditionally cabbies are a unique group of professionals. W.O. was appointed to oversee the daily maintenance of the cabs and to ensure that operations at Hammersmith were conducted with as much efficiency and economy as possible. The National Cab Company's fleet of taxis comprised some 250 Unic vehicles, these French machines being highly regarded for their reliability. French cabs had been part of the scene in London since the arrival of the first motor cab, a Prunel, in 1903. Mann & Overton, the principal supplier in the capital (and subsequently throughout the United Kingdom), had first introduced the Unic to London in 1906 and thereafter the vehicles were popular with both drivers and passengers.

By 1910 motor cabs were replacing horse-drawn hansoms (two-wheelers) and growlers (four-wheelers) at a rapid rate. The Unics in service with the National were painted a distinctive bright red colour and were the company's property. There were several other taxicab operators in London, some having considerably larger fleets than the National, and competition was fierce, hence the need to keep overheads to a minimum. Drivers tended to work for those operators that offered the most work and ran the most popular cabs; offend one or several cabbies and they would seek work elsewhere without notice. Such was the cab trade in London that smaller operators risked being taken over by larger concerns, and it was in the National's interest to remain financially buoyant.

The London cab trade has, over the years, been regulated via the Metropolitan Police under the direction of the Public Carriage Office. The design of the capital's taxicabs has been largely influenced by the 'Conditions of Fitness', a strict set of rulings that demand exceptionally high standards in areas ranging from the pattern of cabs and their maintenance to the licensing and training of drivers. It was within this regime that W.O. found himself. As it happened, his experience of the code of discipline of the railway industry proved to be a good basis for working in the cab trade.

W.O. recalled that the cabbies employed at the National were, on the whole, jovial and honest. As in all areas of life there were a few individuals who would take advantage of any situation if they could, and in W.O. they met their match for he was determined to put a stop to any malpractice. Cabbies were employed by the day or night, and as such were paid accordingly. The night shifts were generally quieter than during the day, after the theatres had closed and the West End trade had diminished, and were used to service the cabs in readiness for the next day. It was W.O.'s responsibility to see that that the drivers were paid their dues and that the cabs were properly overhauled in accordance with Public Carriage Office directives. No cab was allowed on the streets in a dirty or damaged condition, and each had to be maintained to exacting standards. Police had powers to stop any cab and check its condition, and if it failed in any respect it was taken out of service immediately.

On his first day at the National W.O. met those with whom he would be working. The two that made the greatest impression were Colborn, the foreman mechanic, and Hussein, a French mechanic. Colborn was a massive fellow and one that wouldn't stand for any nonsense; Hussein was an engineer with an innovative mind who was able to solve almost any problem that occurred with the fleet of Unics. He had one trait that W.O. found especially undesirable: he was addicted to absinthe. This made him, on occasions, quite violent.

In addition to the daily maintenance of the National's cabs it became W.O.'s responsibility to investigate fraudulent behaviour by a few less-than-honest drivers. It was obvious from the condition of some cabs, and their mileage, that there was some discrepancy between the fares carried and the income submitted to the company. To prove anything was difficult and the last thing that W.O. wanted to do was to accuse drivers, who would immediately leave and work for another firm. Experienced cabbies were difficult to find, which meant that they were always in demand. The situation came to a head when W.O. was visiting Birmingham and he recognised one of the National's cabs by its registration number and distinctive livery. When he checked on the cab's daily record log it appeared that the cabbie had only logged some 45 miles, despite having driven to Birmingham and back.

It emerged that a few drivers were leaving the Hammersmith depot at the start of their shift and driving into some quiet back street where they would change one of the front wheels. Taxi meters were operated via a scroll on the front offside wheel, and by changing the wheel for one without a scroll they could claim to passengers that the meter was faulty. The cabbie would then agree a fare with the passenger and pocket the money. When W.O. arranged for the scroll to be sealed and checked every 24 hours there began a cat-and-mouse situation whereby the cabbies would find another way to prevent the meter from working. The cabbies always seemed to be one step ahead, and at one time it seemed that they had got the better of W.O.

In recalling the efforts to quell the fraud, W.O. commented, 'We sealed the wheel nuts, sealed the (meter) cable, sealed half the nuts in desperation, until the cabs were going round with several pounds of dead-weight lead and wire on their chassis.' Months went by before W.O. realised how the cabbies were falsifying the meter readings. When examining a meter on one occasion he detected a minute hole in the meter glass which was just large enough to accept a fine needle. With the needle in position it was merely a case of delicately turning the dials to show a fictitious reading.

To drill such a tiny aperture in glass called for some intricate and skilled handiwork which could only be achieved by a handful of specialists. With the support of the National's management, W.O. employed an undercover detective parading as a cabbie. Once the cabbies were confident about the new driver in their midst they let him into their secret and sent him to a back-street merchant near to Kings Cross to have the meter modified. When the scam was brought into the open the drivers accepted defeat and got on with their job in the proper manner, there being no repercussions on either side. Nothing was ever said, and the cabbies and W.O. had mutual respect for each other.

Similar scams were probably fairly widespread within London's cab trade, but few taxi operators had the resolve or the resources to find a solution. W.O.'s dogged determination to put an end to the fraudulent behaviour says much about his character and his skills in dealing with what could have turned into a nasty situation. The National's stamping out of the scam would have been known to other operators, so it was futile for cabbies to move to other taxi firms to carry on their contrivances. The cabbies knew when they were beaten, but that did not prevent them from having respect for W.O., who might otherwise have been instrumental in the National proceeding with disciplinary action.

W.O.'s engineering skill was responsible for bringing in a number of money and time-saving measures at the National. He devised ways in which the cabs were off the road for shorter intervals than had previously been the case, and when it came to a vehicle's annual Public Carriage Office inspection, which meant detaching the cab body from the chassis, he negotiated lower fees with the coachbuilder employed to undertake the work. Among the servicing problems with cabs, and the Unics in particular, was the amount of wear on the gears. Instead of replacing worn gears, W.O. devised a method of simply welding on replacement engagement dogs. Fuel costs were always being looked at and W.O. was forced to spend hours adjusting carburettors to achieve the lowest possible running costs.

W.O.'s efforts at the National paid off. The fleet of Unics increased steadily until there were 500 in operation, double the number there had been when he had started work at Hammersmith. When he was not working he was generally enjoying life, living at home in Avenue Road and making the most of the available night life. Evenings would be spent at the Palace and Empire music halls and sometimes rounded off with a late supper at the Piccadilly Grill Room to the accompaniment of the famous 10-piece orchestra of David de Groot. On these occasions he would avoid hailing a National cab to take him home to Hampstead for he knew that his business would be the talk of the cabbies the following day. W.O. made a number of friends but throughout he maintained a particular friendship with Jack Withers, with whom he had spent so many hours motorcycling. Often during an evening W.O. would find himself at Jack's home in Maresfield Gardens, also in Hampstead, and there the conversation would inevitably involve motor cars.

W.O.'s experience at the National was partly to blame for his growing desire to buy a motor car. When he first went to work at Hammersmith he used his motorcycle every day to make the journey, but with earning a salary and having some money to spare, the thought of owning a car was more attractive. Until he had started work W.O. had been reliant on an allowance provided to him by his mother, which was funded through the inheritance of his grandfather, Thomas Waterhouse.

When he did succumb to four wheels, W.O.'s first motor car was a Riley 9hp, the company's first four-wheeler which was built between 1906 and 1907. Employing a centrally-mounted V-twin engine of 1,034cc, the 9hp specified a duplex chassis with parallel tubular mainframe and front and rear cross members. It was also the first car in the world to be fitted with detachable wire wheels as standard equipment. When new the Riley cost £168 with £2 10s extra for the detachable wheels. A spare wheel and tyre was priced at £7 7s, a pair of headlamps £9 9s and an electric tail-light set £2 5s. W.O. bought his Riley in 1910 or 1911, and although there is no record of what he actually paid for the car, it would have cost him around £100.

There is little doubt that the Riley remained one of W.O.'s favourite cars, despite its tricky handling. He did admit, though, that one always has a particular affection for one's first car. As a make of motor car the name of Riley would have been known to W.O. as the firm had long been associated with bicycles, firstly through Bonnick and Company and, from May 1896, the Riley Cycle Company Ltd. William Riley was much involved in the fledgling auto industry before the firm expanded into motor building. The firm supplied wheels to Hispano-Suiza, Mercedes, Napier and Rolls-Royce, and also built the first constant-mesh gearbox. Riley then undertook manufacturing of motor tricycles and motorcycles before announcing the 9hp. That the car displayed some pretty worrying characteristics is shown by W.O. recording that it failed to hold the road very well and suffered from the dreaded sideslip, a characteristic of a number of cars that caused concern among motorists at the time. Acceleration was reasonable, but as for comfort it left much to be desired, especially as it was completely open to the elements.

The Riley was kept for about a year, and after that time W.O. was pleased to see it go. He exchanged it for something rather different, a Sizaire-Naudin. Attracted by the free-thinking approach to engineering of the French, the Sizaire-Naudin was purchased from the firm's London concessionaires, Jarrott and Letts. A single-cylinder machine, the car always started and proved to be highly reliable and economical. Sizaire-Naudin was established in 1903 but no cars were produced until 1905. The firm's first model was unusual in employing a rear axle incorporating three crown wheels and one pinion, thus precluding the need for a gearbox. The chassis, too, was unconventional, and had front stub axles carried in guides, with a transverse leaf spring offering independent suspension. Sizaire-Naudins performed exceptionally well in voiturette racing, something with which W.O. would have been familiar.

W.O. was soon enjoying the all round improvement of the Sizaire; the two-seater's straight-line performance as well as the positive steering and excellent roadholding at speed. Working at the National Cab Company had provided him with a clear insight into engine tuning and it wasn't long before his fine tuning of the Sizaire's engine was paying dividends. When a four-cylinder water-cooled car was produced by Sizaire-Naudin, W.O. took note. Although he was unable to buy a new model he did eventually trade his single-cylinder car through Jarrott and Letts for a second-hand four-cylinder model. While it was well built and much faster than the previous type, W.O. expressed some disappointment in the vehicle and thought the engine to be noisier and less reliable than the single-cylinder unit.

Both A.W. and H.M. showed an interest in W.O.'s work at the National, and although the brothers continued to display a keen enthusiasm for motorcycling they also shared their younger brother's interest in motor cars. Despite having been trained as a chartered accountant, H.M. thought that he might be able to combine this with an interest in the motor industry. There is little doubt that his thinking was largely inspired by W.O., who by now was convinced that his future lay with the internal combustion engine and the absolute freedom that the motor car offered. A.W. also shared such beliefs and had already ventured into the industry in a mechanical sense. There is every reason to believe that had he lived (he died at the age of 28), A.W. would have contributed greatly to W.O.'s future.

Exactly what he wanted from the motor industry, W.O. wasn't sure. Despite being happy at the National and enjoying himself with the daily routine and challenges that went with operating a London cab company, he was nevertheless wanting something more stimulating and challenging. More than that he felt that he wanted to be in charge of his own destiny, working for himself rather than being answerable to others.

W.O. was approaching the age of 24 when his brother L.H., who was then 29 years of age, announced that he intended leaving farming, his chosen career. Farming, he had decided, was too much like hard work, and he had failed to generate any meaningful income from his endeavours. W.O. put his brother's lack of enterprise down to his managerial skills, or lack of them! L.H.'s decision seems to have affected the family as a whole, for H.M. began to try to find an opportunity for his brother in the motor trade.

As it happened, H.M.'s efforts brought little benefit to his brother. Leonard Holt Bentley had been exploring openings for himself, and in the first week of 1912 he found himself in negotiations with a new venture. He had seen a classified advertisement for the position of director for a firm that held the franchise as concessionaires for three makes of French motor car, namely Buchet, La Licorne and DFP. Buchet was a company known as much for its proprietary engines as its cars, which were small and medium-size machines built as four and six-cylinder models. Not particularly regarded for their performance, Buchets were well-built and nicely designed and therefore enjoyed some following in France. La Licorne (Unicorn) was the adopted name of those vehicles built by J. Corre in Paris. Popular in France, La Licornes were rarely found elsewhere.

DFP (Doriot, Flandrin et Parant) was established in Courbevoie near Paris in 1906, somewhat later than the other two makes. Auguste Doriot and Ludovic Flandrin had both worked for Peugeot and, later, Clément-Bayard when they set up in business together. They were joined by the Parant brothers, Alexandre and Jules-René, in 1908. Before 1908 the cars were sold as Doriot-Flandrins, and following the formation of the new company they were marketed as Doriot, Flandrin et Parants. Limiting itself to just three or four models, DFP acquired a good reputation for quality and reliability.

H.M. thought that L.H. might prosper from such a venture. The advertisement clearly stated that the opportunity would suit someone able to invest some capital into the undertaking, and L.H. was looking for a good business proposition. The firm in question was Lecoq and

Fernie, an enterprise that was tucked away in Hanover Court Yard, a converted stables positioned at the rear of a block of flats in Hanover Street within Hanover Court, and the registered address of Lecoq and Fernie was in fact Hanover Court. In addition to selling motorcars, the firm had other interests, G.A. Lecoq being chairman and managing director of Louis Vuitton Trunks, the manufacturer of suitcases.

H.M., it would appear, thought it pertinent to arrange and attend an interview with Lecoq and Fernie on L.H.'s behalf. The interview did not proceed entirely as planned. H.M. quickly discovered that Lecoq knew very little about the motor trade and had little experience of motor cars or the selling of them. He knew much more about suitcases and luggage, and appeared to be content making money from that enterprise. Lecoq was sharp-witted and probably wondered why he should be conducting an interview with H.M. when it was clear that it was L.H. who should have been opposite his desk. The reason why L.H. did not attend the interview is unclear, but it seems likely that H.M. thought he could assess the potential of the situation better than his brother. There was also the matter of farming, and L.H.'s difficulty in making any profit from it. The motor trade and farming were at opposite ends of the industrial spectrum, and a failed farmer seeking a future selling motorcars seemed odd.

Lecoq was unable to provide all the answers to H.M.'s numerous and penetrating questions and invited him to talk to his business partner, Major (rtd) Francis Hood Fernie. Compared to Lecoq's affable manner, Major Fernie was blustering and aggressive. He appeared to know as little about the motor industry as his partner, and H.M. suspected that he succeeded in running the affairs of the firm (not that well, incidentally) by intimidation and bullying.

From his interview with Fernie and Lecoq H.M. established that the two partners had little intention of continuing the franchise for Buchet and La Licorne, there being little evidence that selling these cars was financially viable. The DFP franchise was only just profitable, which is a wonder considering that absolutely no marketing of the car was undertaken, and therefore sales were minimal. That any sales were achieved at all is surprising, and somehow the firm survived selling, on average, one vehicle per month. The sales figures told their own sad tale: without any road testing or effective marketing, those sales that were accounted for were in response to word of mouth and the few mentions the marque received from time to time in Britain's motoring journals. What was intriguing was why Lecoq and Fernie had acquired the concessions to the three cars in 1911 when it appeared they had so little interest in promoting sales.

It was evident to the two directors that H.M. was a much more satisfactory candidate for directorship than L.H., whom they perceived as being someone unlikely to succeed in any business. A chartered accountant who could take over the reins would be all the more beneficial, thus leaving Lecoq to get on with selling his luggage equipment, and for Fernie to continue blustering around and getting nowhere. H.M. was approached there and then to consider taking up the directorship.

H.M.'s knowledge of the motor industry was such that he immediately realised that the DFP was under-marketed. As the car had a good reputation, and sales abroad were relatively buoyant, there was potential for considerably better turnover in the United Kingdom. It also occurred to H.M., and W.O. for that matter, that other foreign makes of car in Britain were enjoying a strong following, and that sales were extremely encouraging. With the right marketing and advertising, selling the DFP could be lucrative.

When H.M. returned to Avenue Road he was faced with a dilemma. He knew the opportunity at Lecoq and Fernie was quite unsuitable for L.H., but on the other hand such a position was eminently suitable for W.O., whose mechanical and engineering training suggested something far more challenging than the routine at the National Cab Company. As for H.M., he was in something of a quandary, for he also fancied the opportunity of buying into Lecoq and Fernie himself.

A family debate ensued at the Bentley home. W.O. was obviously very keen to acquire the directorship but conceded to his brother's seniority and financial astuteness. Both Emily and Alfred Bentley expressed a preference for their youngest son to take the directorship, on the grounds of his experience with automobiles and motorcycle racing, together with the useful contacts that he had made.

The outcome was determined on the toss of a coin. The fact that one person's future should be decided in such a manner might appear to be somewhat wild, but at the time it seemed fair and rational. Possibly H.M. had already accepted that W.O. was better placed to work at Hanover Court Yard, but nevertheless the outcome was going to be a gamble. The tense atmosphere can be imagined at Burbank House as the family watched the future of the two brothers being decided by nothing more than a coin that was flipped into the air. The time it took to reach its apex and fall to the ground must have seemed an eternity.

W.O. won the toss. His investment in Lecoq and Fernie cost him the substantial sum of £2,000, and instead of using monies that he had earned while at the National he dipped into the trust that would be his inheritance on the death of his mother Emily. It was therefore on 15 January that W.O. was elected as a company director, and he took up his position at Hanover Court Yard immediately.

In a number of respects his farewell to the National was an emotional affair. He had made his mark on the operating of the company and had acquired some good friends among both the management and cabbies. In his surviving notes, W.O. succinctly reveals his thoughts on saying goodbye to those at Hammersmith: 'I was to miss certain things at the National, but I was content never again to peer under one of those identical red bonnets at one of those identical two-cylinder engines.'

What should have been a stimulating first couple of weeks at Hanover Court Yard was in fact a period that was desperately depressing. It became clear to W.O. exactly why Lecoq and Fernie had advertised for a director, and in despair he watched his two colleagues conduct their business in a dreadfully sloppy fashion and with absolutely no regard for motor cars, the DFP in particular. Furthermore, to his dismay he found himself the target of Major Fernie's bullying tactics. W.O. stood his ground at being pushed around, and he soon discovered that his aggressor's antagonistic ways were a front to disguise the fact that he knew very little and did scarcely any work. His resolve to resist Fernie's harassment was the cause of some disagreement between the three directors, and Lecoq firmly refused to address the behaviour of his partner. However, on the plus side W.O. enjoyed the camaraderie of company secretary G.P. de Freville, a compulsive pessimist whom W.O. thought the one mainstay at Lecoq and Fernie.

The true extent of the moribund business selling the DFP became all too evident to W.O., who recognised the strengths of this quality French car with its sporting potential. In their native country DFPs were highly regarded, and for very good reason. They were ruggedly built and were capable of sustaining the harsh treatment of the poorly maintained French roads. They were also resilient to the severe treatment typically meted out to them by French drivers. After 1908, when Doriot-Flandrin cars emerged as DFPs, the cars were fitted with proprietary engines that were built by Chapuis-Dornier and were of 2.4 and 2.8 litres according to model specification. A single-cylinder model dating from former ownership remained available until 1910. DFP introduced the 10/12hp with a 1,592cc Chapuis-Dornier side-valve engine in 1910, and the following year this was joined by a 3,617cc 25/30hp model. The firm's fortunes changed in 1912 when DFP began building its own engines, the most highly regarded unit being the 12/15hp 2-litre. An ideal engine for tuning, the three-bearing crankshaft design was equipped with pressure lubrication and offered sparkling performance when mated to the specified four-speed gearbox.

During those formative weeks with Lecoq and Fernie W.O. was able to make an in-depth study of the DFP, and he acquired for his own use a 12/15hp that was in stock. W.O.'s perceptions of the car proved to be wholly correct, and he admired the vehicle's overall 'feel' and roadholding qualities. To use his own words, the two-seater coupé 'possessed the indefinable quality that makes certain cars a pleasure to drive, and always feel "just right".'

While W.O. set about examining ways in which to promote the DFP and build up sales, he was aggrieved by the complete lack of support and interest from his fellow directors. He guessed from their attitude that they would have been happy for him, having bought into the business, to sink to the same level of inactivity as themselves. Realising that if he did nothing to reverse the situation that existed he would quickly lose the money that he had invested in the company, W.O. consulted his brother.

In W.O.'s opinion DFPs had just as much sales potential as other foreign cars being sold by Jarrott and Letts and Warwick Wright. But with Lecoq and Fernie at the helm of the company there was simply no chance of success. During their discussions W.O. and H.M. concluded that Lecoq and Fernie might be agreeable to a buyout, and they decided to make an approach to the directors.

As it happens there is every indication that Lecoq and Fernie had hoped that such an approach would be forthcoming, and they were only too willing to discuss terms. Both directors were highly impressed by H.M.'s business acumen, and even in the short time that W.O. had been at Hanover Court Yard they had sensed his outstanding engineering ability.

Lecoq and Fernie were secretly delighted at the prospect of getting rid of the DFP concession, but not surprisingly decided to claim to be reluctant to lose an important and lucrative business. W.O. and H.M. knew that this attitude was no more than a front to increase the pair's bargaining powers and extract more cash from the potential buyers. Lecoq and Fernie's reluctance to part with the DFP business was in no way convincing, and H.M., taking the lead in negotiations, tried hard to secure the best deal possible. Negotiations on the vendors' part could have been completed quite easily and quickly had they not chosen to wrangle to an exasperating degree.

They seemed to treat the process as some sort of game. Each time H.M. and W.O. were sure that an agreement had been reached, either Fernie or Lecoq would introduce a new demand that would set discussions back.

Reminiscing about those negotiations W.O. once mused that the two directors were highly skilled hagglers who knew just how far they could take the brothers without losing the deal. 'The negotiations were interminable,' W.O. recalled, 'and before we had finished a couple of Lecoq's Vuitton suitcases became involved in the bidding.' It took two months to reach an acceptable deal: H.M. paid £2,000 for Lecoq and Fernie's shares, and in return the DFP concession was passed to W.O. and H.M., along with two suitcases.

With the £2,000 that was paid by W.O. to buy his directorship, he and H.M. were the directors of a £4,000 business that was to become known as Bentley & Bentley Ltd, Automobile Concessionaires & Exporters. Board of Trade papers show that H.M. was elected as a director of the new company on 14 February 1912, and that W.O.'s election was dated one day later. The certificate of Change of Name from Lecoq and Fernie Ltd to Bentley & Bentley Ltd was dated 19 July 1912, the new company having been formed two months previously. Throughout the business transaction Alfred Hardy Bentley (A.H.) conducted all the legal affairs, and as their solicitor remained legal advisor to Bentley & Bentley and subsequent concerns.

The sum of £4,000 in 1912 represented a considerable amount of money. Nevertheless the firm of Bentley & Bentley Ltd was under capitalised, something that was accepted at the time by the two brothers, who were convinced that by sheer hard work and their relative expertise they could provide a substantial income. Again the inheritance

udoun Road Station, South Hampstead, where W.O. would insist on being taken as a child to watch the
presses in and out of Euston. This picture dates from 1879 but the scene would have been much the same
the early 1890s. *(Martin Bourne)*

e Close at Clifton, pictured in 1898. All the Bentley sons went to Clifton, and W.O. attended the public
ool between September 1902 and July 1905. *(Old Cliftonian Society/Tom Gover)*

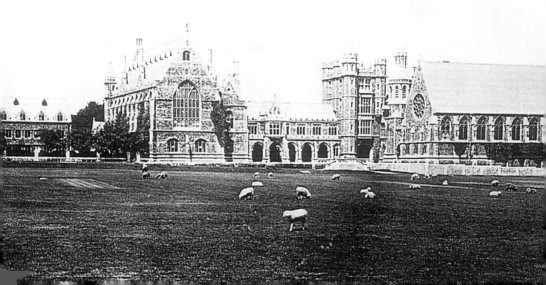

W.O. was passionately fond of cricket and he is pictured here while playing for the Clifton Eleven in 1904. *(Old Cliftonian Society/Tom Gover)*

Oakley's House at Clifton in 1905. W.O. is standing in the middle of the back row, sixth from the left. *(Old Cliftonian Society/Tom Gover)*

The Quadrant motorcycle with which W.O. enjoyed independence. His experience with the machine whetted his appetite for faster and more reliable motorcycles. *(National Motor Museum)*

When W.O. finished his apprenticeship with the Great Northern Railway he took a job with the National Cab Company at Hammersmith. This pre-World War One scene depicts London and its taxicabs at the time W.O. was supervising the National's operations. *(Author's collection)*

In 1912 W.O. and his brother H.M. Bentley acquired the franchise to sell DFP cars. W.O. decided one of the best ways to market the car was to enter trials and hill climbs and he is seen here with Léonie Gore, his fiancée, at the start of the Aston Clinton hill climb in June 1912. W.O. was placed first on time and formula in the Class II event. W.O. and Léonie were married on 1 January 1914. *(LAT Photographic)*

Following their success at the Aston Clinton hill climb with the DFP, W.O. and Léonie took tea with members of the Herts Automobile Club in Tring Park at the invitation of Mr Lionel de Rothschild. *(LAT Photographic)*

O. at the wheel of his DFP during practice for the Isle of Man TT in 1914. Next to W.O. is Leroux, DFP's ench mechanic, and the boy looking on is young Doriot, son of DFP's director in France. *(David Quayle)*

O. and Leroux travelling at speed near Kirkmichael while competing in the 1914 Isle of Man TT. *(LAT otographic)*

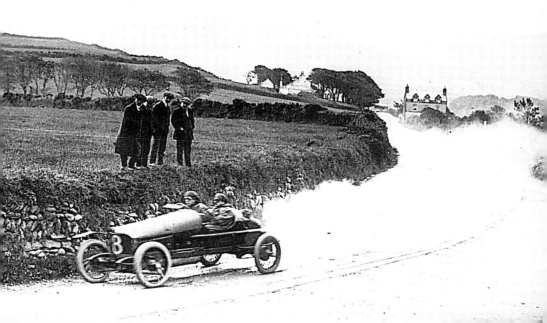

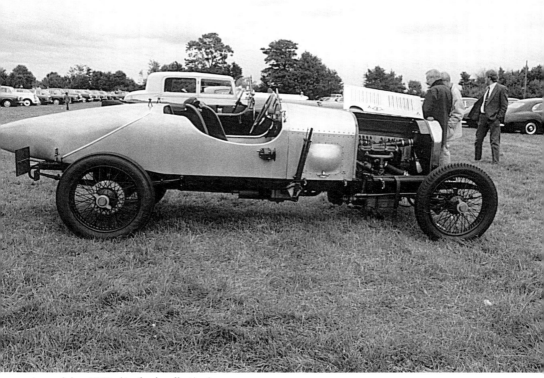

A surviving DFP. *(Author's collection)*

New Street Mews off Chagford Street, where the first
Bentley motor car was built, as depicted in 2002. Today
the premises are used as an office and small warehouse.
(Author's collection)

The plaque on the wall of the New Street
Mews workshop to commemorate the
birthplace of the first Bentley motor car.
(Author's collection)

No.16 Conduit Street. W.O., with F.T. Burgess and Harry
Varley, designed the Bentley motor car in a top floor office.
(Author's collection)

W.O. as photographed in 1919.
*(Jolyon Broad collection, source
unknown)*

The Bentley works at Oxgate Lane, Cricklewood. *(Jolyon Broad collection)*

Inside the Bentley works during the early days of the company. Stan Ivermee (with shock of curly hair) ca be seen centre right. *(Jolyon Broad collection)*

Freddie Gordon Crosby's depiction of a Bentley at speed at a time when the car had yet to be fully designe *(National Motor Museum)*

trust provided under the affairs of Thomas Waterhouse was tapped, which brings the need for some brief explanation.

According to the terms of Thomas Waterhouse's will, the bequest to his daughter Emily was to remain intact, and she should live off the interest for the remainder of her life. Obviously the family, no doubt with Hardy's guidance, overcame certain limitations.

The share capital in respect of Bentley & Bentley amounted to £1,000, of which W.O. and H.M. held £500 each. Along with the premises at Hanover Court the new company rented an old coach house in New Street Mews in Chagford Street off Upper Baker Street. The coach house was the property of the coachbuilding firm of J.H. Easter & Co. of Paddington, and it is there that W.O. established himself a workshop and vehicle servicing facilities. Happily the premises have survived and are now used as a small warehouse and business unit. On the exterior wall is a blue plaque commemorating the production of the first Bentley motor car in 1919. H.M. remained at Hanover Court to conduct the business side of the firm. H.M.'s secretary had her office alongside H.M.'s, and G.P. de Freville transferred from Lecoq and Fernie to be with Bentley & Bentley where he continued as sales manager.

W.O. and H.M. took over the DFP concession in March 1912 when they moved into Hanover Court. There is an interesting debate about exactly when the concessions for Buchet and La Licorne were disposed of: before or after Bentley & Bentley was established? From W.O.'s own notes it is quite clear that the concessions were given up before Lecoq and Fernie sold out to the Bentley brothers. Other sources of reference disagree, and Arthur Hillstead, who took over as Bentley & Bentley's sales manager when G.P de Freville resigned, is equally adamant that W.O. disposed of them very soon after taking over the company. There is every reason to accept W.O.'s account as Hillstead had not at that time joined Bentley & Bentley; furthermore, the moribund state of the business when W.O. and H.M. took over reinforces the fact that it was only DFP that had been of any interest to Lecoq and Fernie.

Whatever happened, the establishment of Bentley & Bentley at Hanover Court and New Street Mews was sufficient to engender great enthusiasm for ensuring some level of success. The brothers certainly had the right talents to make a success of the concern – financial expertise on the part of H.M., and fine engineering ability on the part of W.O.

As far as W.O. was concerned the venture was the most exciting that he or H.M. had yet encountered. Recalling those days years later, W.O. realised just how nervous the brothers had been at the time of signing the document. After all, a £4,000 business was quite substantial, even if the previous owners had been glad to rid themselves of it, and when they took it on it was so static it was almost dead.

If there were any misgivings on W.O.'s part he made sure that there was no evidence of it. Ahead lay a whole new future, Bentley & Bentley and the DFP motor car.

CHAPTER 3

Pistons and Aero Engines

W.O. was convinced that the only way to publicise the DFP was for the car to be seen in competition, and for it to be successful. It was essential to attract attention and acquire an impressive reputation, which, with the right marketing and advertising strategies, would promote the vehicle's reliability and performance.

During those first weeks the working party at Bentley & Bentley maintained long hours, such was the furious appetite for recognition and success. The target was to be able to show a profit, a marginal one even, at the end of the first six months.

Under H.M.'s direction Geoffrey de Freville ably supervised the DFP sales department at Hanover Court. He revelled in the new style of management, going about his duties with a level of enthusiasm that was not evident during Lecoq and Fernie days. De Freville, as it transpired, knew much more about DFPs than either W.O. or H.M. had first thought. Five years older than W.O. and the son of a Kentish clergyman, de Freville had received a classical education and his knowledge of French and German was extensive, which was very much to his advantage in business.

In the opening years of the 20th century the Long Acre Motor Car Company was the largest and best known of importers of foreign cars in the London area, and de Freville had joined its ranks in 1902. Four years later he was appointed manager of the DFP agency. That is the last mention of de Freville and DFP until the arrival of Lecoq and Fernie, when he joined them, complete with the DFP agency.

H.M. and de Freville tended to the day-to-day running and promotion of the business, and in so doing H.M. learnt much about motor cars and, essentially, the DFP. There was a complete transformation of the business: three models of DFP were kept in stock waiting to be sold. W.O. was equally busy promoting the firm and time was spent at New Street Mews preparing his 12/15hp for competition work. The workshop was carefully designed so that every aspect of servicing could be undertaken swiftly and efficiently under one roof.

Prices of DFPs started at £265 for the 10/12hp, which W.O. referred to as 'a pleasant enough little motor car with a well-raked windscreen and a fair turn of speed.' While this might have lacked some of the performance of some of the more sporting machines then available, it was nevertheless a desirable vehicle and one that was keenly priced. At the other end of the market was the 16/20hp, which W.O. virtually dismissed as a 'heavy, sluggish car with little more character than dozens of British-made competitors.' To an extent, therefore, this luxury car costing £550 in its most expensive form lived off the reputation of the smaller cars in the range, but was keenly sought by a select clientele whose demands were more for comfort than for speed. When buying a car of this calibre the customer received a vehicle that was furnished with the finest upholstery materials, including West of England cloth.

Looking back to early motor cars, hide upholstery was standard material, cloth being reserved for only the most luxurious vehicles, whereas today it is hide that is sought after by motorists selecting prestigious motor cars. In common with the motor industry at the time, the usual method of a purchasing a car would be to select a chassis, then to specify a preferred coachbuilder along with the desired style of coachwork. As far as Bentley & Bentley were concerned the coachbuilding methods and materials that were used were all-important. Chassis were imported direct from DFP at Courbevoie, and in order to provide the customer with the widest choice possible Bentley & Bentley were able to offer a standard style of coachwork in addition to that offered by bespoke coachbuilders. It was to J.H. Easter that Bentley & Bentley entrusted their coachbuilding, and from this the firm became closely associated with DFP and subsequently Bentley Motors. From the outset W.O. and H.M. insisted on the finest quality coachwork; to prepare a car to a customer's specification could take several weeks depending on requirements.

W.O. was justifiably proud of the efforts that went into supplying a DFP. Recalling those busy days just before the onslaught of the World War One, he remarked on the labour that went into building a quality motor car, and the fact that all the panel-beating was done by hand. The ash frames and soft trim were formed by carpenters and upholsterers who were dedicated craftsmen and the painting took weeks to accomplish, each of the coats being hand-smoothed with a pumice powder in a cloth bag (a 'pumice bag') and brushed before being finished off with multiple coats of varnish.

W.O.'s favourite DFP was the 12/15hp, and this was the model on which he based the company's fortunes. As the car was a four-seater, few even in its native country would have considered it suitable for sporting events. W.O. was soon to prove its ability to rival some other pretty agile machines, the 12hp Humber in particular.

Soon the company was in need of a mechanic to undertake the firm's servicing work and to prepare both new and second-hand cars for sale. That person's other task – and in W.O.'s opinion the most important – would be to work wonders keeping abreast with W.O.'s sporting commitments, and reliably keeping his car in race-ready condition at all times. Such a Man Friday was obviously going to be difficult to find.

Leroux – he was only ever known as that – was hired from DFP at Courbevoie and arrived in England ready to start work in April 1912. His knowledge of the car was unsurpassed, and whatever problem occurred he managed to produce an immediate solution. As far as the mechanical side of the business was concerned, Leroux was its backbone, always available and never shirking from hard work and exceptionally long hours. He got on well with W.O. and fitted easily into the routine at New Street Mews. He had an excellent understanding of the English language, and there is also evidence that he enjoyed a particular affinity with England and the English. W.O. refers to Leroux with much admiration and refers to him as 'a little wizard', no doubt because of the Frenchman's short and stocky stature.

The fact that Leroux had been released from Courbevoie illustrates the good relationship that Bentley & Bentley had with DFP. Monsieur Doriot offered the closest co-operation with the Bentley brothers and nothing appeared to be too much trouble. W.O.'s eagerness to compete in motorsport events was obviously of some amusement to Doriot, who saw his cars as sturdy and reliable family machines that in France would not have been considered for their performance. He was impressed, too, by H.M.'s advertising and marketing techniques, which did just as much to promote his cars as W.O.'s sporting exploits.

The DFP was put on the map, as far as W.O. was concerned, on Saturday 8 June 1912, when he entered his 12/15hp into the Aston Clinton hill climb near Tring in Buckinghamshire. The event was significant for a number of reasons, one of which was that W.O. enjoyed the pleasure of a companion. Leaving New Street Mews on a warm and sunny Saturday morning, and being waved off by de Freville, who showed none of his usual pessimism, W.O.'s passenger was Léonie Gore, Jack Withers's stepsister.

W.O. had first met Léonie on his visits to Jack's home at 49 Maresfield Gardens following evenings spent in London's West End. The Withers' residence was typical of those in Maresfield Gardens; large imposing Edwardian houses built of attractive red brick. Herbert Asquith, 1st Earl of Oxford and British Prime Minister 1908–16, also chose to live in Maresfield Gardens, as did Sigmund Freud, whose house is now home to the Freud Museum.

Attracted towards Léonie from the beginning, W.O. had only recently finished his apprenticeship with the Great Northern, and his tenure with the National Cab Company was in its infancy. The fact that he was at least earning a living, even if it was with a taxi firm, did at least afford him some credibility. J.E. Withers, Léonie's stepfather, let it be known in no uncertain terms that he expected more for his stepdaughter than W.O. could provide, and that in his opinion he was an unsuitable suitor.

Léonie's father, St George Ralph Gore (he chose to drop the name St George) was born on 21 September 1841 at Kingsholm House, Brisbane, Australia. The Gores were of minor Irish aristocracy with origins in County Donegal. Ralph married Eugenia Marion Caulfeild Browne on 6 April 1876; they had two sons, Ralph St George Claude and Irwin St John, and two daughters, Hilda Grace and Léonie Gore (Gore was a given name in addition to the family name, hence Léonie's full name on her birth certificate was Léonie Gore Gore, such practice being common in aristocratic circles), who was the youngest of the four children. Léonie has elsewhere been erroneously referred to as Léonie Withers, on account of her mother's second marriage to J.E. Withers.

Eugenia was also born in Queensland, Australia, in around 1845 and was the only daughter of the Hon. Eyles Irwin Caulfeild Browne. Her marriage to Ralph ended in divorce, and she married Jack Withers (senior) in 1894. Following the divorce, Ralph Gore returned to Australia, where he died on 17 October 1887 at the family home at Dunrobin, Brisbane.

In his customary fashion W.O. said and did little; he was resolute about his affections for Léonie and decided the only thing to do was to bide his time until the right circumstances prevailed. He was aware, too, that his attraction towards Léonie was not immediately reciprocated, although they acknowledged their Australian family connections. Léonie was two years older than W.O.; she was used to all the comforts of life that wealth, a secure home and a social agenda commensurate with upper middle class society offered. Had W.O. taken the courage to invite Léonie to some concert or dinner engagement, he knew only too well that his advances risked rejection. W.O. recognised that he was totally unable to maintain the standard of living that Léonie clearly expected, and wisely decided on the safest course of action: biding his time.

In time, W.O.'s standing at the National, his penchant for hard work and his sophisticated social life began to make a difference, and Léonie's mother and stepfather grew more agreeable to W.O.'s advances to their daughter. More acceptable still was the directorship with Lecoq and Fernie, and the subsequent acquisition of the DFP franchise in partnership with H.M. During this time Léonie became more receptive to W.O.'s visits to Maresfield Gardens, and she enjoyed the constant chatter about business and motor cars. The pair began to be seen together at concerts and other social functions, and they were on the invitation lists of many well-to-do and highly respected society people. At last their relationship was on a firm footing, and Léonie accepted W.O.'s proposal of marriage.

W.O. was in ecstatic mood as he and his fiancée headed out of London through Hendon and Watford towards the Chilterns. It was a gloriously warm day and the DFP was running beautifully. Content that Léonie was there to give him all the moral support he needed, he was as relaxed as he could be considering that the Aston Clinton hill climb was among the most important events of the season, and attracted some of the most experienced drivers.

The couple were dressed appropriately for the occasion, having called in at Dunhills on the Euston Road some time before the event to collect suitable attire. Dunhill in later years became more associated with smoking paraphernalia: the highest quality pipes, cigars and cigarettes as well as tobaccos and lighters. But at that time the company also specialised, like Gamages at Holborn, in motoring wear, and all self-respecting motorists patronised the store for accessories. Open motoring called for warm clothing, especially in winter, and it was at Dunhills that one could obtain those marvellous fur-lined coats that protected every part of the body, from the neck down to the calves. Even summer driving called for protective jackets and trousers that were lined to keep out draughts.

Despite his confidence, W.O. was all too aware that this was his first motorsport event on four wheels. He knew that his car was in good fettle but he was nevertheless worried about what was at stake, for this was a time when only success mattered.

W.O. was familiar with the routine at motorcycle events and he was familiar with many of the competitors. Motorsport on four wheels was something entirely different, and it was the unexpected that that made him nervous. His worst fears were realised as soon as he arrived at Aston Clinton. There wasn't one person there that he knew, although some of the personalities he recognised through the motorsport journals. The familiarity and camaraderie that was evident among the competitors made him feel an outsider, and the stress of the situation was only relieved when H.M. arrived, having travelled from London to give his brother an extra measure of support.

Looking around at the participating vehicles, W.O. was gratified to note that the majority of them were foreign makes, which boosted his confidence in the DFP's marketing potential. British machines that were represented included Arrol-Johnstons, Straker-Squires and Vauxhalls. A couple of Humbers were in evidence, one of them being driven by that firm's test driver, W.G. Tuck, who enjoyed a formidable reputation. Of the foreign machines, W.O. noted the French Chenard-Walckers, De Dions, Hurtus, Vinots and the little-known Le Gui. There were German Stoewers (which were never fully appreciated in their native homeland but nevertheless remained in production until 1940) and Oryxs, the latter having been taken over by Dürkopp in 1909. Other machines to be reckoned with included Talbots, Hispano-Suizas and Austro-Daimlers. Fully aware that some of the machines were consistently good performers in competition, W.O. was depressed to the extent that he wondered if he was doing the right thing in participating.

W.O. and his DFP were included in the 2-litre Class Two category, along with Tuck and his Humber. Tuck was ultimately disqualified, his Humber being fitted with a non-standard touring type body. *The Autocar* carried the following paragraph which said of the car: 'It was of the very low rakish two-seater type, with the cushions practically on the floor boards… there was no dashboard, the scuttle being open right through to the engine, and the wings were certainly inadequate, being only a little wider than the wheels.' Tuck's feelings at being eliminated from the event can be imagined – he had been favourite to take the lead.

If Léonie sensed her fiancé's apprehension, she refrained from showing it, giving him as much confidence and support as she could. H.M. was also supportive but nevertheless worried on his brother's behalf. To add to his anxiety it was obvious that some very fast times were being achieved by one of the Vinot drivers, and also by Tuck in his Humber. Conscious that he knew little about the Aston Clinton course, and having no previous experience of such events, inwardly W.O. began to resign himself to failure.

As they got into position W.O. and Léonie, ensconced in the cockpit of the DFP, watched the 2-litre cars get away from the start line. There could be heard the burbling roar of flat-out acceleration from the exhausts that every competing driver instantly recognizes. And in the wake of each car a cloud of dust billowed into the air. All too soon it was the turn of the DFP.

W.O.'s experience of hill climbs in motorcycling days proved extremely useful, and watching the other competitors he decided that he needed an early and fast change from first to second gear at very high engine revs in order to combat the initial steep gradient for which Aston Clinton was renowned. Waiting for the flag, W.O. edged the DFP to the white line, pulled on the handbrake and fixed his goggles over his eyes. Watching intently for the flag to drop he was away, flicking the gear lever into second without use of the clutch and keeping the engine speed as high as he dared. As the gradient levelled off he changed up to third and kept his foot hard down on the accelerator as he negotiated the first left-hand bend; still at full revs he took the next incline and the right-hander beyond, and then the finish line came into view.

It was all over. His first test in a four-wheel motorsport event had gone pretty well to plan, but it was the time that mattered more than anything. Hill climbs are all about split-second timing, and a tenth of a second can be the difference between success and failure. But Leroux had worked his magic with the DFP engine; incredibly W.O. made the fastest time of the day at his first attempt and, moreover, he established a new record at Aston Clinton for 2-litre cars.

Léonie was as ecstatic about the result as W.O. She had enjoyed every second of the hill climb, despite the discomfort, and once over the finish line she smiled at him through a mask of grey dust. No longer did W.O. feel alienated; those at Aston Clinton were quick to congratulate him, including Tuck whose Humber had been pipped at the post. It must have been a gruelling blow to Tuck to lose to someone whose experience of hill climb motor trials was, until that moment, non-existent. H.M., too, was on hand to offer congratulations, and there was huge excitement. W.O. left Aston Clinton that afternoon all the wiser, but he was very much aware that Tuck would want to have his revenge for the defeat.

On their return from Aston Clinton competitors were invited to take tea in the grounds of Tring Park, Lionel de Rothschild's home, the occasion adding to the social atmosphere of the event. There is every reason to believe that W.O.'s success was the subject of popular discussion. The event had been something of a family occasion, for Jack Withers had also competed, driving his 27.3hp Austro-Daimler in Class IV to finish in second place.

There was huge elation at New Street Mews and Hanover Court the following Monday morning. Geoffrey de Freville was waiting to greet W.O. and was full of enthusiasm. So was Leroux, who was waiting anxiously to prepare the DFP for W.O.'s next competitive meeting and continued success. The events that weekend proved to be a good launching point for some much needed advertising and publicity, and Bentley & Bentley made the most of the interest surrounding W.O.'s efforts. The DFP, along with accompanying testimonials, took pride of place in the Hanover Court showroom, and a few days later there emerged in the motoring press some advertising praising the performance of the car. For those motorists with a penchant for sport the publicity provoked real interest, which was also noted by a number of motor distributors who saw potential in selling the DFP.

In the period between establishing Bentley & Bentley and his success at Aston Clinton, W.O. had spent much of his time touring the country encouraging motor traders and distributors to sell the DFP. This was something that he found immensely difficult, mainly because he did not possess the flamboyant manner that was often evident in salesmen in the motor trade and other industries. For all his shyness and reserve, however, his genuine character revealed his true personality. The fact that he understood engineering and could talk to company executives at the highest level gave him powers of persuasion that most sales representatives would have found difficult to equal, making him a pretty fair, if unconventional, salesman.

W.O. travelled the length and breadth of the country meeting dealers in dimly lit and smoky hotel bars. Being away from London, his brother H.M. and the hub of the business, not to mention Léonie, did not make for an easy life. There was, however, a good measure of success: dealers were recognizing that the DFP represented a solid financial proposition, and a substantial number of orders began arriving at Hanover Court.

Motoring journalists began to show an interest in DFPs and they were as intrigued by W.O.'s sporting prowess as they were by Bentley & Bentley's advertising. Requests for test cars were received and the reviews that followed made for happy reading, which caused the atmosphere at Hanover Court to become cautiously optimistic. Further advertising was arranged, which really did put a strain on the firm's finances, but this was nevertheless considered essential if the momentum of sales was going to continue.

W.O., meanwhile, was anxious to be at the forefront of competitive events. That same desire to participate in racing he had discovered during his motorcycle days had returned, and he restlessly awaited a proper battle with Tuck and his Humber. He wanted a more sporting car for this test, and W.O. was sure that a car with a purpose-designed lightweight body that met his specifications would enable him to gain extra performance.

W.O. believed Harrisons of Stanhope Street to be among the finest of the London coachbuilders. He approached the firm to build him a two-seater streamlined narrow aluminium body for the 12/15hp DFP. Seeing the coachwork in the latter stages of completion and mounted to the chassis, W.O. remarked that the car looked quite formidable, especially with its streamlined tail and disc wheels. As soon as the vehicle was delivered to New Street Mews, Leroux set about modifying the engine, increasing clearances where necessary and raising the compression.

W.O.'s objective was to take the Class B records from Tuck and his Humber. He practised at Brooklands, his lap times indicating speeds approaching 70mph. Under the right conditions and with fine engine tuning he was sure he could achieve better results. DFPs were entered by others into a number of hill climb events during the remainder of the 1912 season: the results were impressive with five wins and handsome publicity.

The Harrison-bodied 12/15hp was put to the official test on 9 November. W.O. took Leroux in the DFP to Brooklands where they were met by H.M. The speed trials were intended to satisfy two purposes, one being to gain valuable experience on the track to establish the car's potential, the other being to produce some valuable material for the forthcoming motor show. The visit to Brooklands was made shortly after an Arrol-Johnston, which was driven by Reid, a renowned driver, had toppled the record held by Tuck at the wheel of his works' Humber. The recent victory added to the sense of the occasion and inspired W.O. to challenge Reid's record for the 10-lap event, which stood at 60.5mph.

Colonel Lindsay Lloyd was timekeeper for the DFP record attempt, and apart from the usual officials the course was otherwise devoid of spectators. Following a number of practice runs, W.O., confident his car was up to scratch, signalled that he was ready and set off. The result was that he snatched the record from Reid, setting a new record of 66.78mph. This was seen as a fine achievement, especially for someone who was comparatively new to motorsport. Despite breaking the record, W.O. and his team believed that a better result could have been achieved, and although there was every reason to celebrate, they determined to improve their performance.

During 1912 W.O. and H.M. decided it was appropriate for Bentley & Bentley to join the Society of Motor Manufacturers and Traders (SMMT). The expense drained company resources, but it was necessary if the firm intended to exhibit at the London Motor Show. The publicity that the firm had attracted during the year fully justified them appearing at Olympia; no longer was it prudent to rely solely on word of mouth as a means of building recognition and reputation. Moreover, the company felt that exhibiting would capitalize on W.O.'s achievements.

The jubilation at Bentley & Bentley was marred by the sudden death in December 1912 of Arthur Bentley. W.O.'s words provide a fitting epitaph for the brother that had been responsible for his initial participation in motorsport: 'A wonderful personality who seemed always to be overflowing with vivacity and enterprise and high spirits.' Had A.W.'s enthusiasm not persuaded W.O. and H.M. to enter endurance runs with their motorcycles, then W.O. might well have remained in the railway industry. Today A.W.'s death could have been easily prevented. He had suffered an acute throat infection which would have been treated by modern drugs.

There was profound grief within the Bentley family. H.M. and W.O., who had spent so many hours in the saddles of their motorcycles accompanying A.W. on competition runs the length and breadth of the country, were particularly devastated by their brother's untimely and early death. A.W. and H.M. were next to each other in age, and there was a great affection between them.

Characteristically A.W. had left instructions for his ashes to be scattered at Achanalt in Ross and Cromarty, an area of Scotland that had been his favourite and where he had spent many idyllic fishing holidays. Such was A.W.'s romantic outlook on life that W.O. decided that he and H.M. should personally scatter the ashes, using the occasion as an endurance run for the DFP. A.W. would certainly have approved the adventure, something that W.O. noted: 'I knew the idea of a non-stop drive – at that time 600 miles was a very long drive – would have appealed to Arthur.'

W.O.'s diary for that trip provides a clear indication of the harsh driving conditions, and the level of fitness that was needed to endure such a journey. It was raining heavily when the brothers, H.M. driving, headed out of London in the dimness of a wintry afternoon. The conditions had not improved when a stop was made at Grantham, where the brothers filled up with petrol and went into the George Hotel in the High Street for a meal. When they came out, W.O. took over driving, stopping at Doncaster in the hope of replenishing the acetylene. Their search was in vain and they continued the journey with dimmed lights to Newcastle, where they arrived at 2am. Again they there was no acetylene to be had, so they were forced to continue to Berwick, where they took a short break before going on to Edinburgh.

With their supply of acetylene exhausted they had no other means of illumination other than a battery-operated torch, which they strapped to the DFP's front offside wing. Following a hearty breakfast and a refill of acetylene in Edinburgh, the brothers left the city in snow. They spent the entire day negotiating the narrow tracks, which were shown as roads on their map, that weaved northwards towards the Highlands. The route took them via Inverness, which they reached a little before eight in the evening, Loch Garve and Loch Luichart, and they arrived at Achanalt after some 31 hours of driving.

W.O.'s feelings about the drive were clear, although he and H.M. had arrived at their destination in an exhausted state, very cold and cramped. 'I think we had done the right thing,' he noted with some modesty. Notwithstanding the brothers' stamina, the reliability of the DFP itself is worthy of comment, for the car performed perfectly throughout its ordeal of a 1,200-mile round trip in less than perfect weather conditions.

For W.O. the unhappy period following A.W.'s death continued into the early part of 1913. There was, however, much to be optimistic about: the Olympia show had produced some worthwhile results, and the DFP's success at Brooklands remained fresh in the minds of editors and journalists. W.O. rightly concentrated on the competitive side of things, while H.M. and de Freville maintained the business of selling cars. With Leroux's mechanical expertise, W.O.'s DFP was again successful at Aston Clinton, and Bentley and his car were by now recognised as a force to be reckoned with. Shelsley Walsh was another favourite hill climb venue, and it was there that W.O. triumphed again with a time that bettered the majority of larger-engined machines.

W.O. wanted to challenge the most respected drivers of the day at Brooklands, and he realised this opportunity at the Whitsun Handicap held during the middle of May. Bad weather influenced the meeting to the extent that the Benzole and sprint races were cancelled. As for Tuck, he was competing with a new 2-litre Humber that attracted much favourable comment, the car having lapped in excess of 75mph to win the Ninth 70mph Long Handicap, the sixth race of the event. W.O. was among the 18 starters in his first appearance at the Motor Course at the wheel of a car, but failed to be placed.

Later the same day W.O. competed in the ninth race, the Eleventh 70mph Short Handicap, which was run over three miles. Tuck, still fresh from his earlier success, proved to be a formidable opponent and one that was difficult to challenge. As it happened W.O. had an astonishingly good race and held on to Tuck until the very end. Tuck, who spun round twice on the members' banking trying to pull up once across the finish line, conceded victory to Sydney Cumming. W.O.

recorded that he came second, but this is contrary to reports published in *The Autocar* and *The Motor*, both of which state that he finished in third place. Bill Boddy, in his *History of Brooklands Motor Course*, confirms that he came in third. In W.O.'s defence, he did record that the placings for second and third positions were very close!

The Autocar in its publication dated 17 May carried the following report of the race: 'This, as usual, was a very lively affair, but suffered by having too many competitors, whom it was next to impossible to distinguish. Tuck's Humber, having been penalised thirteen seconds and set back to scratch, made a fine show of speed and put up a wonderful fight with Bentley's DFP.' The report ended with the following comment: 'The Humber and the DFP were practically dead heaters.'

How to improve the DFP's performance on the track was the subject of many hours of discussion between W.O., Leroux and H.M. W.O. had confirmed that modifications to the DFP engine resulted in dramatically better acceleration, and a maximum speed well in excess of that of the standard car. During his record breaking attempts W.O., with the bene-fit of Leroux's tuning expertise, had not managed to reach speeds much above 80mph without succumbing to piston failure. Cast iron pistons were prone to cracking, and even the experimental use of light steel pistons usually resulted in broken piston rings. Keen customers were also asking how their DFPs could be modified to provide similar agility to W.O.'s car, and with this demand in mind W.O. travelled to Paris to talk to M. Doriot.

Doriot, who was quite bemused that his cars were so highly regarded by a number of British motorists, did not hesitate to agree to modifications being made to vehicles bound for export to the United Kingdom. He instructed the factory to raise engine compression and make improvements to the engine's induction system and carburetion. W.O. mentioned the idea of improving performance still further, explaining to Doriot that he planned to extend his racing activities with the DFP. Doriot was again surprised that his cars were being viewed by the motorsport fraternity as having levels of performance more associated with the likes of Humber and Sunbeam.

The real turning point in the DFP's racing career came when W.O.'s attention was suddenly caught by a decorative model piston that was being used as a paperweight on Doriot's desk. Clearly the item was made of an alloy material, and W.O. guessed it was a souvenir that had been presented to Doriot at some time. It was in fact cast in aluminium, and was made by the Corbin company, whose foundry undertook DFP's work. Doriot, seeing W.O.'s curiosity, offered the item to him for further examination.

W.O. said little at the time, but he was extremely impressed by what he had seen. Driving home to London he had sufficient time to consider the whole question of using pistons cast in aluminium, something which a number of engineers had tried but which had proved virtually impossible to perfect. By the time he reached Hanover Court he was convinced that this was the way ahead, but it meant converting a lot of people to the cause.

H.M., while hating to doubt his younger brother's integrity, urged extreme caution. W.O.'s mind was nevertheless sure that aluminium held the answer to the problem of the DFP's power, and would lead to substantially higher speeds. W.O. was aware that at the time the French automobile industry was promoting the use of aluminium, not only in coachwork, but also in engine components such as crankcases. It was universally accepted that use of aluminium in manufacturing certain components was giving rise to a number of problems of fragility and endurance. As far as W.O. was concerned aluminium had immense potential, although he accepted that lessons were there to be learned. France was by a considerable margin the largest European producer of aluminium, and was second in the world only to the United States.

Within days W.O. returned to Courbevoie, his intention being to discuss with Monsieur Doriot the possibility of acquiring aluminium pistons for the DFP. Although he was as polite and helpful as ever, Doriot nevertheless argued that the material was unsuitable, and said that the stresses involved for the application Bentley had envisaged would lead to the pistons disintegrating at around 2,000rpm. W.O. equally politely refuted Doriot's claims. He told him he that was wrong in his judgement, and said that he would like to visit the foundry for himself to discuss his ideas. Doriot reluctantly agreed to his request, undoubtedly because he could see that W.O. was not going to be swayed from his belief. After all, it was going to prove that one of them was right!

Corbin, who by this time was well aware of the DFP's success at Brooklands and elsewhere, welcomed W.O. to their foundry. Evidence exists that Corbin had been manufacturing aluminium pistons since

PISTONS AND AERO ENGINES

1910, and that Bentley was not the only engineer to recognise the benefits that lightweight pistons offered. Peter Hull, for a long time the secretary of the Vintage Sports Car Club, advises that while Bentley was the first to introduce the use of aluminium pistons in Britain, firms such as Chenard-Walcker in France and Aquila Italiana in Italy had already gained much experience in this respect. It is further claimed that Panhard-Levassor and Violet-Bogey had also fitted aluminium pistons to good effect.

Corbin listened to W.O.'s ideas and the pair decided it was likely that an alloy based on 88 per cent aluminium and 12 per cent copper would be suitable. Discussions led to Corbin producing some pistons for experimental work, and these were delivered to New Street Mews within a few weeks. Corbin had been very deliberate about the calculations, which prompted W.O. to note 'We never had to alter the formula by even half a per cent, and it remained as the standard right through the war and well into the 1920s in both aero engine and car engines.'

The arrival of Corbin's pistons caused some excitement at Bentley & Bentley. Leroux carefully fitted them ensuring there was plenty of clearance. The first results were encouraging and there was great relief when they remained intact at normal engine speeds. From the outset it was apparent that more power was being obtained than from the original pistons. W.O. decided to lighten them further, again with good results and increased performance.

Even the more cautious H.M. was by now convinced that his brother had been correct all along. In opting for maximum performance, W.O. decided to lighten the pistons still further, and at the same time increased the engine's compression. The outcome was just as W.O. had dared to anticipate – the pistons showed no signs of any problem. If there was any criticism it extended to nothing more than increased engine noise when starting from cold. Aluminium has a greater expansion coefficient than steel and was the cause of something known as 'piston slap'. Even after exhaustive testing everything seemed positive.

Monsieur Doriot expressed extreme pleasure at W.O.'s efforts, despite his doubts that the pistons would live up to the demands made upon them. He then received news that W.O. was to start trials of the re-pistoned DFP at Brooklands, which would surely prove their worth.

The Bentley & Bentley team arrived at the course to take part in the

August 1913 Brooklands Automobile Racing Club (BARC) meeting. The event was well patronised with some 219 entries, and gave W.O. his first motor race win at the venue. Again his challenge was to beat Tuck, and while Tuck's Humber lapped at 81.64mph he was forced into second place by W.O., who lapped at 75.12mph on an easier handicap. Tuck had his revenge by taking all the Class B records with speeds averaging 82mph, which W.O. was determined to retrieve.

Eventually he had his opportunity, but only after a long wait while A.J. Hancock attempted the 12-hour record with his 'Prince Henry' Vauxhall. (Hancock had to retire owing to mechanical problems but nevertheless had taken the two and three hour and 150 and 200-mile records in Class F, and the World's and Class F four to nine-hour and 300 to 700-mile records.) Driving 10 laps W.O. averaged 77.927mph, a considerable achievement when the opening laps were completed at speeds in excess of 80mph. The weather proved to be a problem though, and he was forced to drive at slower speeds in the heavy rain. Despite the conditions, however, W.O. was able to snatch some of the Class B records from Tuck.

A few days later W.O. returned to Brooklands to take the Class B flying half-mile, kilometre and mile records from Tuck. The best speeds achieved by W.O. were 82.38mph over the half-mile and 81.6mph over the mile. Moreover, W.O. was successful in improving Tuck's figures for the Humber over the 10 laps by some two miles per hour. Both he and H.M. were so confident of the DFP's performance that arrangements were put in hand with Doriot to begin supplying the 12/15hp with aluminium pistons. The cars would then be known as the 12/40 Speed model. The more conventional 12/15hp remained in the catalogue.

Getting the 12/15 to this stage of tuning had meant the Bentley team having to work exhaustive hours. H.M. had kept a watchful eye on company expenditure, and his prudence in ploughing profits back into the business had paid off to allow some careful expansion. It was obvious that Leroux was badly in need of some assistance, and in order to provide this, W.O. succeeded in persuading Doriot to agree to his son leaving Paris to work at New Street Mews.

With the London Motor Show looming, W.O. was anxious to have the 12/40 Speed model on display and to be able to take orders for the car. The 12/40 had to have subtle differences from the 12/15 to enhance its sporting appeal. This was achieved by removing the outer wheel discs to reveal the wires beneath, and mechanically the engine was specified with higher compression. What was not disclosed was the fact that aluminium pistons were used.

On the race track, the mechanical changes that W.O. had introduced gave him a huge advantage, and it was clear that his opponents were puzzled by his car's sudden transformation. He was confident that his new records would remain secure for the time being, at least for the duration of the Motor Show. Tuck, however, had other ideas, having undertaken further tuning of his Humber engine. At the Brooklands autumn meeting he reclaimed the 50 and 100-mile and hour records, the latter at an average of 75.78mph.

Not to be beaten, W.O. countered by storming around Brooklands, lapping at speeds in excess of 83mph between laps 3 and 11 before dropping to 82.5 and then to 82mph. The final laps (34 and 35) he took at 76.5mph owing to a low petrol level, but he then had to stop as the car had run out of fuel. His DFP had consumed only 4½ gallons throughout the 94 miles to reveal fuel consumption averaging 21mpg. W.O.'s rewards were the Class B 10-lap, the 50-mile, hour (at 82.15mph), and the 50 and 150-kilometre records.

The autumn meeting signalled the final speed attempts for the Bentley team at Brooklands for the year. The London Motor Show had presented W.O. and H.M. with a heavy work schedule and, moreover, W.O. insisted that serious work was necessary to prepare the DFP for future sporting events. Leroux was kept busy modifying the engine, fitting two plugs to each cylinder, a Bosch dual magneto and raising the compression still further. To lighten the car's chassis, holes were drilled in it. Modifications were made to the transmission, W.O. having decided to fit the rear axle from the 10/12 model in place of the original type, and to use an open propeller shaft instead of a torque tube. An accident at Brooklands, in which racing driver Percy Lambert had been killed following a burst tyre on his Sunbeam, caused W.O. to do away with the differential. Lambert's car had gone into a skid and overturned, and W.O. surmised that, had the car not been fitted with a differential, the driver might well have survived.

There were arguably more important things on W.O.'s mind during the closing weeks of 1913. He was to be married to Léonie Gore on New Year's Day 1914. W.O. was 25 at the time of his wedding, Léonie 27. The ceremony was conducted at the Parish Church of St John,

Hampstead, and the signing of the register was witnessed by Léonie's brother Ralph St George, and W.O.'s close friend, best man and now brother-in-law Jack Withers.

The wedding was a social occasion in the best tradition. The bride wore a robe of charmeuse trimmed with embroidery, and a court train of brocaded velvet with ropes of pearls at the shoulders. Her two young nieces, Joan and Barbara Grigg, acted as bridesmaids. The reception was held at the Withers' home in Maresfield Gardens, and after the ceremony the newly-married Bentleys enjoyed a short honeymoon before moving to 38 Netherhall Gardens in Hampstead. (It is coincidental that while serving his apprenticeship in Doncaster W.O.'s lodgings were in Netherhall Road!) Newspaper accounts of the wedding claim that the honeymoon was to be spent motoring in France, but W.O.'s records reveal that he and Léonie actually honeymooned in the West Country.

The imposing house in Netherhall Gardens was similar in size and architecture to those in Maresfield Gardens, the roads being parallel. In a highly desirable area of London, properties in the vicinity were at a premium then as they are now, and commanded considerable prices. Typically a house like the Bentleys' would have cost around £2,000, approximately £600,000 in present values. A large and splendid property comprising three storeys and a basement, it has in more recent times been converted into apartments. It has, happily, retained its period charm and has been made even more pleasing with the addition of a fine gated entrance and courtyard.

The short honeymoon, whether a touring holiday in the West Country or a trip to France, naturally involved taking a DFP. Léonie well understood her husband's desire to return to London in order to put the finishing touches to the DFP Special and to make arrangements for the new season's events at Brooklands. There were preparations to be made for the Isle of Man Tourist Trophy in June, and there was also the matter of marketing aluminium pistons on behalf of Corbin, Bentley & Bentley being sole British agents.

On St Valentine's Day W.O. returned to Brooklands with the newly-bodied 12/40 DFP. Leroux was there, as were H.M. and M. Doriot's son. W.O.'s aim was 'To finish the Humber off once and for all.' His autobiography provides us with a succinct image of what it was like to chase speed and endurance records, and he demolishes all perceptions that such challenges were romantic, despite the emotive reports that appeared in the press. To achieve the best results the weather conditions had to be exactly favourable, with the wind blowing strongly from the north-east to give plenty of help from behind along the straight. 'It was often a tedious business waiting for a wind that might give you an extra two or three miles an hour, and I just did not have the time to spare to hang around the club-house.'

The thought of waiting around at Brooklands in the hope of the wind changing direction made him impatient, and he asked whether it was possible to drive around the track clockwise rather than anti-clockwise. This put the course officials into a turmoil and they flurried around checking rule books. No one had suggested such a thing before. As there wasn't a rule that prevented lapping in a clockwise direction, W.O. was reluctantly given permission to drive around Brooklands the 'wrong way'.

The DFP's rear axle was minus a differential; the tyres were of the narrowest possible width and the camshaft had cam profiles to W.O.'s own specification. An extremely narrow single-seater body was fitted and was characterised by a well-cowled radiator. Following a number of practice laps W.O. returned to the pits to report to Leroux and H.M. Travelling in the opposite direction proved to be satisfactory, although he did remark that care was necessary when coming down the banking towards the fork and negotiating the rough surface.

Impatience got the better of him, and deciding that he couldn't wait any longer, W.O. set off in pursuit of the speed record. The result was outstanding: not only did he take the flying half mile at 89.70mph, he claimed the kilometre, mile and 10-mile records for his class, bettering even the Class C records. 'I survived the bumps and that nasty turn, and the single-seater behaved faultlessly' he recalled afterwards.

While W.O. and Tuck battled in other areas of motorsport, not always to W.O.'s benefit, Tuck did concede the Class B records to his rival. Jack Withers, having competed in an Austro-Daimler at the 1912 Aston Clinton hill climb, joined forces with his brother-in-law on a number of occasions driving a 12/40 DFP. Bentley and DFP had reached a point where they were synonymous, and in terms of publicity W.O. had earned an enviable reputation.

Despite the demure size of the DFP compared to some other sporting cars, W.O. and H.M. were confident that it could ably compete in the

Tourist Trophy. For W.O. this meant a nostalgic return to the Isle of Man. Entering the event called for hefty expenditure, especially with shipping costs, accommodation and general overheads taken into account. H.M. was sure that it was financially viable. As long as the car could sustain the race, there was every reason to expect the venture to be profitable in terms of potential income and publicity.

The Bentley team arrived on the Isle of Man to take good advantage of the practice time that was allowed. The TT was among the most important and challenging events in the motoring calendar for 1914. It attracted the top drivers of the day, people such as Tony Vandervell, R.S (Dick) Witchell (later to become Bentley Motors' works manager), A.J. Hancock, Frank Clement (later synonymous with the Bentley company and one of the 'Bentley Boys'), Louis Coatalen, Laurence Pomeroy, Cecil Bianchi, Jean Porporato, the Guinness brothers and, of course, W.G. Tuck. Frederick T. Burgess, Humber's chief designer, who was destined to play a major part in W.O.'s career and Bentley history, was also there, with his mechanic Arthur Saunders. Saunders was also to play his part during the Bentley Motors era, becoming head of the racing shop. The Humber TT team comprised three cars, Burgess driving No.2. History has shown the 1914 TT to have collected together a number of person-alities who, after World War One, enjoyed an association with W.O. and the Bentley marque.

The DFP coachwork, which usually accommodated a couple of spare wheels in the rounded tail, had been suitably modified for the TT, the streamlined cover having been removed in order to eliminate time wasted in the event of wheel changing. Two fuel tanks were fitted to the car, the plan being to empty the rear tank first before switching to the front tank. A further modification was to the axles used on the car; those fitted to the 12/40 did not meet the regulation track specification and therefore the wider 16/22 axles were substituted. This was at a cost to the vehicle's overall weight, adding two hundredweight to make the DFP substantially heavier than its competitors.

It has often been suggested that W.O. had a problem in that Leroux did not understand English, and that W.O. and H.M. did not speak French. It has been further suggested that both parties relied on sign language, such as running a hand down the cheek to mean that steel-studded tyres were needed. The truth of these claims must be questioned, since the close working relationship between Leroux and the Bentley brothers has already been mentioned. Moreover, there is no evidence at all that on Leroux's arrival at Bentley & Bentley there were any language difficulties. It is far more likely that a code of signals was arranged so that W.O. and riding mechanic Leroux might communicate to the pit crew from the cockpit of the DFP.

Two DFPs were taken to the Island, one for practice, the other reserved for the race itself. Practising for the TT commenced at 4.30am on Monday 25 May. The weather conditions were pretty awful, for rain lashed down and the mountainous sections of the course were engulfed in dense fog. As well as having to contend with slippery surfaces and reduced visibility, there was always the threat of colliding with animals straying on to the road. More problems emerged throughout the practice period, with numerous complaints made by the locals about the noise and reckless driving.

The race, which was staged over two days, started at nine o'clock on 10 June. Anticipating dry weather for the event, the Island authorities had laid a substance on the roads which, in theory, would have absorbed the moisture in the air to prevent excessive dust from rising into the atmosphere. In fact the weather was decidedly wet, and the substance, akonia, contributed to the dire conditions, making surfaces even stickier than they would otherwise have been. A further problem was the mud: mixed with akonia it penetrated competitors' goggles to cause extreme discomfort to the eyes.

The race began in a fury with the Sunbeams going into the lead. Kenelm Lee Guinness, of sparking plug fame, nearly crashed as he took his hands off the steering wheel to adjust his goggles. He regained control and swept through the first lap at an average of 59mph. His brother Algy was in hot pursuit, finishing the first lap in second place. W.O.'s adversary, W.G. Tuck, was forced to retire during the second lap of day one, his Humber having broken a valve. Burgess managed to survive until the second day, but retired during lap 11 with a seized piston.

W.O. chose to take the course with deliberation and finished the first day in ninth position, behind Burgess and ahead of Frank Clement. After some careful driving in the dreadful conditions earlier in the day, speeds increased as the weather improved and the skies cleared, and Bentley's time at the end of 300 miles was 6 hours, 19 minutes and 25 seconds. That he experienced no mechanical problems whatsoever was a considerable feat.

The second day began with fine weather. W.O. took the opportunity to change the steel-studded tyres that were essential for the wet conditions and to fit conventional non-skid tyres. W.O. referred to Leroux as 'the perfect mechanic to have on such a race'. Unknown to Bentley though, Leroux had severely burnt himself on the DFP's exhaust; such was the mechanic's consideration for his driver that he refrained from mentioning that he was in acute pain throughout much of the day. W.O.'s driving was not without incident. When he took a corner rather more ruthlessly than he should have, Leroux looked at his companion, raised an eyebrow and asked if he was '*un peu fatigué?*' (a little tired?).

The fastest time was that of Riecken, driving a Minerva at 59.3mph. It was insufficient, though, to topple Kenelm Guinness from first position in his Sunbeam. Third was Léon Molon, a garage proprietor from Le Havre driving another Minerva; fourth was the Straker-Squire of Dick Witchell, and fifth was Jean Porporato in the third Minerva, which meant that Minerva took the team prize.

W.O. was placed sixth. For the Bentley & Bentley team, this was an admirable achievement, notwithstanding the fact that only six cars finished from the original 21 starters! When asked what DFP stood for, W.O. reportedly replied 'Deserves First Place!' So although W.O.'s dark red DFP did not qualify for a cup or prize, an award in the form of a special medal was bestowed on the team at a presentation ceremony a couple of days after the race. The excellent publicity that the DFP attracted made up for any trophy, and the increased demand for DFPs kept H.M. and his sales team happy and busy at Hanover Court.

The euphoria in the wake of the TT was short-lived. Bentley & Bentley issued a new catalogue a few weeks after the race which, as well as advertising the more usual DFPs, promoted the Tourist Trophy Model. There was also frenetic activity building the business marketing aluminium pistons, and Bentley & Bentley sought to increase its investment in this respect.

On 1 May 1914 W.O.'s brother-in-law, A.H.M.J. Ward, who was married to W.O.'s sister Edith, was elected to the board of Bentley & Bentley. Ward was later to acquire a majority shareholding in the business, so it is interesting that W.O. seldom referred to him, and he was not mentioned at all in his autobiography. This is particularly odd since during World War One Ward had much to do with the aluminium piston business of Bentley & Bentley.

There is a philosophical element, if not a hint of bitterness, evident in W.O.'s notes dating from this time. 'The ironical thing about our effort in the TT was that the benefit from it lasted a bare eight weeks, and we never gathered our rich harvest.'

The political situation in Europe during the summer of 1914 was bleak, and when W.O. took Léonie on holiday in early August it was obvious that war was inevitable. The couple had arranged to join Léonie's mother, her stepfather and his family aboard their yacht, which was moored in the Solent in readiness for Cowes Week. They watched destroyers being prepared for action at Thornycrofts, and waited in vain for a last-minute breakthrough in negotiations that might prevent conflict. There was none. On 4 August W.O., deciding that Belgium's cry for help to Britain signalled the inevitable call to arms, left Léonie in Southampton with her parents and travelled back to London with his brother-in-law Irwin Gore.

W.O. and Irwin stopped at the Bear Hotel in Farnham for a meal, and it was while they were leaving (W.O. recalled that the manager had politely refused a £5 note in payment) that news arrived that Britain was at war. H.M. and Irwin immediately signed up for duty, leaving Geoffrey de Freville and Ward to carry on the business of Bentley & Bentley along with W.O., who sought to put his technical expertise to best use in the war effort.

W.O. was later to recall the effect that the onset of hostilities in 1914 had on the business: 'I feel it is in almost bad taste to record that World War One killed the DFP.' W.O. had reason to feel rancour – the onset of war meant that Leroux returned to France, and within a fortnight was killed on the battlefields of Flanders. The war was also to claim the life of W.O.'s brother Leonard Holt, who died on 30 May 1918 while serving in the Mediterranean as second lieutenant, ASC. His remains are buried at Hollybrook Memorial Cemetery, Shirley, Southampton.

As for W.O., his engineering experience encouraged him to approach Rolls-Royce to serve in an armoured car division. Rolls-Royce was at the time in consultation with the relevant army department, and he arrived at Nightingale Road in Derby on 9 October. There confusion at recruitment centres around the country, and often men with knowledge of specific trades were dispatched to regiments that had no use for such experience. In W.O.'s case he was sent away from Derby, only to be told to return when the situation had settled down.

Returning to London he found the demand for supplying second-hand cars had greatly diminished, and there was only a limited amount of servicing work. W.O. not only experienced guilt at not fighting for his country, he also dwelt on what use aluminium could be to aero engine manufacturers. As far as he knew, no other British car maker had realised the potential that aluminium pistons offered compared to cast iron or steel, and the fact that the DFP carried these had remained undiscovered. Fitting aluminium pistons to aero engines was obviously feasible and could improve performance and reliability, especially as the alloy material improved heat dissipation with less risk of distortion and related stresses, in addition to reducing reciprocating masses. It appeared that no one apart from W.O. had even remotely considered the use of aluminium.

Appreciating that the utmost discretion was called for, he made various enquiries about the right person to speak to about engine design. Eventually he was directed to Commander Wilfred Briggs at the Admiralty. W.O.'s initial meeting with Briggs was held in the latter's office, located, as W.O. recalled, 'In one of the little temporary wooden huts put on the top of Admiralty Arch.' The Admiralty was responsible for expanding an efficient engine department within the RNAS, and it was Briggs's job to oversee this, and to liaise between the different aero engine manufacturers. From the outset their admiration for one another was mutual and it didn't take Briggs long to realise that the aluminium piston that W.O. had shown him could revolutionise aero engine design. He was intrigued by the fact that the DFP's aluminium pistons had remained secret.

Briggs made it clear at that meeting that W.O.'s ideas for using aluminium pistons would be taken up, and that W.O. should consult with engine manufacturers. To conduct this task, which needed to be handled with total confidentiality, he would need the authority of a King's Commission, which meant that he was made an officer. Within a couple of days W.O. was being fitted out with a uniform at Gieves in South Molton Street. It was with some amusement that he found himself saluted as he left the premises, but Léonie's reaction when he arrived home at Netherhall Gardens was not so positive. She worried for her husband's safety, and seeing him in uniform did little to suppress her anxiety.

W.O.'s first task as an officer was to meet Ernest Hives, who was head of Rolls-Royce's experimental department. W.O. travelled to Derby in the 12/40 DFP, the car being used extensively on Admiralty duties. W.O.'s tour of the engine makers took him around the country including the Midlands, the heart of the British motor industry. Journeys were made to and from Coventry on a regular basis, and often he found that he could do the trip in under two hours according to his mood and travelling conditions. W.O. admitted to pushing the vehicle rather harder than he should have. The demands made upon the car eventually took their toll, and he came to an abrupt halt one evening when a con rod went through the crankcase to wreck the engine.

As engineers both Bentley and Hives were highly qualified. Ernest Hives was two years older than W.O. and had understood motor cars from an early age. As a boy he went to assist a motorist when his car needed repair, which led him to finding employment with C.S. Rolls & Co. at Lillie Hall in Fulham as a chauffeur-mechanic, the motorist having been none other than the Hon. Charles Rolls himself. He then went to work for Napier at Acton before eventually applying to Rolls-Royce at Derby for a job.

Hives was naturally sceptical about W.O.'s claims for the piston that was shown to him, but he nevertheless arranged for his foundry specialist, a scientist named Buchanan, to check the figures and put this revolutionary idea to the test. Nothing was found to disprove Bentley's theories and Hives immediately arranged for some experimental castings to be made. Tests were carried out without delay, and the results were so positive that Hives specified aluminium pistons in Rolls-Royce's first aero engine, the Eagle. The success of the Eagle engine is well known, and, among other applications including powering airships, it was used to propel the Vickers Vimy aircraft that made the famous first non-stop Atlantic crossing in 1919 with Captain John Alcock and Lieutenant Arthur Whitten Brown at the controls.

The relationship between Hives and W.O. was extremely cordial, both engineers recognising each other's knowledge and expertise. W.O. recorded that they got on well together to such an extent that their rapport was not compromised years later when Rolls-Royce acquired Bentley Motors under what can only be described as contentious circumstances.

Without his DFP to use, W.O. purchased a V8 Cadillac and this car in particular gave him a lot of satisfaction. He was impressed at the smoothness of the car's engine, and the torque that enabled the vehicle to be propelled in top gear from near walking speed to its maximum. It was superbly quiet in operation, and W.O. once made the point that the only sound that was audible when the car was running was the engine cooling fan. There were several occasions during the early war years when he made visits to the Rolls-Royce factory at Nightingale Road, and W.O. liked nothing better than to show off the Cadillac's virtues to a workforce who were accustomed to the 40/50hp Silver Ghost, and for whom the car had no rival.

The Rolls-Royce was of course recognised for its quiet running and smooth transmission, a press report having dubbed it 'The Best Car in the World'. The car's legendary performances in the Royal Automobile Club's 2,000-mile trial and later the 15,000-mile reliability trial remained fresh in the minds of all those interested in motor vehicles, but nevertheless W.O. delighted in a little devilment, goading the Derby factory personnel with what was often assumed to be the US equivalent of the Rolls-Royce. The Cadillac was obviously expensive to run, but as the car was being used on government business it was not a major concern.

W.O. liked nothing better than to drive the big 5-litre V8 alone and with the hood down. He was nevertheless critical of some of its characteristics and once remarked that the car's handling was like 'navigating an empty barge along a canal.' The interior of the Cadillac was not as refined as that of the Silver Ghost – W.O. was able to drive one of these cars from time to time, the vehicle belonging to a friend – but it had other qualities such as folding occasional seats which, when in use, increased the passenger capacity to seven.

W.O. eventually tired of the Cadillac and sold it at a profit. He replaced it with another American car, an air-cooled Franklin, which in comparison with the Cadillac he found disappointing in performance. Not only was the car a sluggard, it was expensive to run. Thank goodness the Admiralty was paying the running costs!

With his negotiations with Rolls-Royce finalised, W.O. was sent to Sunbeam at Wolverhampton. There he met his old rival Louis Coatalen, who until he learned about W.O.'s mission had not known why Bentley's DFP had been so successful in motorsport. W.O.'s reputation as an engineer was sufficient for Coatalen to accept the principle of using aluminium pistons in aero engines, and subsequently Sunbeam adopted them for all their engines. Dealings with Sunbeam were more informal than those with Ernest Hives at Derby, and on a number of occasions Coatalen and W.O. ended up reminiscing about their racing exploits.

Although he did not know it at the time, W.O.'s integrity and expertise were tested to the limit when Commander Briggs called him to a meeting which was to change the course of his life. 'I am sending you to Gwynnes at Chiswick who are experiencing problems with the French Clerget aero engine.' At least the commission was in London, which meant that W.O. could get home to Hampstead on a regular basis.

Before the war Gwynnes were acknowledged for their manufacture of marine pumps in addition to a well-constructed and reliable light car. The firm's expertise had much to do with acquiring the concession to build Clerget engines under contract to the Admiralty. The engines were being built in large numbers and were specified for Sopwith and Nieuport aeroplanes. The Clerget was a rotary engine, a design that was largely unfamiliar to British aircraft and aero engine manufacturers who were more used to radial, in-line and V-configurations. The concept of the Clerget rotary impressed W.O., who later said of it 'In a fighter the power/weight ratio coupled with reliability is everything, and the rotary was the lightest form of piston engine for any given capacity.'

One of the principal advantages of a rotary engine over other types is that there was reliance on high compression to raise power output. Cooling was all-important, and the Clerget achieved this by having the cylinders finned and made of thin steel. With a propeller-tip speed of 150mph at cruising revs, there was a need for the cylinder to have effective cooling over its entire surface, which in this instance was not the case. The trailing side was undercooled, and therefore distortion due to uneven heat distribution was inevitable. In attempting to avoid this situation, Clerget had devised a solution by, using W.O.'s words, 'fitting an "obturator" piston ring, which was rather like a leather washer in a bicycle pump, but made of light alloy.'

When he examined the Clerget engine W.O. discovered the obturator ring to be too thin to offer any strength, and consequently it was prone to breaking, causing the iron pistons to seize with devastating results. The average life of an engine was often no more than 15 hours of flying time, and it came as a shock to him when he realised how many pilots were being killed because of a design that he considered to be unsound.

Briggs's instructions to W.O. were clear and succinct. He had to find a solution to these problems, and establish a programme of experimental work that would lead to adoption of aluminium pistons. It was with trepidation that W.O. arrived at Chiswick, where he was greeted by Neville Gwynne, the company chairman. W.O. wasn't convinced that his presence at the works was universally welcomed. Gwynne's attitude left him in no doubt that dealings with the man were not going to be easy, and he wondered how long he could maintain the tact and patience that was obviously required. He need not have been too concerned, however; his daily contact was with the works manager, an engineer named Armitage who was receptive to W.O.'s investigations and who made life as easy for him as possible. It was fortunate for W.O. that he had Petty Officer Aslin assigned to him, a man with an appetite for hard work over long hours, who never failed in his enthusiasm or duties.

The fact that the lives of countless pilots now rested on W.O. finding solutions to the Clerget's unreliability was a huge responsibility and one that he faced with anxiety and some misgivings. Returning home to Hampstead after long days at Chiswick he felt utterly drained. In retrospect, working countless hours between Hanover Court and New Street Mews seemed remarkably stress-free. He realised that he was not always the best of company, and when trying to relax he was more often than not using all his mental resources to find a solution to some nagging problem. He knew that his preoccupations were affecting Léonie, who was suffering from the fact that he was seldom at home, and bearing the brunt of his worries when he was.

One of his first duties was to travel by destroyer to Dunkerque to visit the pilots on the front line in France and Belgium, to see first-hand the conditions under which the squadrons flew and fought. Apart from the matter of failing aero engines, one of W.O.'s first encounters was to experience the difficulties that existed between the RNAS and the RFC, the two bodies representing Britain's air power. The RNAS was administered by the Admiralty, the RFC by the War Office. It was the RNAS squadrons to which W.O. was mostly assigned, for they had the majority of Clerget-engined aircraft. His visits took him as far away as Ypres, and while on mainland Europe he received the help and backing of two officers in particular, Captain Charles Lamb and Commander Frank McClean, both of whom always backed him in any decision and acted as intermediaries during interdepartmental difficulties.

W.O. spent weeks at a time in northern France and Belgium, listening to pilots' evidence and investigating problems. He talked to their squadron leaders, and to the fitters and riggers who kept the aircraft going, sometimes in appalling conditions. Even if he had tried to remain detached from the crews' emotions, their fears and their frustrations, he would have been unable to do so. For the majority of those based on the front lines he was a contact to whom they could easily relate and who understood their cause, unlike bureaucratic figures with little or no technical expertise.

Pilots and mechanics alike appreciated the way W.O. spoke their own language and understood everyday engineering problems. The fact that he could get to grips with an engine, dismantle it and put it back together gave him credibility few others would have possessed. There were times of fear when W.O. would have wished he were back at New Street Mews or putting his DFP through its paces on a hill climb or at Brooklands. One such occasion arose when he and Aslin had investigated a certain problem with a Nieuport 10, having spent several hours stripping down the engine. They were in the final stages of reassembly when the commanding officer arrived on the scene to check their progress. A little too confidently W.O. claimed that he wouldn't mind flying in the machine himself.

W.O.'s confidence was far too good an opportunity for the CO to pass by, and he found himself agreeing to accompany the dawn patrol. This presented a number of problems; he had never flown in an aircraft before and had never had cause to use a firearm, especially not the Lewis gun with which the aeroplane was fitted to protect against enemy fighters. From the rear cockpit, with a Lewis gun on which he had received only a scant pre-flight briefing, W.O. had, as he later recalled, 'plenty of time to think about the icy water 5,000 feet below, waiting to receive me if we had been slipshod in our work the night before.'

It was only when W.O. was safely back on the ground that he realised how near to catastrophe he had been. On checking the engine following his flight he found to his dismay that three of the con rods had overheated to the point that they were blue, and failure was imminent. His thoughts on being so near to death, and for that matter the crews risking their lives several times a day, had a profound effect on him. He later penned the following words: '...the appalling sense of responsibility hung over me and never left me for the rest of the war, the figure of a pilot killed by engine failure leaning over my shoulder, like some ghostly conscience, whenever I was at work.'

W.O. had several narrow escapes while serving in Belgium and France although he modestly claimed that he was never seriously at risk. Among the more interesting escapades was the time when, on the ground, he was forced to flee the bullets of a Fokker flown by German ace Baron von Richtofen. Taking refuge in a canal on the boundary of the airfield he found himself dodging the action in company with Petty Officer Nobby Clarke. Neither of them knew at that time that a future existed building and racing Bentley motor cars.

The doubts that W.O. had had when he first arrived at Gwynnes were confirmed when he tried to put significant modifications to the Clerget engine in place. He had been able to convince Neville Gwynne to adopt the use of aluminium pistons – but in reality the company had little choice in the matter, since it was under Admiralty contract. W.O.'s recommendations for raising the engine's compression were also accepted, but there was fierce opposition to modifying the obturator ring and designing a cylinder using aluminium, incorporating a cast iron liner. W.O. believed that this would resolve the problems of unbalanced cooling, but Gwynnes fiercely opposed him. It transpired that the company was considering building a rotary engine to its own design, and had appointed a French engineer to work on the project. They therefore viewed W.O.'s intervention as unhelpful, and even thought that he intended to substitute the proposed engine with one of his own design.

The atmosphere at Chiswick became charged to the extent that W.O. was forced to seek the backing of Briggs and the Admiralty. Briggs had to convince him to persevere at Gwynnes and produce and test a piston and cylinder of his own design. He reasoned that only then would Gwynnes have the facts. W.O.'s new cylinder design proved itself, but instead of being conciliatory, this success only aggrieved Gwynnes still further. Briggs was very much aware of W.O.'s ongoing problems at Chiswick, and ultimately he recalled him to the Admiralty.

By now Briggs knew that W.O., having resolved to find solutions to the inherent problems of the existing rotary engine, was deeply anxious to develop a rotary of his own design. Anxious is an understatement: W.O. was determined to succeed. Briggs, accepting that a Bentley-designed aero engine had huge potential for aiding the war effort, had purposely been researching the companies that were best suited to building such a machine. W.O. was thus dispatched to Coventry and the firm of Humber.

Leaving Léonie in London to be near to her family, W.O. sought accommodation in Coventry and chose to take lodgings above the King's Head Hotel. He returned home to Netherhall Gardens as often as he was able, usually at weekends. Being parted from his wife after such a short period of married life was obviously painful, but he acknowledged that he was relatively well off compared to those who were fighting the war on the front lines.

W.O.'s pleasure at being assigned to Humber, where he could develop his rotary engine, can be imagined. He had particular respect for this motor manufacturer that had been instrumental in providing for Britain's pioneering motorists, and he had also formed an excellent relationship with a number of key personnel. Firstly there was Frederick Tasker Burgess, his 1914 TT rival; then there was Niblett, the works manager, and his assistant Meason. J.F. Crundle, who had successfully ridden motorcycles for Humber, was chief tester while Sam Wright, an acknowledged Humber driver, presided over the fitting shop.

To W.O.'s relief Petty Officer Aslin was appointed to assist him at Coventry. The two worked easily together, Aslin always managing to be in the right place at the right time with everything to hand. The Humber management was equally relieved to have Bentley on its side. For too long during the war the company had been relegated to churning out large quantities of bicycles and travelling kitchens, a mundane task considering its vehicle manufacturing expertise. The development of aero engines called for imaginative and positive engineering, for which Humber was well equipped.

F.T. Burgess was head designer and a brilliant draughtsman. Known as 'Monkey Burgess' because of his striking facial expression, he had the ability to skilfully translate W.O.'s design theories into drawings. Of Burgess's expertise, W.O. remarked: 'He had the most facile pencil of any man I have known, a pencil that flashed across the board in deft strokes, expressing in lines our ideas as quickly as the words were spoken.'

The engineers at Humber were quick to recognise the effective cooling qualities that aluminium offered. Under W.O.'s guidance it was possible for them to manufacture thick sections of metal without any corresponding increase in weight, and to avoid unequal expansion through overheating. The design which W.O. had perfected at Gwynnes with the Clerget (this time without an obturator ring) formed the basis of his own rotary. Nevertheless he accepted that time was of the essence if his engines were to be used in action, and he had no objection to using the Clerget's valve gear, which had proved exemplary in use. He recognised that duplicating the parts made servicing easier.

W.O.'s approach to devising his rotary engines has been questioned in recent years by those who consider the format to be a copy of the Clerget. There were in fact considerable differences between the two designs, that of Bentley employing a completely modified cylinder pattern and using a different method to attach the cylinders to the crankcase. He certainly made no apology for using proven technology, for to create a completely new design would have been impossible given the time constraints. W.O., acknowledging that he had duplicated the Clerget's valve gear for good reason, was able to perfect the overall arrangement to his own exacting values.

There is nothing to suggest that W.O. merely improved an existing design. In fact he became embroiled in lengthy and bitter correspondence as recently as 1970 regarding letters published in a motoring journal that were aimed at discrediting him. Clearly angry that his integrity was being questioned, he published a blistering reply with clear indication that legal action for libel would be sought in absence of an apology. Of the insinuating comments made of him, he responded 'In the course of a long and full life, I do not think that I have ever read such a malicious, biased and wholly inaccurate collection of innuendo and mis-information as that published…'

Michael Frostick summed the matter up succinctly when he said 'Had W.O. stayed at Gwynnes and had they agreed to his suggested modific-ations, not only to the pistons, but to the construction and metal of the cylinders as well, the engine that emerged would have been a Clerget!' As has been shown, the management at Gwynnes was hostile to W.O.'s approach and decided to go its own way. When W.O. took his know-ledge elsewhere, it was Gwynnes loss. Humber and the Allies benefitted.

The power output of the 9-cylinder Bentley Rotary 1 (BR1) was substantially higher than the Clerget, providing 150bhp compared to 130bhp. W.O. continued in his 1970 reply: 'Regarding the suggestion that I copied the Clerget engine, this clearly originated from those who glanced only at the cam mechanism – the only similar feature – and were incapable of differentiating. The crankcase, crankshaft, method of securing the cylinders as well as their heads on the BR1, were all fundamentally different from the Clerget.'

W.O. devised two engines, the smaller BR1 and the larger and more powerful BR2, and when the drawings were complete he took them to Briggs at the Admiralty. Politics being what they are, Briggs was unable to give the go-ahead for production immediately, despite W.O.'s persuasion. Briggs had done much to promote the idea of a Bentley rotary, and there had been much lobbying on his behalf to even get an agreement for Humber to undertake the work thus far. Briggs advised W.O. to return to Coventry and concentrate on getting the BR1 engine running before going on to the next stage of perfecting the BR2. Unused to the bureaucratic red tape, W.O. returned to Coventry. While not exactly dejected, he nevertheless resigned himself to the fact that there was a long haul ahead, and that it would be some time before his ideas could be put into full production.

Getting the BR1 prototype to a stage where it was running and proving itself in terms of both output and reliability was an exhausting business. It was the early summer of 1916, and the residents of Coventry in the vicinity of the Humber factory were subjected to a roar that continued throughout the day and well into the night. W.O., by now immune to the noise, thought little about the disturbance that was created by testing the engine to its limits, that is until he experienced it for himself as he tried to get some sleep at his hotel lodgings.

When the droning ceased one night he instantly awoke, conscious of the silence and knowing that something was radically wrong. He was dressed and back at the works within minutes to discover that a valve had broken. Repairs were carried out and the engine was restarted, although the same valve failed after only a few hours. More repairs were undertaken, and more testing; failure occurred a third time.

The problem was eventually traced to a crack around the flange supporting the induction pipes where they were bolted on to the cylinder. This was a serious setback and although W.O. was confident the problem could be rectified, it nevertheless delayed the test programme. The cure, he determined, was to lighten the valves, and once this was achieved the running of the engine resumed without further incident.

Humber's chairman, Earl Russell, was clearly agitated by the engine failure, even suggesting that it had 'burst'. W.O.'s response to this can only be guessed at, and luckily for him Russell's confidence was not too badly shaken and he allowed experimental work to progress.

Testing was completed by late summer. A couple of modifications were found to be necessary to improve the engine's performance still further, one being to raise the compression in order to allow the Sopwith Camel to attain greater speed at altitudes above 10,000ft. The other was discovered almost by chance when an engine on test was found to be producing greater power than had been specified. The cause was traced to a leaky induction pipe, which encouraged W.O. to drill a 2mm hole in the induction pipe casting of another engine. The power immediately increased to provide a valuable extra 11hp, and after further testing which confirmed the phenomenon, the modification was adopted.

Before BR1 could be put into production it required Admiralty inspection, which was conducted by an inspector from the Aircraft Inspection Department (AID). The inspector was none other than S.C.H. 'Sammy' Davis, who had been assigned the duties. The engine passed its inspection, but the discussions that took place that day, and the memories of men, motorcycles and motor cars that were recalled, can only be guessed at.

The BR1 went into production that August at the Humber factory in Coventry. By 1917 its use in service was mainly confined to the Sopwith F1 and 2F1 Camels. Whereas the Clerget-engined Camels could attain no more than 15,000ft, those machines using the Bentley engine were capable of flying at 19,000 to 20,000ft. In his account of the Bentley aero engines, Donald Bastow makes the point that these figures differ from those officially published, but would vary with the state of fuel load. The official figures are those taken on a certain day, at a certain temperature, in a certain aircraft flown by a certain pilot: they always differ!

The BR1, once in service, did cause W.O. one major problem. While in France he was given the news that four of No.4 Squadron's aircraft had failed to return owing to engine failure. Two of the aircraft had crash landed on the beach near Dunkerque, and W.O. was rushed to the scene to inspect the damaged engines. The fault, he ascertained, lay with a fractured spring in the oil pump.

Late in the evening W.O. was back in England, having summoned Humber engineers who worked throughout the night re-treating springs that had been supplied too hard by an outside contractor. Early in the morning W.O. was on his way back to France aboard a destroyer carrying a suitcase full of new, correctly-tempered springs.

Working throughout the night and delivering the new components was only part of the problem. When the Admiralty's administration uncovered the fact that W.O. had bypassed a number of regulations in order to deal with the matter effectively and quickly, the official view being that he had virtually hijacked a naval vessel, he faced disciplinary action. Not only did he receive a written warning, he had to attend an interview and was chastised for bypassing procedures. The fact that he had saved lives hardly seemed to matter.

Work began immediately on the BR2, which being similar to its sister engine was more straightforward to develop and used a number of inter-changeable parts. Producing 230bhp power from its 24.9 litres, it was suitable for the Sopwith Snipe 7F1 Mk1 and the 7F1A Mk1A, along with the ground attack Salamander TF2. The Snipe was widely thought to be the best fighter available to the Allies in the closing stages of the war.

Building both the BR1 and the BR2 put too great a demand on Humber, with the result that Daimler and Crossley were contracted to construct the latter. The engine did not enter production until very late in the war, but nevertheless some 120 units were built on a weekly basis. The RNAS and the RFC were amalgamated to form the Royal Air Force in April 1918, by which time the superior design of Bentley aero engines was fully recognised. The aforementioned Baron von Richtofen, one of the most celebrated pilots of World War One, is said to have been a victim of a Bentley-powered Camel: his Fokker triplane was shot down and von Richtofen, 'The Red Baron', was found dead. There remains a question mark over this, however, as the bullet that killed him came up through his seat. The success of the BR2 resulted in the placing of orders totalling 30,000, which were cancelled following the Armistice.

W.O.'s patience was tested to the limit when, shortly after the formation of the RAF, he was ordered to take over the post-production experimental work on a new engine, an air-cooled radial. It was to supplement the BR2, but W.O. recognized at once flaws in its design which, he warned his commanding officers, would lead to failure. His views were not well-received; he was told that he was tired and prejudiced, and ordered to get on with the job. In his autobiography

W.O. confirms that his worst fears were realised when an engine did indeed fail, killing the renowned test pilot H.G. Hawker. The circumstances surrounding Hawker's death are indeed controversial, and it is known that he was suffering from incurable spinal tuberculosis. Despite evidence that flames were seen coming from the engine, the coroner's report reveals compelling evidence that Hawker experienced a sudden and massive spinal haemorrhage before impact, causing his legs to become paralysed at the aircraft's controls.

At the end of the war the manufacture and use of aluminium pistons was well-established. As well as being used by most major manufacturers, they were used in all Rolls-Royce aero engines and were fitted to the company's 40/50hp (Silver Ghost) motor cars on the resumption of production in 1919.

The question of aluminium pistons is somewhat ironic as far as W.O. and Bentley & Bentley are concerned. With both H.M. and W.O. on war service, the day to day running of the firm was entrusted to A.H.M.J. Ward and Geoffrey de Freville. While there was some trading in used cars throughout the war there was insufficient work to rely solely on DFPs, and therefore the firm existed buying and selling whatever came along. The mainstay of the business, however, revolved around aluminium pistons, Bentley & Bentley being agents in Britain for those produced by Corbin.

Difficulties arose when the delivery of pistons from France became unreliable. To ensure the supply of pistons for the British aero engine industry, Bentley & Bentley essentially became manufacturing agents and formed a separate concern, the Aluminium Piston Co., the pistons being cast at Rowland Hill's foundry in Coventry, near Humber. Neither W.O. nor H.M. was a director, since it would have been unwise for W.O. to profit from the company seeing that much of the firm's output was destined for Bentley rotary engines. The Register of Directors shows that Ward was the sole director.

The Aluminium Piston Company's products were marketed as Aerolite Pistons, the Aerolite Piston Company having been formed on 29 August 1916. The registered office was in London at Hanover Court Garage, Hanover Court.

Geoffrey de Freville was put in charge of the work on behalf of the Aluminium Piston Co. but it appears that when piston manufacturing was still at its experimental stage, de Freville decided to part company with Bentley & Bentley to establish his own piston manufacturing business. This was the Aluminium Alloy Piston Co., and from British Aluminium records it is evident that de Freville engaged the Coan company to cast his pistons.

British Aluminium's files add that the Bentleys' Aluminium Piston Co. was supplying Aerolite pistons solely to the services, the products having been adopted by the Ministry of Munitions. De Freville's Aluminium Alloy Pistons Co. was blacklisted because of his actions, along with the delay in experimental work that ensued.

When de Freville left Bentley & Bentley, Ward appointed Arthur Hillstead as salesman. Ward had previously interviewed the young Hillstead in response to a letter he had written to the company seeking employment in the motor trade. Sensing that Hillstead was keen to join the firm, he invited him to keep in touch in the event of there being a suitable position at a later date. Ward was, however, instrumental in arranging for Hillstead to work for Ernest Lyon, a motor trade colleague in Wigmore Street. Having made it his business to keep in contact with Ward, Hillstead was accordingly summoned to Hanover Court and given a job.

Hillstead hadn't long been employed at Hanover Court when he met H.M. That meeting, incidentally, was in Hillstead's words 'the beginning of a friendship which endured many years.' It was some time before he made W.O.'s acquaintance. Ward had already warned him that the two brothers were of opposite temperaments, but Hillstead had to find out for himself how their personalities differed. It was at a time when W.O. was experiencing a number of difficulties with the quality of pistons, and the day that he called into Hanover Court his mind was preoccupied.

W.O. caught Hillstead examining a set of pistons that he had laid down on a desk. Asked by W.O. what he was looking at, Hillstead immediately recognised a condition in the material that he termed 'that awkward malady known as *blow-holes*'. W.O. was not impressed, and gave Hillstead a look which, he recalled, 'would have withered a jelly fish!'

Hillstead does, however, provide a cameo of W.O.'s personality. Certainly he was known for his wry humour, and for being obstinate at times and caring little for protocol. Although in the services he found it difficult to remember to salute a senior officer, otherwise he remained the perfectionist he had always been. Hillstead found it difficult to believe that H.M. and W.O. were brothers; he says of the two: 'Whereas H.M. was of average height, well-built, neither dark nor fair, cheerful, ready to crack a joke and possessed of a decided twinkle in his brown myopic eyes, W.O. was short, stocky, dark, inclining to ocular fierceness, deliberate, monosyllabic and decidedly dour.'

During the war W.O. never rose in the ranks and remained a junior officer. His salary during the period was abysmal and in order to supplement his income he applied for a £1,000 tax-free gratuity, which was funded by the Admiralty on the recommendation of Commander Wilfred Briggs. The payment was made in recognition of the expenses W.O. had incurred going about his duties, as well as the additional living expenses he had while he was living in lodgings away from home. He recalled later in life that he was never officially demobbed, and indeed there remained some question of his actual rank. According to his own notes he was a lieutenant, and yet elsewhere he is referred to as Captain Bentley.

The war was not quite over when he left the services to take some desperately needed leave. He returned home to Netherhall Gardens, his mind filled with all sorts of ideas, mainly about engines and motorcars.

CHAPTER 4

A Bentley is Born

RETURNING to a home life after four years with the Admiralty took some adjustment, for both Léonie and W.O. Being separated because of war the couple had been denied any real married life and, as far as W.O. was concerned, spending weeks at a time away from his wife and his Hampstead home and existing in lodgings or hotel rooms when he wasn't actually working was hardly the basis for a secure and pleasurable existence. Léonie, at least, had received the support of her mother and stepfather, who were living nearby in Maresfield Gardens, and she looked forward to her husband's infrequent visits. When the Zeppelin bombing raids on London were at their height W.O. had, whenever possible, commuted by train from Coventry in order to stay overnight at Netherhall Gardens.

His absence from Bentley & Bentley and his distance from activities relating to DFPs had caused him to think about the direction the motor industry might take once the war was over. His association with Humber and working alongside Frederick Burgess, in addition to his dealings with Sammy Davis and others, had nurtured a number of ideas, which he resolved to further when circumstances allowed. He anticipated that motoring would no longer be confined to the wealthy or the sporting fraternity and believed that car ownership would become much more widespread. A demand would therefore exist for more affordable vehicles. While this was to be welcomed, W.O. nevertheless foresaw a risk that the specialist hand-built motor car would fall into decline. Having assessed future motoring trends W.O. was convinced a market would exist for a quality sports car that would be the choice of enthusiasts.

It emerged that Burgess shared W.O.'s outlook, and the initiative to design and build a pedigree sporting machine of the highest standard and incorporating traditional values came from long discussions at Coventry that often continued well into the small hours.

Burgess had already conceived plans of his own to develop a post-war car, but one that was more affordable, to appeal to the popular market. Following their discussions and arguments he abandoned such ideas in support of W.O.'s proposal. W.O.'s vision was for a dependable and resilient machine that was capable of providing comfortable high-speed touring over long distances. He was unhappy that, in general terms, the future of British car design opposed the direction that some European manufacturers were taking. Rolls-Royce and Vauxhall satisfied the demand for high quality machines, as had Argyll, Arrol-Johnston and Napier before the war.

It was W.O.'s aim to design a car that could sustain speeds in excess of 60mph over virtually any type of road surface. To this end he looked to some of the cars that were native to mainland Europe and which were designed for Continental touring; machines such as Minerva, Bugatti, Chenard-Walcker, Darracq, Hispano-Suiza, Lancia and Fiat, among others. During the 1920s and 1930s, incidentally, 'Continental' coachwork was in vogue and was applied by a number of coachbuilders, especially on chassis such as those built by Rolls-Royce. The image was of a close-coupled car that featured, in the French style, a separate luggage trunk rather than one integral to the body. Moreover, W.O.'s philosophy was that new cars would be owner-driven rather than chauffeur-driven, and therefore the requirement for constant maintenance should be minimal. In W.O.'s own words, his aim was to devise a machine that would be 'A fast car, a good car, the best in its class.'

He also envisaged developing a smaller and less expensive model, a 'bread-and-butter' car as he described it, at a time when the initial sports car had been in production sufficiently long to be showing a meaningful profit. In all probability this was the type of car that Burgess had proposed.

Returning to civilian life W.O. became far more engaged in producing his own car than perpetuating the business of Bentley & Bentley by selling and promoting the DFP, which remained in production in France. He nevertheless needed and got the support of his brother H.M. – if the new venture was to succeed it was important that Bentley & Bentley should continue to do well. H.M. believed in his brother's vision and he rapidly put in hand a strategy for financing W.O.'s enterprise.

While Bentley & Bentley had profited selling DFPs courtesy of W.O.'s motorsport activities, W.O. firmly believed that a car such as the one he had in mind should not be marketed as a racing car, although experience gained from motorsport should be reflected in the design in the interests of maintaining both durability and reliability. In his deliberations W.O. was influenced by the performance of the DFP, although he recognized that in order to satisfy his design criteria the engine had to be considerably more powerful, around 3 litres.

During the months before the Armistice, Bentley & Bentley, in the safe hands of Archibald Ward and Arthur Hillstead his young assistant, became more involved in the acquisition and selling of DFPs. H.M., now promoted to lieutenant colonel, and W.O. made more frequent appearances at Hanover Court.

In the lean war years Bentley & Bentley had deemed it appropriate to venture into any motor-related business that offered profitability. One such opportunity arose with the selling of farming equipment when the company established itself as a sub-agency for Emerson Tractors. The Emerson was a giant of a machine (which like others ran on paraffin once it had been started on petrol), and on paper at least promised ideal performance. When H.M. and Hillstead had arranged for demon-strations to be conducted in Hampshire and on the Isle of Wight, their confidence quickly evaporated when farmers remained unconvinced that the machine could achieve better and cheaper results than either the horse or the steam engine. Accepting that their hopes for the Emerson were unfounded, H.M. ruthlessly sold out.

The same determined manner was shown when, in 1918, H.M. called Hillstead into his office and told him that it was in his and the company's interests to locate and sell every DFP they could lay their hands on. Obviously there was an urgent need to bolster the finances, although on the exact reason for this H.M. remained silent. Instead he gave assurances that a boom in selling motor cars was imminent and that the company should be well-placed to profit. Hillstead suggested that the company buy and sell other makes of car in addition to DFPs, as being reliant upon a single marque could prove restrictive. H.M., whose knowledge of cars extended solely to DFPs, was unsure, but he was nevertheless sufficiently confident in Hillstead's expertise to allow him to vet cars for their condition, and decide whether they were saleable. For his forethought and enthusiasm Hillstead had his salary doubled.

The future of Bentley & Bentley was often the subject of discussion at Hanover Court. Answers to continuing speculation remained unforthcoming, however, and Hillstead recalled that whenever the matter was raised Ward would become tight-lipped. H.M., when he called in, was equally reticent, and to get anything from W.O. was simply impossible.

The ever-ebullient Hillstead did in fact glean some information from Ward's wife Edith, sister to W.O. and H.M. W.O., she assured him, was answerable to no one when it came to engineering. In other matters, such as funding his racing activities, he had been governed completely by the limited amounts of money H.M. would allow out of Bentley & Bentley's resources, H.M. being particularly astute when it came to financial affairs.

Hillstead's confidence that he could broaden the company's activities was boosted by the fact that Bentley & Bentley had taken on a young mechanic, Leslie Pennal, whose mechanical knowledge of cars, together with a deftness in the use of tools, stood him in good stead for future activities. Hillstead guessed that this sudden burst of activity to rake in cash had everything to do with W.O.

It had, of course. Bentley & Bentley achieved much in those first months following the Armistice; sales of second-hand DFPs were boosted by the demand for any motor car, whatever its type. When production of DFPs resumed at Courbevoie in the autumn of 1919, Bentley & Bentley acquired as many chassis as possible. The quality of the car was, sadly, not nearly as good as it had been pre-war, and there was evidence of cost-cutting and the use of inferior materials. Bentley & Bentley did what it could to make the product more superior, a practice that paid off because there was an influx of orders following the Motor Show that was held at Olympia in November. Sales remained buoyant into 1920 for the reasons stated, but there is little doubt that the car's pre-war reputation had much to do with demand.

When deliveries of DFPs were delayed because of difficulties experienced with the French railways, H.M. and Ward organised the ferrying of chassis from Courbevoie to London. Hillstead was co-opted to assist the operation, along with William, the eldest of the Bentley brothers, and Hugh Kevill-Davies, who had been employed as a junior salesman. Between them they ferried a considerable number of chassis from the outskirts of Paris to London via Dieppe and Newhaven by road and sea.

W.O., it has been recorded, was particularly impressed by the rate of deliveries, even if he had been infuriated by not being able to park in his usual place at Hanover Court because of the abundance of vehicles and the lack of storage facilities. In a relatively short time the money raised through Bentley & Bentley that was necessary to help finance W.O.'s project amounted to £20,000. His frequent appearances at Hanover Court, and the countless discussions between him, H.M. and Ward in secret behind closed doors, only served to heighten the intrigue about what was going on.

W.O.'s plans were finally exposed when Alfred Bentley visited Hanover Court and inadvertently made it known that his son was preparing to go into business building quality sports cars to his own design. He told Hillstead that much depended on raising sufficient capital and finding suitable investors, and he would be wise to invest in the venture.

Again Hillstead provides an insight into W.O.'s personality. It is evident that the two were not the best of friends, but Hillstead did at least have the courage to tackle W.O. directly about his proposals. On one of his visits to Hanover Court W.O. was intercepted by Hillstead who asked him if he could have the job of sales manager. Hillstead's memoirs indicate that W.O. was not at all receptive to the idea, but he nevertheless didn't give up and invited W.O. to lunch. In accepting Hillstead's invitation W.O. was bombarded with questions that he was reluctant to answer, and avoided doing so despite his host's tongue-loosening efforts, which took the form of plying W.O. with copious amounts of alcohol. W.O.'s adeptness in evading Hillstead's determined probing provoked the latter to recall that 'We talked, we talked, and we talked; we also went round in circles. When I brought the conversation back to the main issue, W.O. shot it off at a tangent and started on a lengthy discourse on an entirely different subject.' W.O. remained immune to Hillstead's tactics until the question of investment was broached, together with the possibility of Hillstead finding potential investors.

From that point on W.O. was quick to develop his ideas and to collect together a team that could produce the Bentley car. The essential character of the machine had in many respects already been conceived. Those discussions in Coventry had materialised into a collection of drawings and sketches, but it is important to emphasize that these had originated from W.O.'s ideas, and had been committed to paper by Burgess. So great was Burgess's admiration for W.O. as an engineer, and so sure was he of the proposed car's success, that he willingly surrendered his position as chief engineer at Humber in order to work for W.O. and the fledging Bentley Motors. According to various accounts by those who were associated with W.O. during the formative years of the company, W.O. spent hardly any time at the drawing board. He was not a draughtsman, but he did understand drawings and was able to add to the interpretation of a design. Burgess did not move to London until October 1920, although he did spend much of his time in the capital working on the project. Nevertheless, the timescale indicates that some of the formative design work on the Bentley car was carried out in Coventry, at Burgess's home.

The one other person closely involved in the embryonic Bentley project was Harry Varley, the designer of the 3.4-litre V12 Vauxhall engine and architect of that company's motif. Before he joined Vauxhall, Varley had served an apprenticeship with Lloyd and Plaister, a company which, pre-war, had designed and built fire-engines in addition to motor cars. Harry Varley possessed a truly sophisticated approach to engineering and was a highly skilled draughtsman. Years later Varley was in the planning department at Rolls-Royce's Crewe factory.

Unhappily for W.O., Burgess and Varley were not exactly compatible in temperament. Both were volatile, which made for an interesting state of affairs when they worked in close proximity to each other, and it often fell to W.O. to maintain a fragile peace. On at least one occasion W.O. was overheard to say that he could happily work with either of them separately but not together!

W.O.'s and Burgess's proposals to produce a true sporting car had determined that they would employ some of the ingredients of those pre-war machines that had established particular standards. Essentially they looked at the 1912 Peugeot, the 1914 Grand Prix Mercedes, and Burgess's own creation, the 1914 TT Humber.

The Peugeot was interesting because its engine was designed by the Swiss engineer Ernest Henry (there is confusion here regarding the spelling, some references being to Ernest Henri), whose understanding of engine technology was at the time very much advanced. The camshafts of Henry's engine were housed in aluminium while the spark plugs were located centrally in the cylinder head, between the inlet and exhaust valves, which was formed from a single casting. The 3,995cc Peugeot engines delivered 100bhp at 3,200rpm, a figure that W.O. and Burgess found interesting and which satisfied their own design calculations.

W.O. had been involved in the affair concerning the 1914 Mercedes Grand Prix car. One of the team cars was discovered in London in 1915, and when arrangements were made to transport it to Derby, W.O. had been present when the engine was dismantled and examined by Rolls-Royce engineers at Nightingale Road. The link between the Mercedes and W.O. is Roy Fedden, the Old Cliftonian and future technical chief of Bristol, who was responsible for preparing the 1914 TT Straker-Squire cars and was a friend of Commander Briggs at the Admiralty. Briggs's acquaintance with Fedden, and the former's close working arrangement with W.O., was sufficient for Bentley to be invited to Derby when the machine was tested.

W.O. was prudent enough to record the results of that test, which showed the engine to have a maximum power output of 100bhp at 2,500rpm. When the engine speed was increased to 3,000rpm, which denotes an exceedingly high piston speed relative to the engine's stroke of 165mm, the output dropped to 99bhp.

That W.O. subscribed to the ideas behind Burgess's design arrangements for his 1914 TT Humber is shown by the fact that similar front and rear axles, chassis frame and gearbox were adopted for the first of the Bentley designs.

The Bentley motor car was effectively conceived on 20 January 1919, when W.O., Varley and Burgess occupied a small office on the top floor of 16 Conduit Street which, incidentally, was in close proximity to Rolls-Royce's London headquarters, which remained operational until the late 1990s. It was there, under W.O.'s direction, that the three engineers persevered for nine months drawing up designs and blueprints from a series of notes, sketches and ideas. What eventually emerged was the Bentley 3-litre.

While W.O. led the design work it was Burgess's responsibility to translate W.O.'s theories into working practice. Burgess additionally concerned himself with the chassis arrangements, especially the rear axle and transmission. Varley was responsible for collating the designs and creating the drawings from which the necessary components could be manufactured. Much of the work was carried out not particularly by scientific calculation, but rather by experience and ingenuity. The designers' abilities were sufficient to ensure that some over-engineering was evident, and thus began the 3-litre's hallmark: longevity.

Funding the 3-litre might have been easier had W.O. received the recognition and remuneration he deserved in connection with his rotary aero engines. The low pay he had received as a serving officer in the services, while not leaving him in dire circumstances, forced him to make economies. With the knowledge that contracts for the BR2 engine had been cancelled in the wake of the Armistice, along with the prospect of losing a substantial amount of potential income as a result, the outlook for the future was not as comfortable as he might have hoped.

W.O. thought it right to progress a claim to recompense him for the loss of revenue from his inventions and designs, and for the incalculable hours that had been spent developing his rotary engines. He accepted, nevertheless, that such a route through the tribunal system was going to be a protracted affair. As it was, it was two years before anything like a settlement seemed feasible, and ultimately he was invited by the Royal Commission on Awards to make a claim, the hearing having first been heard in December 1919. It continued a month later and was presided over by Mr Justice Sargant.

W.O. found the entire business harrowing, despite benefiting from the services of a highly reputable barrister, Douglas Hogg KC, the future Lord Hailsham and Conservative politician. While W.O. received the backing of Commander Briggs, in addition to a number of noted pilots and high-ranking officers, the case did not proceed in the manner that he and his counsel had anticipated.

Commander Murray Sueter RN told the Commission that Captain Bentley was employed under the Admiralty, and was not initially employed designing engines. He went on to say that, having been approached by Briggs, he had given permission for Bentley to design engines that made extensive use of aluminium for pistons and cylinders. Sueter added that the Admiralty was desperate for engines, and that Bentley's work was creative and outside his normal duties.

A claim was also made by Gwynnes, who argued that the company was entitled to claim for compensation, since the Bentley rotaries, which, it was acknowledged, were vastly superior to any other engines used during the war, were initially developed on their premises. However, to W.O.'s credit, it was stated that the Bentley engines had convincingly boosted morale among the squadrons using them, and had positively aided the war effort as well as saving many thousands of lives.

A witness for the Treasury, Captain C. Fairbarn, refused to accept that Bentley rotaries had anything particular to do with air supremacy. He was head of the Historical Records Branch of the Air Ministry, and he stated that as an experienced pilot, with some 1,000 hours flying time up to 1917, it was his opinion that British air supremacy had been established in the early stages of the war before being temporarily lost and subsequently regained.

The amount that W.O.'s counsel claimed amounted to £107,000, which represented an annuity for the rest of his life on a little larger scale than a Cabinet Minister's salary. The Attorney General made it very clear that while he would want to see Bentley receive a reasonable sum in recognition for his work, there was the very serious problem of government departments being faced with other equally large claims, which might damage the country's finances. Counsel for the Treasury asked whether the Commission was satisfied that Bentley's work could not have been done by any one of half a dozen people in the country, a question that Douglas Hogg thought particularly mean considering his applicant's expertise and engineering acumen.

Mr Douglas Hogg's response was to the point. He submitted that Bentley's expertise had enable him to design an engine using technology previously unknown, and that the Allies had received a new and reliable engine which was specified for the 1919 campaign, had that been necessary. The value of the engine lay in its ability to fly higher than other aircraft, and the fact that it required fewer spares and less maintenance.

The Commission granted W.O. £8,000. Relative to the nature of his inventions, this was nothing less than an insult. W.O.'s, and his counsel's, sense of injustice was compounded by the knowledge that Gwynnes, who had put in a claim for £150,000, had been awarded £110,375.

To make matters worse, W.O. was expected to pay income tax on his award. He prepared to fight the case, and a couple of days before the matter was due to go court the Inland Revenue capitulated. As for Douglas Hogg, he was so incensed about the outcome that he greatly reduced his fee. Rightly, W.O. felt that justice had not been done, and this unpleasant episode rankled with him throughout his life. W.O. did at least receive some recognition for his services: the MBE was conferred upon him on 1 January 1919.

Bentley Motors was established on 18 January 1919, the date that the Registrar of Joint Stock Companies put his signature to the Certificate of Incorporation. The solicitors acting for the new company were Druces & Atlee of 10 Billiter Square, London EC3, the firm with which Hardy Bentley, and later his son John, practised over many years.

The Articles of Association make for interesting reading. The share capital had originally been stated as £13,000, but was raised to £20,000 almost immediately. The establishment of the company was, in fact, the precursor to the forming of a second Bentley Motors, which was established six months later on 10 July 1919, the date that one Birtles as Register of Joint Stock Companies signed the Certificate of Incorporation.

The essence of the first Bentley Motors was that it was formed in order to transfer from Bentley & Bentley the work and the designs that had thus far been established in preparing for W.O.'s motor car, for the sum of £7,000. No monies actually changed hands of course, the agreement having been made to allow payment to be made for the work undertaken. The £7,000 was in fact equally distributed in the form of £1 shares to the three named directors – W.O. and Archibald Ward taking £2,333 each, while H.M. took the extra share to make his holding £2,334.

W.O. was nominated managing director of Bentley Motors, and H.M. and Ward were directors. That all three were directors of Bentley & Bentley was noted in the Articles of Association, as was the fact that Ward was a director of the Aerolite Piston Co. There were also some special conditions: W.O. was to be paid £2,000 per annum royalty in recognition for his patents for the Bentley motor car, and in return he was prevented from competing with Bentley Motors or indeed leaving the company.

There is no doubt that Hardy Bentley had much to do with the legal aspects of the formation of Bentley Motors. The agreement had been worded in such a manner that in effect it was no more than a holding company formed for such time as was necessary to raise further capital and establish a firm footing. Once the infrastructure was in place the company could be restructured at the earliest opportunity. This occurred on 3 July, when an Extraordinary General Meeting of the company was called, which approved the winding up of the business and the formation of a new company. The new Bentley Motors was registered by Hardy Bentley on behalf of Druces and Atlee, the Articles of Association including the matter of purchasing the assets of Bentley Motors in liquidation for the sum of £30,000.

A capitalisation of £100,000 had in fact been agreed, and was subsequently increased to £200,000, but as the call was for ten shillings (50p), realistically the capital was only £50,000. Deducting the £30,000 for fees to the directors for work carried out, the effective working capital was reduced to £20,000. In real terms, therefore, the company was under-capitalised from the very beginning, but for all that the directors, and W.O. in particular, had very positive aims and ideas, all of which called for the taking out of substantial mortgages. To apply the phrase that W.O. himself was fond of using, Bentley Motors was 'batting on a sticky wicket'.

In assessing the formation of the second Bentley Motors it is important to take a look at what was happening behind the scenes. Firstly, it has to be questioned whether there was any real need to acquire offices in Conduit Street. They were on the top floor and had limited facilities, factors which would have attracted a relatively economical rent, and certainly the address was impressive, but the cost might be considered an unnecessary expense. The hub of the business remained at New Street Mews and Hanover Court.

Arthur Hillstead also gives clues as to what was going on. Finding investors proved a problem, largely because the end product was still on the drawing board. W.O.'s reputation did, nevertheless, account for much, as did Bentley & Bentley's track record of successfully marketing the DFP. In addition to investment provided by W.O. and H.M., input came from two of H.M.'s business acquaintances, General Whittington and Colonel Wolfe Barry. Hillstead, too, invested a limited amount of money, and he was responsible for introducing Martin Roberts, the director and proprietor of an engineering business in Rochester Row. Roberts believed the investment to be sound because he thought that he might receive work from Bentley Motors. Finally there was Archibald Ward, who continued to look after the DFP operations.

Never the academic, W.O. was also shy of speaking in public. One of the few occasions that he did do so was at Verrey's restaurant in Regent

Street. Verrey's was a favourite haunt of the Bentley brothers (a branch had once existed in Hanover Court), and often they would lunch there, H.M. using the venue to conduct business. In this instance prospective investors had been invited to a promotional luncheon, and they were treated to a rare oratory performance by W.O., who outlined the state of the immediate post-war motor industry and his plans for a high-quality sports car. He spoke too about the growing need to address safety with regard to motor design, and, not surprisingly, revealed his plans for racing the Bentley, both to promote the marque and to apply the benefits of the results to production models. His speech, which was filled with passion and vision, obviously impressed those present, for there was an immediate promise of funds. Needless to say, H.M. and Hardy were on hand to support their brother by providing the necessary legal and financial support and by answering any difficult questions.

Unfortunately, when Martin Roberts realised that work was not coming his way he made it known that he was withdrawing his capital, which would have been a minimum of £2,000. His actions influenced Whittington and Barry, and when all three requested the return of their monies H.M. was put in a difficult position. Their investments were returned to them, but exactly how H.M., working in close liaison with Hardy, achieved this has never been revealed. Hillstead did divulge H.M.'s and Hardy's fondness for golf, both being active members of Stanmore Golf Club (H.M., incidentally, financed the building of a new club house), and it was there that much of the business of shielding W.O. from the daily financial worries was conducted so that he could concentrate on technical affairs.

The days of Bentley & Bentley were numbered. After the formation of the first Bentley Motors, W.O. took little or no interest in the affairs of the company with which he had achieved so much. His efforts were totally concentrated on getting the Bentley 3-litre off the drawing board and into production. H.M., too, was preoccupied, and was happy to leave Ward to get on with the business of selling DFPs. It was H.M. who was responsible for getting Arthur Hillstead transferred to Bentley Motors as salesman, thus leaving Ward to conduct affairs on his own, aided by a couple of salesmen. Ward was convinced that a future selling DFPs remained secure, and he eventually bought out both H.M. and W.O., transferring the business to North Audley Street. Eventually matters came to a head when DFP's business at Courbevoie collapsed.

The sales operation of Bentley Motors, if that's what it can be termed, was undertaken entirely by H.M. and Hillstead. The loyal customer base that had been built up selling DFPs was obviously a good starting point, and help came from other sources following a notice in the *The Autocar* on 8 March 1919 to the effect that W.O. and F.T. Burgess were engaged in the design of a new car. A far more comprehensive announcement of the proposed Bentley appeared in the same journal on 17 May 1919. This was the first time that details of the 3-litre had been divulged, and the piece was accompanied by an evocative drawing penned by Gordon Crosby (who designed the original Bentley winged B emblem), depicting the car at speed in exactly the idiom that is now synonymous with the marque.

Details of the car made for enticing reading. It would have a monobloc engine with four cylinders (80x149mm) and four overhead valves per cylinder developing 65 horsepower, a four-speed gearbox, a Ferodo cone clutch, 820x120mm tyres on wire wheels, a 9ft 4in wheelbase, 4ft 8in track and electric starting and lighting.

The report intimated that the car was to be built primarily for speed and was intended to satisfy the sportsman of the motor world with its sporting appearance. Its performance would provide the feel of absolute control that was a feature of genuine racing machines of the period. The final paragraph of the feature was sure to attract customers looking for a car that promised performance and quality above all:

> A two-seated, four-seated, or saloon body can be fitted to the chassis, but all will be on sporting lines, so as to be in keeping with the character of the car. With four passengers it is guaranteed that the machine will lap Brooklands track at 75mph. A lighting dynamo and starting motor will be fitted, and the chassis, with running boards, front mudguards, five lamps, five wheels and tyres, a revolution counter and speedometer, and tool kit, will be priced in the neighbourhood of £750.

Almost immediately enthusiasts keen to get a glimpse of the Bentley were beating a path to Hanover Court. Enquiries arrived daily by post, and eventually it was possible to form a waiting list for the car.

Having Burgess's expertise was one thing, but W.O. was keen to get down to some positive hands-on design work. Within a week or two of efforts having got under way in the drawing office in Conduit Street, there arrived at New Street Mews one of the three TT Humbers. It was the vehicle that Burgess had driven, and the intention was to use it as a template for the 3-litre Bentley, and to improve upon its design. Hillstead, having seen it at the Mews, was obviously perplexed, and he said of the Humber that 'It was too light on the front wheels, which made corner work far from accurate; the gears were incredibly harsh and noisy, while the engine was fantastic.' He need not have worried, for the Bentley ultimately proved to be so superior that not even the first experimental model inherited any of the Humber's shortcomings. Having the Humber at New Street was to cause a huge amount of interest, especially when the engine was dismantled to expose its finely engineered components.

With his motorsport experience, together with knowledge amassed during the war years at the Admiralty, W.O. had formed some influential relationships with a number of highly qualified engineers and mechanics. Firm friendships had been established, and he purposely went out to collect together a team that would form the basis of Bentley Motors' technical force. Among the first to arrive at New Street Mews were Nobby Clarke, Jimmy Jackson and Clive Gallop.

Leslie Pennal's role during the formative days of Bentley Motors has already been mentioned. W.O. remembered Petty Officer Nobby Clarke's mechanical talents from his ventures on the front line, and recalled how he had deftly applied them to aero engines. Nobby remembered W.O. too, and the ex-chief mechanic of No.4 Squadron wrote to him suggesting they meet up. W.O. replied offering him a job, as head mechanic of Bentley Motors. Jimmy Jackson was an ex-pilot who had flown Sopwith Camels; he joined Bentley Motors as company secretary. Clive Gallop was also an old friend: he had worked for Peugeot, had raced at Brooklands and had flown as a pilot with the RFC. Gallop also understood engines, and he and W.O. had spent many hours together talking about engine design. W.O. recalled that the first time the two had met was on a train while travelling to the Midlands. It was with the aid of Gallop's engine expertise that W.O. was able to perfect the design of the Bentley 3-litre's camshaft.

Although the design of Bentley Motors' first car was progressing well on paper, there were serious problems getting the machine together physically. The post-war boom had meant that engineering companies were over-burdened with orders; delivery times were extended, not merely to weeks but more often several months. Unlike at later periods when proprietary components were largely available, each and every part that was contained in Burgess's and Varley's drawings had to be made. That meant that the engine, gearbox, clutch, bearings, axles, differential, springs and much more were all reliant on a proficient engineering contractor being able to manufacture them to a very high standard of quality and accuracy, but with the limited capital that Bentley Motors had at its disposal, things were obviously very tight.

However, there was a silver lining to W.O.'s frustrations in acquiring components, for Cosmos Engineering in Bristol were able to assist, although this was only possible with the help and determination of one of their employees, Peter Purves. Had it not been for his tact, intelligence and ability to get things done, coupled with his aptitude for getting the best out of people, deliveries of the Bentley parts would have been much delayed. The outcome of Purves's labours was that W.O. invited him to work for Bentley Motors in a liaison capacity, a post he held for many years.

The building of the first Bentley motor car was undertaken at New Street Mews, the DFP service centre having been adapted for the purpose. The hayloft, which had previously been used as an engine fitting shop, was converted into the engine assembly area, while the ground floor workshop served to build the chassis. The components began arriving from Cosmos Engineering during the middle of the summer, and it was Nobby Clarke's responsibility, along with help from Pennal and Jackson, to build them up. Nobby, however, was in charge of assembling the engine, and while this was being completed the chassis was taken to Easter's coachworks elsewhere in the Mews, where the body, which W.O. and Burgess had jointly designed, was to be built.

Naturally the operations in the hayloft were labour-intensive. A manually-operated grindstone was installed and it was Pennal's job to work the treadle. Recalling his efforts, Pennal was convinced that Nobby Clarke had kept him pedalling for far longer than necessary just for the hell of it! The only other items of equipment were a hand drill, which was used for delicate work, and a separate machine that was capable of heavy-duty drilling, known as the 'gut-buster'.

Finally the day arrived when the engine was ready to be started. W.O. was obviously anxious to see how his design performed, and he was joined by Burgess, Varley, H.M., Hillstead and Clive Gallop, together with anyone else who could justify themselves as being part of the Bentley team, in the hayloft. The atmosphere was tense with everyone conscious of W.O.'s emotions and aspirations, and it could have been no more charged if it were a child that was about to enter the world. The excitement was tinged with an air of concern should everything not go according to plan.

Some eight people were present in the hayloft which, considering W.O.'s aversion to anything approaching a jamboree, represented a crowd. The engine, very new and polished and without an exhaust manifold, was supported on a wooden trestle; alongside was a series of batteries that were connected to the starter.

Starting the engine proved more difficult than anticipated. When everyone was in place W.O. waited until he received assurances from Nobby Clarke that everything was ready. As W.O. pressed the starter switch it engaged the bendix pinion with the toothed ring on the flywheel. As the starter operated with a clatter and turned the engine, everyone present willed it to fire immediately. When it failed to do so, W.O.'s face remained expressionless, although his annoyance and frustration were felt by every person in the room. Again the starter switch was pushed; still nothing. By then the tension in the room was almost unbearable.

Amid much consternation, and probably with some ripe language being muttered under his breath, Nobby tried again to fire the engine, to no avail. All the while the electrical power was being drained, which jeopardised further attempts. W.O.'s expression visibly blackened, no one dared utter a word. Clive Gallop, with an air of nonchalance, played with the throttle as if nothing was particularly amiss, which plainly irritated W.O. all the more. Others shuffled uncomfortably, anticipating the worst and expecting any moment to hear the full force of W.O.'s wrath. When he did speak, W.O. brusquely called for some Benzole.

The tension at least had been broken, and within seconds an orange-coloured can was produced. Assisted by Gallop and Nobby Clarke, who were relieved to be doing something positive, W.O. set to work draining the float chamber and refilling it with the can's evil-smelling contents. A quantity of Benzole was also added to the fuel supply tank before another attempt was made.

W.O.'s face remained impassive as he pressed the starter switch. As the starter engaged and turned the crankshaft a blinding flash was followed by a roar as the engine burst into life. To the relief of everyone present a gradual smile came over W.O.'s face. The roar of his engine responding to so much design and careful manufacture was the sweet sound of success. Once it was evident that the engine was running smoothly and without faltering, all misgivings and worries gave way to joyful elation.

The noise of the engine running in the upstairs hayloft was deafening, and the intense vibration was excessive to say the least. The commotion was sufficient for the matron of an adjacent nursing home to arrive promptly on the scene in a state of some fury, complaining about the tumult and the distress it was causing her patients, one of whom was dying. She threatened to call the police unless the racket ceased immediately, but W.O. was far too preoccupied to worry about such matters, which in his opinion were trifling when a motor car was beginning its life. Clive Gallop, having been told by W.O. to tell the lady to go away, had the arduous task of pacifying her. Meanwhile W.O. opened the throttle to its fullest extent for several glorious seconds to demonstrate the most raucous noise imaginable before shutting it down and returning the loft to some tranquillity. It would appear that W.O. recognised that he had been over-zealous. With tongue in cheek he suggested that the roar of his engine was quite a sound to die to! W.O. ultimately used his charm to calm the poor matron, because testing continued on a regular basis without further complaints.

The completion of tests and other work associated with perfecting the engine's design took some weeks, and by the time it was ready to be fitted into the chassis the coachwork had been delivered from Easters. Getting the heavy engine out of the hayloft was a tricky business calling for the careful lowering of the complete unit by block and tackle through a hole in the floor to the workshop beneath. Once on the ground it was manhandled into the chassis and bolted into place to allow the finishing process of fitting the radiator, hoses and ancillary equipment.

W.O. should have been first to drive the Bentley, but he missed out on the occasion owing to a fit of enthusiasm by his workshop personnel. Just as the final adjustments to the running gear were being made, Clive Gallop arrived on the scene and was so excited to see the complete chassis he suggested the lightweight body be attached to it using clamps to secure it as a temporary measure, rather than drilling and properly bolting it to the frame. One thing led to another; a cushion was used as a driver's seat perched on a couple of boards across the chassis. As Nobby Clarke, Pennal and Jackson clambered aboard, Gallop started the engine, selected first gear and eased the car out of the workshop and into the Mews, all the time extolling the virtues of the brakes, the gear change and everything else about the machine. As it happened the tail of Gallop's dust coat became caught in the prop shaft and dragged him down into the chassis. He was disentangled by his colleagues before any serious harm was done. Later, when W.O. arrived on the scene, a measure of guilt came over those who had taken this illicit joy-ride, and while he said nothing they were unsure whether he was aware of the antics that had taken place.

Amid the excitement there was also frustration. As potential orders for the car were arriving at Hanover Court, an erroneous report in *The Motor* of 3 September told readers that the first year's output had already been sold. If only it had! Although a few firm orders had been received, the majority of enquirers were reluctant to commit themselves without having seen the finished product, or having some reliable information about its true on-the-road behaviour. Bentley Motors by this time was already financially stretched, a situation that might well have been avoided if deposits had been accepted and a more substantial capital raised. Furthermore, the subscribed capital was only sufficient for the construction of two experimental chassis. W.O. believed that once these were on the road it would be relatively easy to secure further capital in addition to increasing numbers of orders.

Combined with the elation and anticipation there was also sadness. The day between Bentley Motors having been registered and that of work progressing in the Conduit Street design office, Alfred Bentley, W.O.'s father, died aged 78. Alfred and Emily Bentley had moved from Avenue Road to a smaller but equally prestigious property at 39 Lancaster Gate, off London's Bayswater Road. Alfred's affairs were conducted by his solicitor son Alfred Hardy, the effects amounting to £409 16s 9d. Following her husband's death Emily eventually moved to an apartment at the near by Leinster Court Hotel, also in Lancaster Gate.

Then, within three months of Alfred's death, W.O.'s wife Léonie succumbed to the severe epidemic of Spanish influenza that swept across Europe in the first months of 1919, dying on 6 March as a result of complications that led to acute dilatation of the heart. She was 32 years old. W.O., understandably, was devastated by her death, although he seldom talked of his grief other than to his family and closest friends. W.O. was unable to register his wife's death himself and left the arrangements to H.M., who was living at Melcombe Court in Marylebone, not far from New Street Mews.

There are few clues as to W.O.'s state of mind during his time of grieving, such was his quiet nature that revealed little about himself. His involvement in the 3-litre's development and the constant pressure of work, not to mention the continual worry of financing the project, did at least help him to take his mind off his personal tragedy. Life had to continue, and W.O.'s determination meant that much progress was made in preparing the Bentley car for production. It was not long before, with the help of H.M. and Hardy, W.O. began to take a wider interest in life, making the acquaintance of Audrey Morten Chester Hutchinson, the daughter of Christopher Clarke Hutchinson, a respected barrister. W.O. refers to Audrey, who was seven years younger than him and a spinster, as Poppy, and the two enjoyed a whirlwind romance before announcing their engagement. They were married at Holy Trinity Church, Brompton, on 7 April 1920. Audrey was given away by her brother, while Clive Gallop acted as W.O.'s best man. Following the marriage W.O. left Netherhall Gardens and moved with Audrey to 7 Pelham Crescent, South Kensington, Audrey having previously lived at 1 Pelham Crescent.

The marriage was destined not to last. W.O., who was desperately unhappy following Léonie's sudden death, had remarried believing that a sound relationship existed between himself and Audrey. The constant attention to his work, the relentless pressure at Conduit Street and at New Street Mews, the search for suitable factory premises, and the persistent worries of keeping Bentley Motors afloat during its formative months, all took their toll. In later years W.O.'s involvement in Bentley racing activities took up much of his time and he was often away from home for lengthy periods, which increased domestic disharmony.

Audrey was a society girl whose interests did not lie at the race track, nor with the gritty daily life surrounding the manufacture of motor cars, even fine ones. She was never happier than when on the social circuit, entertaining and being the perfect hostess. W.O. was not part of that scene; he resented having to be sociable and he was more comfortable leading a homely existence without the endless parties and chitchat that Audrey so adored.

The relationship between W.O. and Audrey was never sound and the couple eventually drifted apart, leading their own lives to a great extent. The differences between them were mainly due to W.O.'s preoccupations, and it became evident that both realised marriage had been a mistake. Although they were temperamentally ill-matched, the marriage survived for 12 years before ending in divorce. W.O. seldom referred to Audrey, and in his autobiography she is not mentioned.

Their marriage certificate shows Audrey's second given name as Morton, which is incorrect and should have been written as Morten, something that was noted in the divorce papers. Audrey began divorce proceedings on 20 June 1932, the day that W.O. moved from Pelham Crescent to take up residence at 54 Queens Gate, South Kensington. The media became interested in the divorce, *The Times*, among other newspapers, carrying details of the case. The grounds for divorce were that it was alleged that W.O. frequently committed adultery with Mrs Margaret Roberts Hutton, the two having been introduced by Audrey, who was an acquaintance of Margaret's. The marriage was dissolved with the decree nisi dated 12 December 1932, and the decree absolute dated 15 June 1933. The divorce, which was a messy business, was heard in the High Court of Justice before the Right Hon. Lord Merrivale. It was agreed that W.O. would pay Audrey maintenance of £888 annually, the order being modified on 21 August 1936 after Audrey's marriage to Ernest Herbert Cooper. With effect from 1 July 1936, the maintenance payable by W.O. was reduced to £250 per annum.

Margaret Roberts Hutton, named in the divorce, was married to Charles Alan Hutton (he used Alan as a name in preference to Charles), a motor engineer from Truro in Cornwall. The couple had two children, Joan Margaret who was born on 11 June 1915, and John Murray, born 20 March 1918. It is clear from Public Record Office files that the marriage suffered serious difficulties and was, in effect, over. On-going quarrels had meant that Margaret had been terribly unhappy, and in desperation she left her husband, choosing to live with her mother in London. For a long time she had put off leaving Alan for fear of emotionally harming their children. Margaret had been living in London for around two years before she met W.O.

Margaret wrote to Alan (whom, for reasons that are unexplained but are presumed to be of affection, she refers to as 'My dear Peter') from

19 Queens Gate Place, London SW7, on 1 May 1932, explaining that after their separation she could never contemplate returning to him. When they had first separated Margaret did not consider that she would ever want to remarry, but after meeting W.O. she recognised the true love that existed between them, and marriage to him became what she wanted more than anything else.

On arriving in London Margaret had taken a job which had meant that she was on her feet for most of the day. That, and the worries of her personal situation, had caused her to be ill and in need of surgery, which she had put off all the time she was reliant on her employment for an income. Following her mother's death, however, Margaret's financial worries were largely eliminated.

In her letter to Alan Margaret appealed to her husband's better nature: 'I am not going to ask you to let me divorce you, but I am going to ask you to divorce me because I think that is only honest and fair.' Margaret also asked to be able to see her children whenever possible, such as during school holidays, and asked Alan to consider seeing W.O. to talk over the matter of the divorce. 'Will you see Bentley and talk it over with him? He would come down and see you and would be glad to. If possible you could perhaps arrange to meet him at Launceston on a Saturday afternoon as soon as possible. If you want to see me, you know I will.'

Margaret also raised the matter of money. 'I would really like to help you financially. I can't offer to give you money, but would you allow me to send so much a year for John?' Presumably Joan was by then old enough not to be a dependant. Signing herself as 'Margie', Margaret added a postscript to the letter. 'I would just like you to know that Mother knew and immediately liked Bentley. She was sympathetic too about his divorce and very glad he was getting a fixed job which would make it possible for him to get free. If you would prefer to see Bentley at Truro he would go down there any day during the week if you would fix it.'

The reference to a 'fixed job' applies to that period, to be discussed in a later chapter, when W.O.'s tenure at Rolls-Royce was somewhat uncertain following that company's acquisition of Bentley Motors' assets in 1931.

Alan Hutton replied on 4 May 1932. Not only did he refuse to see W.O., he was adamantly opposed to a divorce, intimating that he would delay proceedings indefinitely as well as taking legal advice about preventing Margaret from having access to the children. He was also reluctant to allow the children to meet W.O., and referring to his wife's relationship with him, he wrote: 'I cannot see in any case what possible grounds you might have had for divorcing me, and as regard the alternative, that is my divorcing you, what reasons should I have for doing so, as I am perfectly satisfied you have not at any time lived with this man.' Hutton ended his letter: 'I only hope you have not made this man's wife as so unhappy as you have made me, and that you may not regret the step you have taken.'

On 5 June Margaret wrote again to her husband:

Dear Alan,

I am writing to repeat as I have told you before that I shall not live with you again. I stayed with Bentley at the Grosvenor Hotel last week and enclose the hotel bill.

Yours,

Margaret

The Grosvenor Hotel account, incidentally, covering the period from 27 May until 4 June, amounted to £42 10s 9d. It is apparent that Margaret and W.O. resided together at the Grosvenor largely for legal reasons, in order to provide evidence of adultery.

W.O. acknowledged his affair with Margaret, and wrote to Audrey in a brief and matter-of-fact manner on 4 June 1932. It would seem from the cool tone of the letter, which was addressed from London's Grosvenor Hotel in Victoria, that W.O. was acting on his solicitor's advice:

Dear Audrey,

Our marriage has not been a success and it is no use to pretend any longer.

I have met and am in love with Mrs Hutton and we have stayed together at this hotel since 27 May.

Yours affectionately,

Bentley

Having received no reply to her letter of 5 June, Margaret wrote again to her husband on 24 October:

Dear Alan,

It is now nearly six months since I wrote to you saying I wanted you to divorce me so that I can marry again.

Bentley and I love each other and wish to get married. He will soon be free and I am anxious to know if you are going to take any action. I wrote in June giving you evidence, but as I have heard nothing at all from you I am writing again.

I cannot believe that, as you know the circumstances and that as our married life together is completely at an end, you can persistently be cruel enough to refuse me divorce. I will remember your disgusted opinion of Mrs Oakshott when she refused to divorce her husband.

As time goes on I am more and more certain of my feelings and definitely know that I am making no mistake.

I do not wish to think that spite is your reason for taking no action and yet I cannot think of any other motive.

Margaret R. Hutton

Charles Hutton ultimately cited W.O. in divorce proceedings, the case having been set down on 20 March 1933. He chose the case to be tried by judge and special jury, requesting damages from W.O. of £5,000. There is every reason to believe that Hutton, knowing exactly who Bentley was and supposing him to be extremely wealthy, decided to gain as much as possible financially. W.O. was represented by Druces and Atlee, with which firm his brother Hardy was a partner. The outcome was that the amount claimed by Hutton was substantially reduced, W.O. having to pay £1,000, which he settled in two instalments.

The divorce court heard that W.O. and Margaret had 'co-habited at 4 Mount Beacon, and at 41 Sydney Buildings, Bath; also at "By The Pines" in Nelson Road, Bournemouth, and at diverse other places.' The decree nisi was granted on 11 July and the decree absolute on 17 July 1933.

CHAPTER 5

Cricklewood

THE Bentley Motors prospectus had allowed for the acquisition of a showroom and works, although how this could be achieved with such limited capital was unexplained at the time. Shareholders, too, were concerned that W.O.'s aspirations were rather adventurous, and on a number of occasions made their feelings known. This situation, in effect, led to a conflict between those who appreciated that all possible resources were needed if the aims of the company were to be successfully fulfilled, and parties who were more interested in seeing a quick return on their investments without any real regard for achieving the desired end product.

Investors with a clear understanding of business matters would certainly have realised that expectations of early profits and substantial dividends in this instance were unrealistic given the capitalisation of the company. In retrospect it is barely credible that backers were willing to speculate; but they did nevertheless, although many were motoring enthusiasts buying relatively small blocks of shares, who were keen to be involved in the project.

The qualification to become a director of Bentley Motors has already been explained, along with the named directors on the establishment of the second company in July 1919. Martin Roberts resigned his directorship in early June 1920, and a couple of weeks later Archibald Ward also resigned. Walter Keigwin, one of W.O.'s associates at Clifton, became a director, replacing Roberts, and Charles Stead was elected in place of Ward. Charles Boston was also elected, and for a time he served as company chairman. Boston resigned in July 1922, when he was replaced by Carl Breeden; in the same month Stuart de la Rue of the De la Rue printing group was elected a director, and later became chairman after Boston. F. Prideaux Brune was already a shareholder in the company, and when he substantially increased his subscription he, too, was elected a director from June 1923. Other directors were Hubert Pike, who was appointed Bentley service director and manager of the Bentley service station, and Guy Peck, who had been appointed general manager, both of whom joined the board in March 1922.

Before his appointment in 1920, Peck had worked with Major Frank Halford's Airco company. As general manager Peck's position was one of co-ordination, ironing out any difficulties in liaison that existed or arose between the various departments, and supporting W.O. and H.M. in the daily running of the business. He did an outstanding job, was seldom given to being argumentative or bad-tempered, and always maintained an unruffled air. Likewise Hubert Pike, who subscribed generously to Bentley Motors, saw his investment eroded away over the years. For all the capital that he lost, he maintained a sense of humour, and the good of the company always remained his objective.

In addition to constant boardroom arguments, W.O. had other pressing matters on his mind. Before any thought could be had of actually putting the Bentley into production, sufficient firm orders were required to make the whole venture worthwhile and profitable. The London Motor Show was scheduled for the autumn of 1919, and W.O. was insistent that Bentley Motors should not only have a stand at Olympia, but should also have something positive to display.

Mention has already been made of the efforts that were put in to preparing the first experimental chassis, retrospectively known as EXP1, and how it was assembled at New Street Mews. A second chassis, EXP2, was laid down at the same time as EXP1, and it was this that graced the Bentley stand at Olympia.

Preparing the chassis for the event proved to be something of a nightmare. It had been barely a month since the episode at the Mews with the faltering start of the Bentley engine, and in that time W.O. feverishly worked his staff to meet the deadline. There was no question of the workforce not complying with his wishes, and they willingly toiled day and night, working unreasonable hours. At the end of it all what the visitors to the show saw was a polished chassis, which in fact was unfinished, some of the components being merely mocked up and quickly fabricated for the event.

The chassis was nevertheless handsome in its gleaming black paint and with the inside channels painted red. The engine was no more than an empty shell, partly because the machining of some of the parts had been problematic and they were not ready, and partly because there had been insufficient time to fully assemble it. There was no crankshaft, and the wooden starting handle was simply pinned to the crankcase. The dummy starting handle led to a potentially embarrassing incident when a young boy visiting the show tried turning it to gauge engine compression. The unsuspecting lad abruptly came to grief, pitching over the front near-side wheel with the handle clasped firmly in his hands. The flywheel was fastened on a dummy mandrel located in the rear main bearing, and the gearbox was fitted with a glass cover for show purposes. The rear axle and differential were complete.

The quest to have a stand at Olympia was made all the more difficult because of the lateness of Bentley Motors' application to the SMMT, the show organisers. Being the first of the post-war shows it was heavily subscribed, mainly because a vast number of engineering firms had sought to diversify into motor manufacturing, with the result that along with some established names there were those that were unknown. From some of the would-be manufacturers, many of which quickly vanished from the scene, there emerged designs that were eccentric as well as highly impractical.

Stand 126 was the only site the SMMT could offer Bentley Motors. While it was small and confined to a corner, it sufficiently accommodated the single EXP2 chassis. Positioned below the gallery in a side alley, Bentley's stand was, ironically, opposite DFP's display, which by comparison was spacious, having ample room to exhibit two complete vehicles in addition to a 12/40 chassis. If W.O. would have preferred a larger and more prestigious location, H.M. was nevertheless happy with the arrangement, which allowed him to trip between the two stands to gauge public opinion and interest.

In addition to efforts in preparing the chassis there was also the matter of devising a suitable brochure, a task that fell to H.M. and Arthur Hillstead. The respected publicist Frank Corbett was approached, and his artwork and layout were of such high quality that his services were retained thereafter by Bentley Motors. The catalogue's colour frontispiece was Freddie Gordon Crosby's drawing of a Bentley at speed. Inside the brochure chassis details were reproduced in the form of pencil drawings, and while this might have suggested an air of quality the arrangement merely hid the fact that photographic material was simply not available. Detailed drawings of Bentleys in a variety of coachwork styles were included, and while his name is not mentioned, these also have been attributed to Gordon Crosby, who, incidentally, was responsible for a Bentley mascot that was registered but not used as an emblem on the cars, for a number of reasons including copyright infringement. Depicting Icarus, the majestic design did, however, appear on some of the first catalogue editions. Close inspection of Crosby's design detail of Icarus's wings shows them to be very similar to the wings adorning the Bentley winged B emblem, which was also Crosby's work and which has graced Bentleys for 80 years and more.

W.O. was impressed by the overall design of the catalogue but saw two drawbacks. The design and content were so beautifully produced that copies were snatched up from the display, leaving a shortage for serious customers. It was also discovered that it was particularly popular with schoolboys, and the numbers of copies that were given away had to be severely rationed.

Gordon Crosby was a personal friend of W.O., and the famous Bentley radiator shell design is attributed to him. At the time of Crosby's rendering for the Bentley catalogue, a radiator design did not exist, and W.O. left it to the artist to prepare an appropriate sketch of the car at speed. W.O. had of course previously discussed his ideas with Crosby for the type of car that he envisaged, and when he saw the drawing he instinctively knew that the artist had anticipated an ideal radiator shape. It was following his completion of that particular sketch that Gordon Crosby produced the winged B emblem. The Bentley radiator shell that graced EXP2, along with all the early production cars, was a magnificent affair which was hand-built in German silver by Gallay Ltd of Scrubs Lane in Willesden, north London.

W.O. was disturbed to discover that the Bentley catalogue, with its pencil drawings, was seized upon by some rival manufacturers who were keen to spread rumours that the car did not exist beyond the drawing board, and that the chassis was no more than a wooden fabrication. The problem of models being displayed that never became production cars was all too common at the time.

The Olympia show attracted phenomenal interest. Over-subscribed by exhibitors, visitors flocked to the event in record numbers, which at times caused much discomfort for both show personnel and customers. Throughout its nine days' duration, W.O. was never absent from Olympia, spending as much time as was possible on the Bentley Motors' stand. He was assisted by H.M. and Hillstead, who between them amassed a sizeable waiting list for the car, prospective customers paying deposits of £10. As well as the enthusiasts there were pessimists who believed it impossible to manufacture a chassis of the type for the price, while others perceived the car as a racing machine that provided little in the way of comfort.

W.O. had appointed Leslie Pennal to keep the Bentley display tidy and polished, a task that the young mechanic found wholly rewarding. Having little knowledge of the chassis details he nevertheless listened to his peers as they talked to clients, and he quickly picked up the necessary information, repeating what he had heard parrot-fashion on the occasions that he was questioned. Eventually he was caught out by W.O. while indulging in his unofficial sales patter, but he must have been convincing because W.O. chose not to reprimand him, merely smiling and walking away when Pennal told him how he had acquired his knowledge.

The show itself had an exhausting daily routine. Each morning the stands and exhibits were thoroughly cleaned before the deluge of visitors made their appearance at 10 o'clock. Conditions within Olympia quickly became oppressive, especially when the atmosphere filled with tobacco smoke. For the show personnel it was a matter of endlessly talking, smoking and drinking; in rest periods trying to get refreshments from the catering areas was often virtually impossible.

The show ended on a euphoric note. W.O. was delighted with the interest that was shown in the Bentley, although at that time Bentley Motors was without any manufacturing facilities, tools or premises in which to build cars for which orders had been taken.

Finding suitable showroom premises proved to be a lot easier than locating a factory. The fact that Hanover Street had served Bentley & Bentley well, and that Hanover Court had become synonymous with the Bentley name, was sufficient for W.O. to secure a 21-year-lease on No.3 Hanover Court, across a yard from the DFP showroom. Previously a dress shop, the new showroom promised more than the old DFP premises could offer, and it had window space. The premises were architecturally interesting, the pillars adjacent to the front door (smaller pillars were a feature of the façade on the upper floors) providing a majestic appearance.

Converting the dress shop into a car showroom and offices called for some innovation on the part of W.O., with assistance from H.M. and Hillstead. Access to the window space was restricted because it was at a raised level and partitioned off, the space behind having been used as fitting rooms, and there was no way of displaying a chassis. Instead, as a temporary measure, the window was dressed with Gordon Crosby's watercolour of a Bentley at speed, some catalogues, a framed photograph of chassis EXP2 on display at Olympia, a reprint of the first descriptive article that had appeared in *The Autocar*, and a BR2 cylinder mounted on a wooden plinth. Within the showroom itself the furniture was mustered from the homes of W.O., H.M. and Hillstead, and the fitting rooms were used as office space.

When EXP2 was completed following its display at Olympia, W.O. and H.M. sought to redesign the showroom to accommodate the chassis of EXP1, that car's body being assigned to the second of the two experimental chassis. It should be explained that for a long time it was thought that it was EXP2 that was displayed at Hanover Court, when in fact it was used extensively for testing purposes, much of the time in the hands of Frank Clement. Installing a window that could be opened to provide access from the street proved to be too expensive an operation, and therefore it was decided to create a ramp to enable a car or chassis to be manoeuvred into the window position from within the premises. The fitting room-cum-office was demolished, and a mezzanine floor with a veranda was constructed, along with a staircase, to provide an obstruction-free sales area. The basement, which had previously provided storage facilities for the dress shop, was converted into additional office space for use when business commitments, and expenditure, permitted. The sales side of the business at the time was without a typist, or indeed typing facilities, which meant that H.M. popped next door to DFP whenever he was in need of secretarial services. With the improvements concluded, EXP1 was wheeled into the window space, which it shared with a complete BR2 aero engine courtesy of the Admiralty.

The question of where to establish a factory was complicated by the fact that W.O. was beset by advice from those directors who believed that they knew best in such matters. He spent weeks considering the ideal location, and would have known that at least a couple of motor manufacturers were moving to the huge complex at Slough in Buckinghamshire that was once the facility inaugurated by the War Office for the repair of thousands of redundant and damaged military vehicles. Taken over by a consortium headed by Percival Perry, who had previously been the head of Ford's UK operations, and Noel Mobbs of Pytchley Autocar, the site was destined to become one of the largest trading estates in Europe.

W.O. was then advised that he should establish his works in the Midlands, close to the traditional home of the British motor industry. He was adamantly opposed to this, considering it far better to stay as near to London as possible. Then another director suggested that he clear some of his own industrial buildings and lease them to the company, in return for a consideration of course. There were several problems with such a situation, not least the unsuitability of the buildings and their location, which was some 200 miles north of London.

Through one of H.M.'s contacts at the Air Ministry W.O. became aware that Tangmere Aerodrome was available, and H.M. and Hillstead were despatched to Sussex to investigate. Their initial impressions of the aerodrome and its complex of buildings excited them, especially the vast hanger that had once accommodated Handley Page bombers. The aerodrome was the size of a small town, and was equipped with its own power station and railway network, as well as having a dedicated test track that was on a par with Brooklands.

W.O. was consulted, and he too was initially enthusiastic about the prospects offered by the aerodrome. However, the Bentley brothers knew that the facilities on offer were too extensive for the purpose they envisaged. That did not deter them – here was an opportunity to lease some of the buildings and land to other interested parties, much in the same way that Perry and Mobbs had done at Slough. From the outset H.M. knew that the purchaser of the aerodrome would have to buy it as a whole: leasing or buying individual plots or premises was out of the question. Having got caught up in the general excitement surrounding the aerodrome, an offer was made for the estate, which to everyone's surprise was accepted by the Air Ministry. Still with an eye firmly on the future, Hardy Bentley was summoned and instructed to negotiate with the Ministry's solicitors.

The extent of the commitment the company had made was eventually realised. The sheer scale of the overheads made H.M. and W.O. nervous, and it soon became apparent why the Ministry had been keen to find a buyer. Although the purchase of Tangmere Aerodrome seemed a feasible solution to the need for suitable premises – one of the hangers, along with the test track, would have been more than adequate for the purpose – there remained many unanswered questions. If it proved impossible to sell or lease the remaining premises and land, the company would incur colossal maintenance costs. The power station alone represented a huge liability, especially given the unknown state of its condition and the anticipated running costs. Eventually the enormity of the situation and the foolhardiness of continuing with the project became all too obvious. Steps were taken to pull out of the deal, which luckily was achieved with the minimum financial loss thanks to Hardy's skills as a lawyer.

This unhappy episode had left Bentley Motors no further forward in finding a suitable manufacturing base at a time when orders taken at Olympia meant that the 3-litre needed to be put into production as soon as possible. Worse still, the affair had left a hole in the company's already fragile financial resources.

Meanwhile W.O. had been testing EXP1. Later on the same day that Clive Gallop and his associates at the Mews had taken their illicit ride on the vehicle, W.O. had taken the chassis for a test drive himself, believing of course, as was proper, that he was the first to do so. It was some years later that he learnt the truth! For W.O.'s outing the chassis was not temporarily clothed in its lightweight body as it had been for the earlier joy-ride. Bearing in mind that this was the first official test of a prototype car, W.O. was harshly critical of its noise and roughness, and made a diary note to the effect that the experience was almost indescribable. For W.O. excessive noise in a vehicle was intolerable, and it was always his aim that his cars should be as quiet as possible.

The car must have undergone some serious fine tuning, for a couple of weeks later on a Saturday, with the open four-seater body fitted, W.O. took it for a longer and more demanding trial and was accompanied by Gallop and H.M. Again he was critical, although at this early stage in the vehicle's development there is evidence of cautious optimism.

The test route covered some 80 miles, the destination being St Albans in Hertfordshire. W.O. noted to Burgess that the car's road holding was good and that it steered well, although he would have preferred the steering to have not been quite so low-geared. Changing gear proved difficult because of the strength of the plunger springs on the gear-shift mechanism, and the carburetion required attention as the induction pipe remained too cold. There were also noticeable problems on snap throttle openings. The problems of noise remained to a certain extent, W.O. having identified the pump or bottom cam drive bevels as the culprit.

The engine ran too cool, and W.O. recorded that the dial on the water gauge was reluctant to get anywhere near the optimum temperature. On the plus side he found the car's suspension to be excellent, despite the fact that the front springs were too weak; the brakes, too, were exceptional for the time. Although the foot brake was sufficiently responsive, W.O. noted that the leverage could be improved.

The engine was satisfactory and W.O. found it wonderfully smooth; hill climbing presented absolutely no problem, and acceleration in top gear from 10mph was easily achieved, up to a maximum of 60mph before performance tailed off owing to poorly set up carburettors.

Overall, W.O. was convinced that the prototype was up to standard and that it had excellent potential. The handling was ideal, and the car behaved beautifully both in traffic and at speed on the open road. He was undoubtedly very pleased with it; in his opinion it was better than a DFP.

Further testing ensued. On one occasion W.O. took the opportunity to drive H.M. and Hillstead to Bury St Edmunds in Suffolk in order to inspect a DFP. Hillstead mentions the trip in his autobiography *Those Bentley Days*, recalling how his tall frame was cramped in the rear seat, and contrastingly how capacious the cockpit was, with plenty of leg room and a deep scuttle providing ample protection. He commented on the steering wheel with its thin rim, which was raked at exactly the right angle. Of EXP1 he wrote: 'She seemed perfect, yet when I look at her photograph today (over half a century ago!) I am reminded of something archaic; certainly motor car fashions change rapidly.'

If W.O. had been critical about EXP1, something only to be expected from an engineer who was satisfied with nothing but perfection, Sammy Davis, when writing in *The Autocar* in the issue of 24 January 1920, was full of praise. Sammy lauded the 3-litre's performance and its potential for high-speed travelling. EXP1 had been registered on 11 December 1919 and carried the registration number BM8287. So as not to antagonise British authorities, Sammy's words about full-throttle driving actually suggest that the car was tested in France, on the national highways where there were no speed limits. The opposite was in fact true, the road test having taken place in rural England.

Anyone reading Sammy Davis's report with a penchant for a real sporting car could be forgiven for wanting to get their hands on the Bentley immediately. He wrote of the hand-built car that it had only recently been completed, and that it remained unaltered and untuned. He described its power and the rugged test body, which lacked a hood but accommodated four people.

The engine, having instantly responded to the electric starter, emitted a steady roar from the exhaust, and following a couple of movements on the accelerator – Brooklands style of course – the car was off without any real effort. The real test came when the car was subjected to positive acceleration and speeds in excess of 70mph: 'The landscape leaped at us, wind shrieked past the screen, while the flanking trees and other objects seemed, not definitely and sharply contoured, but a blurred streak hurtling past as the roar of the exhaust rose to its full song.' Anyone who has driven a 'W.O.' Bentley, will understand Sammy's words, for the 'Bentley experience' remained little changed throughout the cars' production run. Sammy accepted that a car in its development stage could never be entirely perfect, and this allowed him to be modestly critical of an unidentified noise from within the engine, which, he supposed, could have emanated from the scavenge pump in the dry-sump oil system. He also made a passing reference to an excess of oil that was sprayed on the exterior of the engine – 'problems', he said, that were 'inseparable from the production of a new design that would be solved before series production started.' Concluding his report, Sammy was emphatic that the best feature of the car was its effortless speed and total suitability for Continental motoring. Quite simply he considered the Bentley to be a car *par excellence*.

The question of engine noise persisted for some time, despite all sorts of remedies having been tried. Harry Varley eventually diagnosed the problem, which was one of applied geometry that he had missed at first. The angle of the pump gear had been incorrectly calculated, and when modifications were eventually put into practice, the problem was solved. The initial design featured a dry-sump oil system, the oil tank being scuttle-mounted. However, W.O.'s quest for quiet running led to his decision to revert to a wet sump system, thus doing away with the potentially noisy scavenge pump, and this was adopted for production.

The clamour for the Bentley in the wake of Sammy's report in *The Autocar* can be imagined. The Hanover Court showroom was besieged by enquiries, and Hillstead was later to recall that the sales department could have sold many cars on the strength of the article alone. Even the rise in the price of the 3-litre chassis, which had been quoted as £750 at the time of the Olympia show and subsequently increased to £1,150, did little to deter potential customers. The reason for the price increase was the fact that components had to be sourced from outside suppliers to Bentley drawings, and Bentley Motors had little control over some of the costings that were accordingly imposed. When suppliers increased their prices, there was no alternative but to add the additional cost to the chassis price.

Among the many enquiries at Hanover Court there were, inevitably, some that did not come to fruition. One such was from a group of so-called businessmen from the north of England whose investment, if placed, promised the funding of manufacturing facilities. W.O., possibly suspecting the nature of the deal, declined an invitation to drive EXP1 northwards to meet the proposed investors, and instead delegated H.M. to undertake the journey. H.M. did not relish the thought of travelling so far on what might have been a wasted journey, so the task fell to Arthur Hillstead. As it happened the investors were quite incapable of providing the necessary finance, and clearly did not appreciate the finer aspects of the Bentley. The journey was not entirely wasted, for one of the party had already subscribed to shares in Bentley Motors, and was sufficiently impressed by the car's performance to increase his share-holding in the company. Hillstead had also been able to get to know EXP1 intimately, which increased his enthusiasm for the car.

The search for factory premises came to a head when W.O. heard of land being released for sale in north-west London. The area then was largely rural, amid farmland and rolling countryside, and the plots that had become available were adjacent to the Edgware Road at Cricklewood, then little more than a village south of the Welsh Harp reservoir. The land that W.O. settled on extended to four acres, with double road frontage bordering the Edgware Road and Oxgate Lane, the latter being a country byway. It makes for a stark comparison to the present day. Oxgate Lane is now overshadowed by the North Circular Road at its junction with the M1 motorway. Purchase of the land was made possible by taking a mortgage with the London Joint City and Midland Bank Ltd, and the completion of the works amounted to around £22,000 including the freehold.

With the establishment of the works on the Cricklewood site, Bentley Motors' prospectus provided for the production of five chassis per week, with deliveries commencing in June 1921. A further provision was the profit margin of £200 per chassis, thus allowing a profit estimated at £50,000, a sum sufficient for the company to pay a substantial dividend while maintaining an adequate reserve. The figures were in fact academic, since the net profits for 1919 and 1920 amounted to a deficit in excess of £16,000, with a further deficit of a fraction more than £7,400 in 1921.

In acquiring land at Cricklewood W.O. had won the battle with Bentley Motors' shareholders by keeping the company near to London. It had also been suggested by some shareholders that the manufacture of Bentleys be put out to contract, something that W.O. fought vehemently against. Winning the argument meant that he was able to control production and maintain quality, the latter being one of marque's hallmarks.

Building contractors began preparing the Oxgate Lane site at the end of 1919, and during the early part of the following year construction of a two-gabled brick building commenced. This was the engine test shop, access to which was by wooden sliding doors. As soon as it was complete W.O. made provision for a move from New Street Mews to Cricklewood, the premises serving additionally as a store and assembly area.

Nobby Clarke, who was among the first to occupy the building and who was provided with a small wooden office within its centre, recalls the difficulties in negotiating the rough track leading from the Edgware Road onto the Oxgate Lane building site. W.O. was a frequent visitor, always checking building progress and naturally interested in getting the test shop into operation as quickly as possible. Sometimes he would arrive in a DFP, but as soon as EXP1 was on the road that became his favourite mode of transport. On one occasion the mud was such that the Bentley became firmly stuck in the quagmire and many hands were needed to free it. To avoid a similar situation W.O. arranged for old railway sleepers to be laid along the track, only to be caught later as one them broke in half when EXP1's front wheels rolled onto it. The offending piece of wood struck the underside of the car, damaging the radiator and causing it to leak.

Again W.O. faced problems when fitting out the test shop. Directors and shareholders were worried about the expense of purchasing and installing a Heenan and Froude dynamometer, which, as far as W.O. was concerned, was absolutely essential to check the power output of each engine built. Fortunately common sense prevailed. The only other piece of machinery available at the time, apart from the bench drill and grindstone that had been transferred from the Mews, was a drilling machine that was huge and quite unsuitable for the type of work that was being undertaken. Nobby Clarke likened the beast to a 'coffee grinder with a huge great wheel at the top'. The machine was superfluous and never used, and it ended up being moved around the works to be out of the way. No one knew who had been responsible for its purchase, and the culprit never admitted it.

When Clarke, Pennal, Gallop and Jackson moved to Cricklewood their main worry was the lack of proper tools and equipment. It was some time before all areas of the works were supplied with electrical power, and for some of the operations there was no alternative but to use hand drills. W.O. was only too aware of the plight that his staff experienced and once recalled the dreadful situation – the board opposed any expenditure, and argued that everything the company strove for could be achieved 'on the cheap'. W.O. knew that in order to build a first-rate motor car only the best tooling would suffice. He was also aware that there were certain directors who would have been happy to see a lesser car produced. Obviously, for some, profits came before quality.

It had been W.O.'s intention to install a foundry and welding equipment at an early stage, but the cost was too enormous to consider and the latter only became available after some years. The economies were wide-ranging, to the extent that mechanics and engineers would be instructed to collect and deliver components to and from different engineering companies. Some of the items were bulky, such as tyres, and exhaust pipes that had been welded to form a single item. Works transport was unavailable, and whoever had the task of conveying the items had either to walk or go by bus or tram. There were occasions when money was so tight that there were insufficient funds to meet the coal and coke bills, and the fuel company refused to deliver supplies. Such was their loyalty to W.O. that staff remained at work in the depths of winter even when there was no heating in the workshops. They carried on without any fuss, merely donning scarves and thick coats. The formative days at Cricklewood meant working, on occasions, around the clock, often to include Saturdays and Sundays. W.O. spent countless hours at the works, when he wasn't doing battle with the directors.

Mention has been made of W.O.'s sombre moods, his dismissal of trivial matters, and that dark gaze when he wasn't pleased. He had a way of chastising people quietly and in a civilised manner, often ending a potentially unpleasant encounter with a smile. His philosophy was that he would never expect anyone to do something that he would not, or could not, do himself. There was also a side to his character that was compassionate and utterly modest. When, on one occasion, Leslie Pennal's fiancée was seriously ill and her doctor appeared not to be concerned, W.O. took it upon himself, at his own expense, to arrange for a noted specialist to see her. When it meant Pennal taking the young lady to a sanatorium, W.O. let him have his own car for the weekend while he travelled home on an open chassis.

W.O. was a stickler for punctuality and good time-keeping, and he expected the same from his staff. When they continually erred he made it his job to seek the reason. The compassionate side of his nature came to the fore if there was genuine hardship or problem, but if it were a case of sheer laziness on the individual's part they were left in no doubt as to what the future held for them. Punctuality and discipline had been part of W.O.'s regime during his schooling and apprenticeship; if he could manage to get up and be at work at an early hour, then he took the view that there was no reason for others not doing so. Apart from a few exceptions, the team that W.O. had amassed around him were all youngsters and desperately keen. Inevitably there were some high jinks that were mainly aimed at the older and more experienced staff. Such joviality seldom led to any harm being done, and resulted in a happy working arrangement. High spirits could only be expected in such a working atmosphere, but were usually confined to times when W.O. was not around. Not that W.O. did not understand; he knew only too well what was going on, and took the view that as long as work was not compromised by such actions, then no harm was done.

He was also a person of habit. Each morning he would arrive at Cricklewood at a precise time, to be met by Harry Haggard, whom

Leslie Pennal refers to as W.O.'s own man, who had been employed by the Bentley family for many years. Haggard would be waiting for W.O. to arrive, a hosepipe at the ready in order to wash his car. The routine was the same each day: W.O. would stop the car, get out and have a few words with Harry before going to the other side of the vehicle to lift out his little Blenheim spaniel dog. Tucking it under his arm, he would disappear into the works. The spaniel was a constant companion, it went everywhere with him, even to race meetings at Brooklands and the Isle of Man.

It was W.O.'s habit to wear a long white silk scarf while driving, a throwback to his motorcycling days and early racing career. On one occasion while testing EXP1, the scarf was nearly his downfall when one end became entangled in the spokes of the rear offside wheel and threatened to strangle him. Luckily for him the scarf unwound from around his neck, but it was a lesson to be learnt, and one that Frank Clement, who witnessed the incident, was keen to pass on to all other drivers. W.O. often opted to fit discs to the rear wheels, not only as a precaution against such incidents, but also to reduce the car's drag.

Soon after the move was made from New Street Mews to Cricklewood, W.O. arranged for a wooden army hut to be erected alongside the engine test shop. This provided temporary administration accommodation, W.O. and Burgess occupying an office at one end, and Harry Varley having his drawing office at the other. In between the two departments was the general office. No doubt the arrangements were orchestrated by W.O., to keep Varley and Burgess apart!

Once the move was complete, W.O. took on more staff. Bob Tomlins was acquired from Vauxhall and progressed to become vehicle tester; Frank Clement, who had also worked for Vauxhall, and before that Straker-Squire, Napier and the Star Engineering Company, was appointed works manager. Clement and W.O. had much in common, both having raced before the war, and immediately following hostilities Clement had been appointed head tester of aero engines designed by Roy Fedden. W.O., incidentally, had invited Clement to join him in 1919 when the two had met at Olympia. Because of contractual arrangements in force at the time, it was not until 1920 that he was able to accept the offer.

Walter Hassan joined Bentley Motors in 1921; no more than a lad, he arrived fresh from technical school and joined what became the experimental department, by then headed by Clement. Wally Hassan had, in fact, trained as a marine engineer, but when opportunities in that business were unforthcoming he looked to the motor industry for employment. His father knew the service managers at both Sunbeam and Daimler, the former's offices also being located at Cricklewood. Having attended an interview at the Sunbeam factory he decided to approach nearby Bentley Motors, where he was interviewed by Frank Clement. Arthur and Wally Saunders, father and son, were also incorporated into the Bentley empire, Arthur having been part of the 1914 Humber TT team. Wally followed his father into the motor industry, first working as a teaboy in the machine shop at the Iris Motor Company, and then at Napier from 1914 as an improver. He was with Napier for only a few months before he transferred to Clement-Talbot, staying there until the end of the war in a reserved occupation. The paths of Wally Saunders and Wally Hassan often took a parallel course, both of them being closely associated with Bentley racing.

Frank Clement's appointment as Head of the Experimental Department followed Clive Gallop's departure from Bentley Motors. It was through Clement's intervention that Dick Witchell, whom he had worked with at Straker-Squire, was appointed works manager, Witchell having attended Clifton at the same time as W.O. as well as serving with the RFC. Clement and Witchell, despite being opposites temperamentally, worked in close harmony, the former's come-what-may attitude contrasting with the latter's steady and utterly fair-minded manner.

In addition to Wally Hassan, Clement, with W.O.'s approval, was responsible for engaging several mechanics and engineers who were to emerge as the backbone of the company in all areas, including racing. Among them were Puddephatt, Howard, Martin and Pryke. Of those that Clement hired there were two in particular who made their mark at Bentley Motors: Stan Ivermee and Jack Sopp. Ivermee stayed with W.O. throughout the life of the company, following him to Rolls-Royce, and later to Lagonda. His work on the experimental side of the business was unparalleled and he was responsible for much of the work perfecting the 4½-litre and 8-litre engines. Jack Sopp was of the same mould, W.O. referring to him as one of the finest racing mechanics of all time.

It is remarkable that so many of those who worked for Bentley Motors stayed with the company through thick and thin, the great majority remaining until 1931 and the Rolls-Royce takeover. There were a few who decided not to continue, however, one in particular being Clive Gallop, who departed in order to work for Count Louis Zoborowski, who was perhaps best known for his aero-engined racing cars and, more latterly, Bugattis. Clive Gallop was sorely missed by W.O., and in effect it was Frank Clement who took over the work that he had started.

By the autumn of 1920 work had progressed building the first of the production shops, which was linked to the test shop to form the plant's nucleus. The method of construction was relatively simple and inexpensive. Buildings were steel-framed with concrete-block walls and corrugated roofs were formed from glass and steel. Asbestos was also widely used, the dangers that this material presented being then unrecognised. Writing in 1964, W.O. commented that the buildings were well put together, and appeared exactly as they were during the Bentley Motors' era. Fronting the Edgware Road were the stores, which were, according to W.O., 'proudly and assiduously attended by Fred Conway.'

Much of the work was completed by 1921, the engine-erecting shop being adjacent to the test shop. The chassis-erecting shop adjoined the store and bordered both the Edgware Road and Oxgate Lane, and was also used for testing purposes. The experimental and racing shops also adjoined the test shop, but these were later absorbed into the engine-erecting facilities. Across the yard from the test shop and its adjacent boiler house was the test shop for finished cars. Once production was under way, chassis were despatched to the relevant coachbuilders, and when the bodies had been fitted they were delivered back to Cricklewood as completed vehicles, for extensive checking and road testing.

The machine shops were not constructed until around 1929, and at about the same time the administration block was built. It was there that W.O. had his office, and next to the building was a private walled garden, which often served as W.O.'s retreat.

Both EXP2 and EXP3 were completed at Cricklewood. EXP2 was registered on 25 March 1920 and given the number BM 8752, and EXP3 received the registration BM 9771 in September that year. As for EXP1, this was used as a test vehicle until late in 1920 when it was rebuilt and fitted with a new four-seater body that was dark grey in colour. In its rebuilt state EXP1 became known as 'The Fire Engine' owing to its claret colour. The vehicle remained in service with Bentley Motors as a company demonstrator until 1923, when it was sold to W.J. Dowding.

EXP2 was put through its paces by Frank Clement, who was Bentley Motors' first and foremost professional driver. He participated in nearly all of the company's racing events until 1930, and his name is synonymous with Bentley lore. In addition to testing EXP2 at Brooklands, it was usual for him to use a particular stretch of the Edgware Road for speed tests, the road then carrying very light traffic. Another of his favourite venues was Brockley Hill in Stanmore, which he would often drive up at full speed in third gear.

W.O. and Clement were frequent visitors to Brooklands with EXP2. Much work testing the car's carburetion was undertaken there, Wally Hassan often accompanying the test runs in an effort to try out and tune different carburettors to achieve optimum performance. W.O., in fact, was a master at carburettor tuning, something which stemmed from his DFP days and his work on aero engines. EXP2 had originally been fitted with a single Claudel-Hobson carburettor before a five-jet Smith type was used. It was the experience with EXP2 at Brooklands that helped set Bentley Motors on its route to its racing successes, together with a mention in *The Daily Telegraph* of 24 February 1921, when W.O. let it be known that he anticipated entering a Bentley for selected racing events at the track.

Within three months W.O. had EXP2 entered at Brooklands for the Essex Motor Club's Short Handicap over 5¾ miles scheduled for Saturday 7 May. EXP2, to be driven by Frank Clement with Arthur Hillstead as passenger, was in good company, as other competitors included Woolf Barnato driving his Calthorpe, Lionel Martin in an Aston Martin, and Malcolm Campbell in his Talbot. The field also included Douglas Hawkes, who was later to drive for Bentley, and Cambridge undergraduate Raymond Mays, later synonymous with ERA and BRM and a lifelong Bentley enthusiast. During practice EXP2 was lapping at around 83mph, which pleased W.O. to the point that he placed a significant bet with the Brooklands bookkeeper, an individual known as Long Tom. Clement's fine performance immediately before the race was encouraging, and his get-away from the start line was meteoric, but on changing into top the engine went on to fail, a plug having oiled up, forcing Clement and Hillstead to abandon the race.

They were met by a stony faced W.O. in the paddock – the fact that he had lost a substantial amount of money to the bookie accounting for some of his bad temper.

A little over a week later EXP2, with Clement and Hillstead on board, was back at Brooklands, entered for the Whitsun Short Handicap and Junior Sprint Handicap events. W.O. had forgotten his annoyance and was confident that his car could outpace its rivals. In the first of the two races Clement was again in the company of Campbell and Barnato in addition to Henry Segrave, John Duff, Count Zoborowski and Humphrey Cook. EXP2 lapped in excess of 84mph yet finished unplaced, much to W.O.'s disappointment.

If, at the start of the second race, a short handicap in which Clement drove unaccompanied, everyone was nervous because of W.O.'s agitation, they need not have worried. Although the initial lead was taken by a Douglas driven by Sawers, Clement edged ahead on the straight, increasing the distance between the two cars by four lengths, winning the event at an average speed of 72.5mph.

Bentley's racing career had begun and W.O., of whom it is said that he did not show much pleasure at his team's win, had at last proved that he was a force to be reckoned with. In actual fact W.O. was elated at the car's performance, thanks to Clement's driving skill. It was thought that W.O. would announce that the car would compete in the Grand Prix of the Automobile Club de France on 24 July 1921, but sadly the car could not be prepared in time.

In March 1921 EXP2 was fitted with a new body supplied by Easters. In this guise the vehicle was a regular competitor at Brooklands and elsewhere, and it was sold to J.E. Foden in September 1923. It is ironic that, while driving home to Cheshire after collecting the car from Cricklewood, the new owner experienced piston failure. The car was repaired and sold to T. Heaton, who in 1925 was competing at Kop Hill as part of the Essex Motor Club's hill climb events.

EXP3 was registered on 16 September 1920 as BM 9771. Known as 'The Cab', this was W.O.'s personal car and was fitted with a lightweight Harrisons Allweather body. The car was Bentley Motors' sole exhibit at the White City motor show in 1920 and was more representative of production Bentleys than either of the earlier experimental cars.

W.O. took sole charge of The Cab. He monitored its performance closely and would not even allow it to be washed until it had completed 20,000 miles, although the reason for this was never explained. W.O. visited Brooklands with the vehicle on several occasions, sometimes in the company of his old friend Sammy Davis, the two delighting in tackling the track's test hill. EXP3 was retained by Bentley Motors until 1924 when the car was sold to E. Taylor with a five-year guarantee applicable to the engine only.

The introduction of a five-year guarantee was another example of W.O.'s insistence on absolute quality, and was extended to the car as a whole. Such a warranty was quite unique and remained unmatched by other manufacturers. He was right in believing that such a pledge would prove an incentive to buy the car, and customers appreciated the assurance. If any of the directors were unhappy at the arrangement, which could have caused the company to be liable for relatively large sums of money, they took some comfort from the conditions that were attached to the scheme. A charge of £5 was made to inspect a vehicle before the balance of the guarantee was transferred to a car's new owner, and should any work be found to be necessary the work had to be undertaken and paid for before the transfer was complete. This undoubtedly brought in some income and secured the company's reputation for quality. There is evidence, nonetheless, that losses to the tune of £10,000 per annum were experienced throughout the years 1924 to 1930.

EXP4 was fitted with an open tourer body, registered ME 2431 and assigned to F.T. Burgess. The three earlier experimental vehicles had carried Bedfordshire registrations in order to display the letters BM. W.O. had tried to get Bedfordshire County Council to make a block of numbers available for company use, but the registration authority had refused.

It would appear that the engine fitted to EXP4 was a prototype 4½-litre unit, and the car was rebuilt in the mid-1920s when it was equipped with a production 4½-litre engine. Experimental cars were constructed as a matter of course throughout the era of Bentley Motors. Some were sold, as has been indicated, while others were rebuilt and remained in use within the experimental department.

In September 1921 W.O.'s long-nurtured aspirations to build a fast, high-quality production sports car materialised when the first 3-litre was ready for delivery. That this was a momentous occasion goes almost without saying. Reaching this stage in the career of the car, and the company, had taken nearly three years. In that time there had been some desperately low points when W.O. and his team could well have surrendered all hopes of achieving their goal, the nagging financial worries being ever-present. A member of the Bentley family recalls how H.M. was sometimes forced to provide the cash for the wages, and how, on more than one occasion, the money came from his personal funds. There were the high points, too: the experimental cars performed much better than could ever have been expected, and EXP2 won a race before production had commenced.

W.O. attached a lot of importance to the choice of Bentley's first customer. He thought that the owner of the company's first production car should, ideally, be well known and have a good standing in society, as well as being an enthusiastic motorist, preferably one with racing experience. Of those potential customers who were attracted to the marque it was Noel van Raalte that W.O. considered the best candidate. Van Raalte was exceedingly wealthy and a clever engineer who happened to be a major shareholder in KLG Plugs; he was the owner of Brownsea Island in Poole Harbour, which was just one of his many properties, and he had begun motor racing while an undergraduate at Cambridge University.

W.O. was keen for van Raalte to head the Bentley customer list, for he knew that his authoritative manner when discussing the car with others would compliment the business. He knew too that anyone able to afford over £1,000 for a motor car would appreciate its qualities, and that van Raalte would report on its progress together with any complications that might arise.

On a morning in September 1921, therefore, van Raalte arrived at Cricklewood to take delivery of his car and was met by W.O. himself. Bentley's first customer took care to look over the vehicle in every detail, checking the coachwork which had been constructed by Easters, and lifting the bonnet to inspect the engine. Satisfied that everything was in order, with due ceremony he drove out of the works.

The sale of the car was a huge morale-booster for the Bentley personnel. With the first 3-litre safely in the hands of its discerning owner, the workforce got on with the job of preparing the next batch of chassis.

Witness accounts of the early production era indicate that mainly as a result of sound design and thorough testing, few problems were encountered. There were teething troubles of course, but these were addressed as they were discovered or notified by customers. Some of the problems were caused by the rush to get the car into production, which led to neglect of what might have seemed obvious, such as overlooking the height of the bottle jack supplied, which was too tall to fit under the front axle. The need to produce an owner handbook had simply not occurred to anybody, so when the deficiency was discovered it was W.O. who produced the publication over several nights, the typewritten document eventually being supplied with each car.

Noel van Raalte did indeed prove to be the ideal customer. His enthusiasm for the car became greater as he used it, and in correspondence he described it as superior to any of the many cars that he owned or had owned, including Rolls-Royces.

CHAPTER 6

The Bentley Boys

A FTER the 3-litre's achievements at Brooklands and elsewhere during 1921 W.O. had determined to compete in the 1922 Isle of Man TT with a team of three cars. The event had not been staged since 1914 and therefore W.O. presumed it would attract the leading teams and cars of the post-war era. By entering the race W.O. must have been convinced that a Bentley stood a good chance of success, hence his maxim of never entering an event unless he thought he could win.

All the more adventurous was W.O.'s decision to enter the 1922 Indianapolis race in America, which was scheduled for 30 May, three weeks before the Isle of Man TT. Competing in both events meant that it was necessary for four cars to be prepared, putting a considerable strain on the newly-established racing team.

The decision to compete in Indianapolis proved to be a major error on W.O.'s part. Not only was the exercise of sending a car and racing team to America very expensive, which ate into Bentley Motors' limited funds, but it also failed to provide the company with a positive result, although the car did at least finish in a commendable 13th position. The timescale for building the Indianapolis car was almost impossible, and at one stage it looked as if the project would have to be cancelled. That it was finished in time was something of a miracle; it was crated and delivered to Liverpool where it was loaded aboard the SS *Olympic* to arrive in the United States a couple of days before the race. Douglas Hawkes had been nominated as driver, his riding mechanic being Bert Browning, who had gone to America ahead of the car to prepare for the event.

It had been W.O.'s idea to promote the Bentley marque in America.

Although the car performed reasonably well at Indianapolis, and impressed some of the American competitors, the episode really did very little to establish Bentley sales across the Atlantic. Recalling the event, W.O. admitted that the car simply wasn't fast enough compared to the American machines, some of which were averaging over 90mph.

W.O. had placed Frank Clement in charge of preparations, and in turn Clement appointed Arthur Saunders as foreman, along with mechanics Browning, Leslie Pennal, Wally Saunders, Wally Hassan and Jack Bessant. Most of the preparation work was conducted in that part of the experimental department that became known as the racing shop. The racing team was responsible for the entire preparation of the cars, the necessary special components being made available through the works' stores. The exception to this arrangement was the building of the gearboxes, which were built under Nobby Clarke's supervision within the works.

Hawkes and Browning arrived back in England just in time for the TT, arriving on the Isle of Man a couple of days after practice had started. Their car, however, was delayed, and did not return to Cricklewood until early July. W.O. had already decided that he would drive one of the three specially prepared cars, while Clement and Hawkes would drive the other two. There had been some question about whether Hawkes would actually be available for the race, especially if his return journey from America was delayed. W.O.'s contingency plan was to have Arthur Hillstead as reserve driver, which excited Hillstead but annoyed a number of the Bentley Motors workforce. Hillstead said that there were 'others in power who felt they had been passed over and the affair developed into a first-class row.' Such arguments were rare among the usually content crew at Cricklewood, and ultimately W.O. made no provision for a third driver should Hawkes not arrive in the Isle of Man in time.

Frank Clement's version of the row was somewhat different. W.O. had asked him to visit Malcolm Campbell and to ask him whether he would agree to be the reserve driver. Clement, quite naturally, felt awkward at having to approach Campbell in this manner with such a question, wondering all the time why W.O. had not asked him personally. Campbell was very gentlemanly about the affair; he agreed to drive, but not as a reserve!

W.O. appointed Pennal to be his riding mechanic, a task that he proudly and very willingly undertook. Clement's mechanic was Arthur Saunders, and Browning rode with Hawkes. EXP2 was also taken to the Island, and as well as serving as a practice car, thus relieving some of the pressure on the racing machines, was on hand in case any parts were required from it, such as the engine, springs and anything else that could be cannibalised.

The Bentley team was accommodated at the Prince of Wales Hotel on Ramsey's south promenade. The other teams were based nearby and during the evenings leading up the race proper it was not unusual to find drivers and their mechanics getting together to enjoy a relaxed social life.

The arrival of the competing teams attracted the local girls and, as can be imagined, much revelry ensued, the Bentley contingent included. One particular night Wally Saunders and Bert Harper, who was the Bentley team's tyre fitter, arrived back at the hotel at a particularly late hour after a dance to find the doors locked. Having attempted all methods of gaining access, including trying to scale the exterior wall with the help of knotted sheets lowered from an upstairs window by Arthur Saunders, they admitted defeat and decided to spend the night in W.O.'s car, with his Blenheim spaniel as company.

W.O. realised what was happening and dealt with the situation in his own way. Conscious that some of the young mechanics were at risk of compromising their daytime work performance because of too much socialising at night time, he arranged for them to meet him at nine o'clock the following evening in one of the bars. Without more ado he ordered them to go to bed to catch up on some sleep and escorted them to their rooms. Pennal, recalling the events later, believed that W.O. was also going to his room early, and was therefore surprised to see him later descending the back staircase that led to the bars!

The three TT cars carried several modifications to the standard production 3-litre. In addition to the streamlined bodies that had been prepared by Ewarts, high compression pistons were fitted; the carburettors were Claudel-Hobson designs, and the exhausts were modified as outside systems. The most striking feature of the cars was the design of radiator, a flat affair similar in style to that of the Bugatti and very different to the pattern seen on production cars.

W.O. had devised the radiator shape following discussions with the National Physical Laboratory. He had thought that a reduced frontal area with less resistance would enhance the car's performance in maintaining higher speeds; and there was also the question of economics, the modified radiator being cheaper to produce than the more familiar type. There was a downside, however. The production radiator would have emphasised the Bentley marque more appropriately, and might well have served as a worthwhile sales feature.

It was mentioned at the time in the motoring press that the TT modifications amounted to an extra £25 on the chassis price, and that these were available on a production chassis to order for that additional amount. The truth was more complex, as the chassis featured lightened flywheels and special radiator mountings and shock absorbers, not to mention larger 22-gallon fuel tanks in addition to the original 11-gallon tanks to avoid refuelling during the race. From surviving records there is evidence that few customers ordered the modifications.

Practising for the TT was conducted early in the morning, beginning at around five o' clock so as not to inconvenience the island's inhabitants. For W.O. the reacquaintance with the island was a nostalgic pleasure, even though the dismal weather and downpours made the event itself something of a nightmare. Nevertheless the pleasure was tinged with an element of pathos, for missing from the occasion, partly due to the war, were some of the colourful characters and personalities that had been part of the scene in 1914.

In the race Bentley took the team prize with Clement in second place, W.O. in fourth and Hawkes in fifth. First position was taken by Jean Chassagne driving a Sunbeam, and third went to Oswald Payne in a Vauxhall. W.O. could take comfort from his cars' performance, despite some problems. The radiator plug in Hawkes's car had become detached, so he lost all the coolant, and some 20 minutes were wasted while water was added to the red-hot engine. When he continued the race, it was with a champagne or medicine bottle cork compressed into the drain hole. The floorboards on W.O.'s car worked loose after only a few laps: without any ankle support, and with his legs held up by the pressure of his feet on the pedals, he was subjected to a lot of discomfort. There was worse to come. A joint opened in the exhaust pipe just ahead of the cockpit, engulfing the occupants with choking fumes; when the rear section of pipe eventually fell away Pennal would have been roasted alive by the scorching heat had it not been for the rain.

The incessant rain and problems with his car were enough to depress W.O.'s enthusiasm sufficiently to put him in a sullen mood. Whatever Pennal did to try and make things more comfortable was met with a growl or a look of disdain. When Simon Orde, who was Bentley's pit manager, put out a 'faster' sign for him, W.O. chose to ignore the message, an action which lost him third place in the race to Oswald Payne by six seconds, despite having plenty of reserve in hand. Commenting on the incident at a later date, W.O. recalled that 'I was so cross that I got the sulks and never glanced at the pit again until the end of the race.'

For a number of reasons this was W.O.'s last race as a driver. Not only did he concede that running a business at the same time as actively racing constituted too much stress, his insurers were also adamant he should divorce himself from personally competing in events. W.O.'s position within Bentley Motors as chairman and joint managing director (which included the role of racing manager) was intrinsic to the success or otherwise of the company. To personally engage in competitive events, which were considered highly dangerous, represented too much of a risk in the insurers' estimation. Had W.O. been killed or incapacitated, the loss of his expertise would have put the future of the company in jeopardy. Moreover, W.O. was financially tied to Bentley Motors (and was in fact its most important asset), so his death or serious injury behind the wheel in a racing event would have compromised the company as a whole.

The Bentleys, unlike the other larger cars in the race, were without front wheel brakes. W.O. was very much aware that he and Clement and Hawkes were forced to brake ahead of the competition, thus losing valuable seconds, and even the Bentleys' superior road holding in the dreadful weather conditions was not sufficient to regain lost time. If the TT did nothing else, it prompted W.O. to develop front wheel brakes for his cars.

The performance of the Bentleys was responsible for the establishment of one of the first Bentley agencies outside London. Watching the race was George Porter, a well-known car dealer from Blackpool, who was so impressed by the cars that he was willing to sign up for the Lancashire dealership there and then. As it happened, Porter remained a loyal advocate of Bentleys until his untimely death in the mid-1920s, while driving one of the TT cars that had been purchased from Bentley Motors by one of his customers. George's wife took over the Bentley agency and she successfully increased its turnover.

The Bentley team travelled back to Liverpool aboard the *Castle Mona*. During the voyage W.O. was introduced to H. (Bertie) Kensington Moir, who had put up a fine performance with his Aston Martin 'Bunny' before retiring through a broken valve. The two spent the night crossing in deep discussion about motor racing. They drank well too, W.O. savouring his favourite whisky.

Bertie was a generous man in all respects. Tall and rotund, he was a model raconteur, always full of good humour and endless stories. There was never a dull moment with him around, and his loud raucous laugh became his trademark. That he and W.O. established a special relationship during their passage across the Irish Sea is shown by the fact that when they arrived in Liverpool W.O. invited him to join Bentley Motors, an offer that he enthusiastically accepted. In the ensuing years Bertie Kensington Moir became an intrinsic part of the company, at the wheel, during race meetings and in the general running of the business.

W.O. had a particular assignment in mind for Kensington Moir. With production of cars under way he knew that the company was in need of a well-equipped service station at Oxgate Lane, and he wanted a proficient person to run it on a day-to-day basis.

One of the first London Bentley agents to be appointed was the well-known racing driver Captain John Duff. In 1921 he had driven his giant 1910 10-litre Fiat at Brooklands, where he achieved speeds in excess of 105mph, eventually selling the car to John Cobb. In the same year Captain Duff arrived at Brooklands in the famous 18-litre Fiat 'Mephistopheles', which he had bought for £100 after discovering it in a Fulham mews. Another London agent was Jack Withers (W.O.'s friend and brother-in-law) of Osnaburgh Street, opposite Great Portland Street underground station, who advertised himself as London's largest Bentley distributor.

Duff had met W.O. at Brooklands and elsewhere on various occasions and had ordered a car from Bentley Motors, chassis 141, which carried the registration XM 6761. Some time previously Duff had established his own company, Sporting Cars Ltd, and made it known that he wanted to operate a Bentley franchise. Because W.O. was insistent that Duff should have appropriate premises in which to sell and service Bentley cars, he approached an old friend, W.J. Adlington, from which association emerged Adlington and Duff Ltd in Upper St Martin's Lane in London.

It was with his already well-raced 3-litre Bentley that Duff put up an incredible performance at Brooklands on 28 August 1922. He took the one, two, three-hour, 100 and 200-mile and 100, 200, 300 and 400-kilometre Class E records, the hour being at 86.24mph and the others from 85 to nearly 87mph.

Then came another of those milestones that punctuate the history of the marque, for Duff wanted to compete in the first Le Mans 24-Hour race that was scheduled for 26 and 27 May 1923. However, when he approached Bentley Motors about the company's support, hoping to have his car suitably prepared and Clement as co-driver, W.O. was not entirely convinced it was such a good idea.

The concept of the Le Mans 24-Hour race was arrived at by three men: Georges Durand, who was wanting to promote the reliability of touring cars, Charles Faroux, editor of *La Vie Automobile*, and Emile Coquille, the French agent for the Rudge-Whitworth centre lock detachable wheel, who agreed to donate 100,000 francs in addition to presenting a trophy, the Rudge-Whitworth Cup.

When W.O. considered the format of the race he was not impressed. While he agreed that such an event was ideal for showing his cars to their best advantage, given that it was a long and gruelling race over a course that included a long straight, he remained unconvinced about its 24-hour duration. Such a contest, he argued, was ridiculous; no car could survive such treatment.

Duff was equally resolute and ultimately W.O., much against his better judgement, agreed not only to prepare Duff's car but also to release Clement. He further agreed to manage Duff's pit, and assigned Arthur Saunders and Jack Bessant as mechanics and pit crew. Driving the car that was entered for the race, the four-man team departed for Le Mans some days before the start of the race in order to prepare for the event. W.O. had declined to personally support the team and had arranged to stay in London for the duration of the race. Then, on the Friday, the day before the event, he had a sudden change of mind and called for Arthur Hillstead, telling him to pack an overnight bag. Hillstead did not have to be asked twice, and the two caught a late afternoon train to Newhaven, which connected with the night sailing to Dieppe.

The journey from Dieppe to Paris and thence to Le Mans was a miserable experience. The train was crowded, there was no restaurant car nor any refreshments, and not even a sandwich or a drink was available. It stopped at every station, and the time taken to reach the destination seemed unending. W.O. sank into one of his moods, and however Hillstead tried to make light of their situation he was met at best with a growl but mostly with either silence or a blank stare. Having not eaten anything since leaving London, they were both hungry and thirsty, and to compensate for the monotony they smoked throughout the entire journey. By the time they left Paris their mouths were parched and throats sore.

Waiting to greet them at Le Mans railway station were Duff and Clement, who were in optimistic mood because the Bentley was performing beautifully. The race facilities at Le Mans were not ideal: it was evident that the meeting was held too early in the season, as hailstones rained down at the start of the event. The road surface was poor and began breaking up during the first few hours, and tents made do for pits. The race started promptly at 4pm and no sooner was it under way that W.O. underwent a complete change of heart and realised this was just the sort of event that Bentleys were suited to.

Duff and Clement put up a heroic performance. The lack of front wheel brakes was all too obvious, but nevertheless the car held its own despite some formidable opposition from the Chenard-Walcker team. Duff was first to take the wheel, handing over to Clement at the first refuelling at around 8pm. The weather was pretty awful, the heavy rain resulting in a lot of mud on the road surface. Throughout the rain Duff and Clement drove without headgear or goggles, which gave rise to the French believing the drivers would retire through cold and exhaustion.

Just as it was getting dark a stone thrown up by a competing car damaged one of the Bentley's headlamps and put it out of action for the duration of the race. Night driving with a single lamp took its toll, and while the Bentley team were in second place, the distance between it and the leading Chenard-Walcker increased to 20 miles. With the coming of daylight Duff and Clement were able to reduce the French car's lead, and lap speeds in excess of 64.7mph by Duff and 66.69mph by Clement were sufficient to secure the first lap record at Le Mans.

At one stage the Bentley was going so fast at the end of the long Mulsanne Straight that the car's brakes were insufficient to slow the car down, and Duff was forced to take the escape road. The consequence was that Duff, who had been in sight of taking the lead, lost it to the Chenard-Walcker. Then, just before midday on the Sunday, disaster struck when a stone holed the Bentley's fuel tank. Duff had to leave his car and walk back to the pits, but the race jury agreed that Clement could requisition a French soldier's bicycle and ride to the stricken car with two bidons of petrol attached to his shoulders. The crowds of spectators cheered with encouragement as he pedalled the 'wrong way' towards the car, at times risking being knocked over by approaching competitors.

There were even louder cheers as Clement limped the Bentley into the pit, the 'vélo' safely accommodated in the *tonneau*. Emergency repairs were carried out to block the holed fuel tank with soap and cork. There were fears that the repair would not be sufficiently effective for the car to continue for the remainder of the race, but it did. The car finished strongly in fourth place, so strongly that shortly before the finish Clement recorded the race's fastest lap at 67mph.

W.O. was delighted by the 3-litre's success, especially considering the course of events, which could so easily have put the machine completely out of the race. He wired the good news to Hanover Court before departing for a well-earned bath and shave, a prelude to a night of celebrating and drinking too many spirits.

Within two months W.O. was back in France to watch the French Grand Prix at Tours and to witness Segrave, driving a six-cylinder Sunbeam, win Britain's first such event. This was the first national Grand Prix won by a British driver in a British car. On this occasion W.O. had insisted on taking his car, EXP3, not trusting the vagaries of boat and train travel. He took with him Clement and Hillstead.

The trio wanted to put EXP3 through its paces and there was a considerable amount of good humoured banter between them, until in a rare lapse Clement caught a hub cap a glancing blow with a small boulder while driving away from a hotel yard in Louviers. They lunched there, and had delighted in a bottle of red *vin de pays*, although W.O. had insisted on drinking whisky, which had not been to his liking. That, and the incident with the boulder, put him in a morose mood for a number of miles, and his temper was tested when Clement took the wrong road and became lost. By then it was getting late and W.O. became all the more fractious at the thought of having nowhere to enjoy a meal and spend the night. Eventually they arrived at Nonancourt, found a suitable hotel and all was well again.

Arriving at Tours W.O. met Henry Segrave and John Duff. The five went to the hotel where Segrave was staying and took a long lunch along with some wine. One thing led to another and the party went off to find a club that Segrave had recommended, the revelry continuing into the early hours of the following morning. Returning to the hotel, W.O., Clement and Hillstead discovered it to be fully booked, their reservation having been transferred to an annexe, which in this case was no more than a *chambre d'hôte* on the edge of town. W.O. was not in the least impressed and refused to move. Moreover he took the attitude of preferring not to converse in French, although he could speak the language quite capably. It was only when Clement was able to encourage the driver of a horse-drawn landau (who was the worse for wear through drink but nonetheless appreciated a few extra francs) that the three were conveyed to their lodgings, waking the owner from his slumbers.

On the journey home, with Hillstead and Clement taking turns to drive while W.O. tried to catch up on some sleep in the back, EXP3 was suddenly engulfed in flames. The two drivers had been putting the machine through its paces, with the accelerator pushed firmly to the floorboards for much of the trip. Under W.O.'s weight, not to mention the rough passage over the bumpy surfaces, the wooden inspection cover over the rear axle had become detached. It had slipped to one side to allow the seat cushion to dip into the hole and make contact with the hot exhaust pipe where it arched over the axle. The heat from the exhaust finally caused it to combust into thick pungent smoke. Clement and Hillstead were too preoccupied with the car's performance to realise what was going on behind them, but as soon as W.O. awakened he let out a fearsome scream that made Hillstead quickly pull the car up. With the horse-hair cushion on the verge the trio looked around in vain for water – they were not carrying a fire extinguisher – and finding none resorted to the call of nature to quell the fire!

John Duff continued racing his 3-litre Bentley, competing in the Touring Grand Prix of Guipuscoa in Spain in late July. He retired when he crashed into a wall, badly damaging the car. In early September he raced at the Boulogne Circuit, his car being one of three Bentleys, the other two being entered as a works' team and driven by Clement and

Bertie Kensington Moir. Duff was forced to retire following problems in practice when he collided with a cow; Kensington Moir experienced carburettor problems and finished the race as a tail-ender. Clement also retired when one of the magnesium alloy pistons he was trying burnt out.

Production of the 3-litre accounted for 145 cars in 1922. 204 cars were built in the following year, increasing to 403 in 1924. The latter figure represents the greatest number of cars built in any year up to 1931. The Bentley customer was discerning and by virtue of the car's price had to be substantially wealthy. Among the early customers was W.O.'s old friend, the artist Gordon Crosby, who bought chassis number 153 with Vanden Plas coachwork. Despite his being able to depict Bentleys at speed so deftly, Freddie Gordon Crosby was in fact a very staid driver who seldom drove his car in a very spirited fashion. Another distinguished customer was Prince George (later King George VI), who was the owner of several Bentleys. An indication of times past is that the Edgware Road and the North Circular Road were used for test runs, traffic conditions then allowing vehicles to be used at speeds far above those normally encountered.

W.O. was back at Le Mans for the 1924 24-Hour race in the middle of June. Duff's 3-litre was the only Bentley entered but since its last outing it had been equipped with four-wheel brakes and stone guards to protect the headlamps and fuel tank. Frank Clement was again nominated co-driver. It was Burgess who had undertaken much of the development work to make four-wheel braking possible, and in addition to it having been fitted to Duff's car, EXP4 – Burgess's own car – was also equipped. Burgess delighted in demonstrating the braking system to the press on a rough stretch of road opposite the Cricklewood works, and the system was made a standard feature for 1924 models.

Avoiding the painful fiasco of the previous year, on this occasion W.O. was determined to make the journey by car, taking with him Hillstead, Witchell and Kensington Moir. More significantly that journey gave W.O. the opportunity to fully evaluate a new chassis with a 6-cylinder 4½-litre engine. Known within the company as 'The Sun', the car was in fact a prototype machine which heralded the introduction of the 6½-litre Bentley in 1925. For some time W.O. had been concerned that the performance of the 3-litre model was being compromised by the fitting of commodious saloon bodywork, despite the fact that the car had not been designed for this purpose. A longer wheelbase chassis had

The 3-litre chassis design as portrayed in the Bentley catalogue. *(National Motor Museum)*

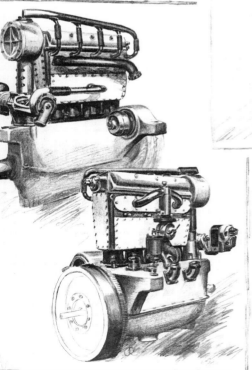

Details from the Bentley 3-litre catalogue depicting the car's components. *(National Motor Museum)*

An illustration from the Bentley 3-litre brochure depicts Icarus. The origins of the Bentley emblem can be appreciated. *(National Motor Museum)*

THE THREE LITRE
BENTLEY

W.O. at the wheel of the first Bentley motor car, EXP1. *(LAT Photographic)*

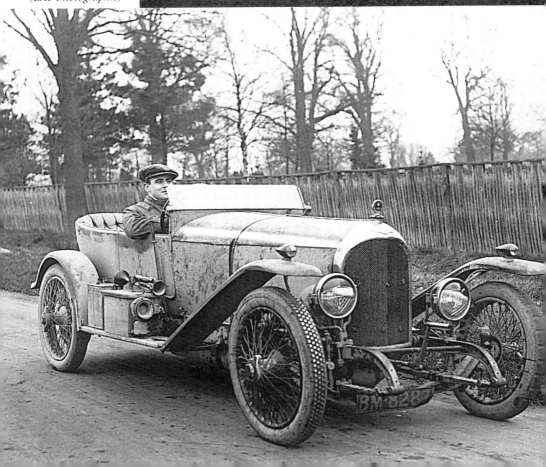

...O. and *The Autocar*'s correspondent Sammy Davis testing EXP1. Sammy produced a glowing report
...out the car in the magazine's edition dated 24 January 1920. *(LAT Photographic)*

...ne of the earliest Bentley advertisements. *(Author's collection/ Andrew Minney)*

BENTLEY

THE OWNER-DRIVER'S IDEAL
15.9 H.P. SPORTING CAR

Extreme flexibility on top gear — walking pace to 80 miles
per hour. 65 on third, 50 on second. Practically silent.
Remarkable ease of control. Chassis lubrication just
once every 5,000 miles — one greaser.

THREE OUTSTANDING GUARANTEED FEATURES

1. Every chassis GUARANTEED to attain 80 m.p.h.
2. Petrol consumption GUARANTEED 25 miles per gallon.
3. Every part GUARANTEED for five years.

PRICE

Chassis, with electric starter, dynamo, etc.,
Klaxon horn, complete tool kit, four 820 × 120
Pirelli tyres & spare detachable wire wheel.
£1,050

Four-seater Saloon Model (as illustration).
£1,500

e : Mayfair 2356

BENTLEY MOTORS, LTD.
3 Hanover Court, Hanover St., London, W.1

W.O. entered the 1922 Isle of Man TT with three cars. W.O. is driving No.9 with Pennal beside him; Hawke and Browning are in No.6 and Clement and Arthur Saunders in No.3. *(Jolyon Broad collection)*

W.O. at the wheel of his 3-litre. Leslie Pennal is riding mechanic. *(Jolyon Broad collection)*

e 1922 Isle of Man TT team. Left to right: Hawkes, Clement, W.O., Pennal, Browning, Saunders. *(Jolyon* *ad collection)*

Mans, 1924. W.O. with the victorious 3-litre. Frank Clement is on the left and Captain John Duff on the ht. Behind the car is Arthur Hillstead. *(Rolls-Royce & Bentley Motor Cars Ltd)*

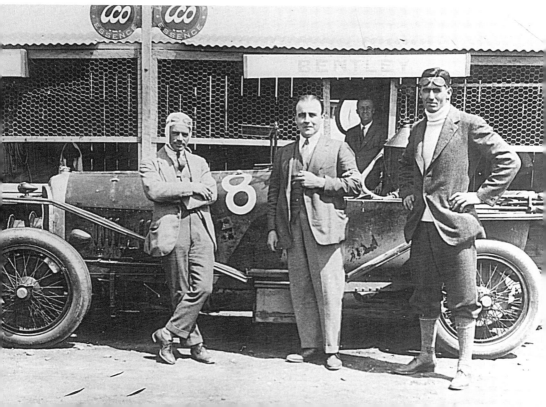

When Woolf Barnato took charge of Bentley Motors in 1926 the company opened new showrooms at Polle House, Cork Street. The photograph, which was taken in 2002, shows that the premises have changed little since the Bentley era. *(Author's collection)*

Bentley Motors used this fine illustration to depict the 6½-litre when it was introduced in 1926. *(National Motor Museum)*

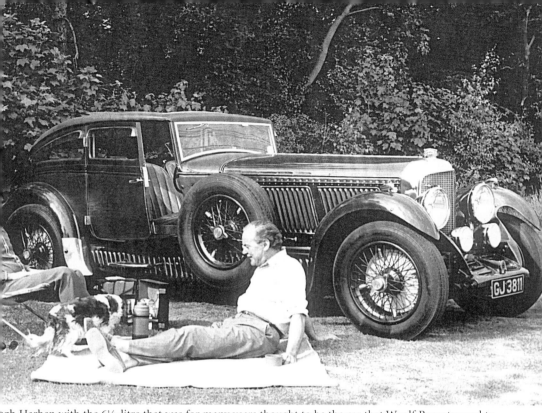

...gh Harben with the 6½-litre that was for many years thought to be the car that Woolf Barnato used to ...e the *Flêche D'Or* from Cannes to London. *(National Motor Museum)*

...me of the Bentley Boys. This picture was taken in around 1927 and shows (left to right) Sammy Davis, ...O., Frank Clement, Dudley Benjafield, Leslie Callingham and George Duller. *(Jolyon Broad collection)*

BENTLEY MOTORS L^{TD}
Introduce the
4½ Litre
BENTLEY

Speed Model only

LE MANS ⸱ 1927
Record Lap. Speed 73·01 m.p.h.

1st 24 HOURS GRAND PRIX DE PARIS
Winner of Grand Trophy and Challenge Cup

Prices from

| 3 Litre Chassis | £895 | 4½ Litre Chassis | £1050 | 6-Cyl. Chassis | £1575 |

DUNLOP TYRES STANDARD

BENTLEY MOTORS, LIMITED, POLLEN HOUSE, CORK STREET, LONDON, W.1

WILL YOU KINDLY MENTION MOTOR OWNER WHEN REPLYING TO ADVERTISERS

Publicity material that Bentley Motors used to introduce the 4½-litre. *(Author's collection/Andrew Minney)*

The Bentley S

A FRESH TRIBUTE

"I have now had my 6 cyl. car nearly a year and have done 10,000 miles on it . . . . It is ev the best car I have ever been in I would not change it for any o Many congratulations on your workmanship and material."

(Sgd.) J.
23rd September,

Full details of the new season's n on application.

STAND 126 OLYMI

BENTLEY

NEW SEASON'S PRICES
6cyl. CHASSIS
£1,575
4½-litre CHASSIS
£1,050
3-litre CHASSIS from
£895

BENTLEY MOTORS LIMIT
Pollen House, Cork Street, London,
Telephone : Regent 6911. Telegrams : "Benmotlim, Phone,

WILL YOU KINDLY MENTION MOTOR OWNER WHEN REPLYING TO ADVERTISERS

The Bentley Six (6½-litre) provoked this testimonial, but who was JC? *(Author's collection/Andrew Minney)*

The Hansom Cab

3-Litre Bentley

LONDON at night sixty years ago! . . . gas lamps shining on the roofs of hansoms, spanking smartly along Piccadilly, carrying the young bloods of the sixties.

In those days the hansom was the height of fashion. There was always a gay and luxurious air about it, with its smart horse, elegant build and easy going, and nobody would drive in the sober four-wheeler if they could only get a hansom.

To-day the slim and luxurious Bentley is the aim of every one who desires the last word in cars. Exquisitely proportioned ; powerful engines running silkily and silently ; subtle, swift, distinguished, the Bentley is fashion's favourite. And nobody would own another car if they could own a Bentley.

3-Litre CHASSIS 6-Cylinder CHASSIS
Prices from - £895 Prices from - £1,150
Dunlop Tyres Standard

BENTLEY MOTORS Ltd., Pollen House, Cork St., London, W.1
Phone : Regent 6911. 'Grams : "Eenmotlim, Phone, London.'

BENTLEY
FIVE YEARS GUARANTEE

WILL YOU KINDLY MENTION MOTOR OWNER WHEN REPLYING TO ADVERTISERS

Another piece of emotive advertising, this time at the end of the 3-litre's career. *(Author's collection/Andrew Minney)*

already been made available to accommodate such coachwork, but a more powerful engine was deemed necessary.

'The Sun' had been fitted with voluminous six-light coachwork courtesy of Freestone & Webb, and to disguise the car a different design of radiator was fitted without any badge or emblem. The foursome left for Le Mans via Newhaven, and it was on arrival at Dieppe that the car was the cause of a problem for W.O. French customs were not convinced that the car was a Bentley. W.O. regularly travelled to France and he used the Dieppe sailings often enough for his cars to be recognised. Eventually clearance was allowed, but only after protracted bureaucracy and W.O. having to pay duty on his English cigarettes, something that made him somewhat grumpy.

Not only did W.O. cover huge distances in his cars in the United Kingdom, he amassed considerable mileage on the Continent, and was especially fond of France. His holidays consisted of testing his cars and he sought few other pleasures. He admitted to being a Francophile, an admirer of the nation's cuisine and fine wines, and loved the language. While he could converse in French quite fluently, he seldom chose to do so in the company of other English people, even to the extent that while travelling with company associates he often insisted on them doing all the talking, another example of his inherent shyness.

When W.O. arrived at Le Mans he was greeted by a number of minor but nevertheless irritating problems. Leslie Pennal was preparing the Bentley and complying with Duff's and Clement's many demands, later recalling that he had only a few hours in which to carry out work that would normally have taken around two days. Duff, recalling the previous year's incident when the car was left without fuel, insisted that a spare petrol can be fabricated. This was undertaken by a small garage in Le Mans, and attached to the side of the car on the running board as part of its tool kit. During the lead-up to the race Pennal worked alone, seeing to the tuning of the engine and making any adjustments that practice runs had shown to be necessary. The worst of it was that he knew little or no French, and therefore found conversing difficult. The fact that the hot weather and burning sun made for unpleasant working conditions added to his discomfort.

Not the least of his worries was that the scrutineering on the day before the race seemed to be biased against the Bentley, which was the only non-French car competing. The scrutineer was insistent that the 3-

litre's front wings did not comply with specifications, being too narrow by a fraction of an inch. Before the car could be passed it was necessary to tack a thin strip of steel along their edges, as a result of which not only did Pennal have to work all day without a break, he continued well into the night.

After dark W.O. found Pennal hard at work in the pits. He stood there for some time watching the mechanic at work on his own. Pennal was well used to W.O.'s habits, for he would often arrive on the scene so quietly that his presence would go unnoticed. W.O., realising the efforts that were necessary to prepare the car in time for start of the race, suggested to him that the Bentley entry be withdrawn.

Poor Pennal. He was obviously exhausted but he was in no mood to accept defeat. Uncharacteristically he challenged W.O.'s opinion; he told him that his colleagues back at Cricklewood would see him as having failed, having got the car all the way to within an inch or two of the starting line. He knew that he was out of order to contradict W.O., but at least the circumstances of the situation led him to show his true feelings. If W.O. was annoyed at being confronted in such manner he refrained from showing it. He did, however, tell him he would consider the matter further. In fact W.O. respected Pennal for being so honest and determined, knowing that he would have felt exactly the same in a similar position. Having left the mechanic on his own for a few minutes he went back to tell him to get some sleep and to continue his preparations in the morning when he was refreshed.

Recalling the incident at a later date, W.O. insisted that he wasn't exactly considering withdrawing from the race, but merely testing Pennal's reactions to see whether the car would be ready in time. 'I had obtained the confirmation I needed – both about the man and the machine.'

The car did start the race although the first few laps were taken in a somewhat tardy fashion. Its performance improved as the race continued and second place behind a Lorraine-Dietrich was achieved by the early hours of Sunday morning. Forty minutes were lost when a coachbuilder's staple became wedged in the gearbox and jammed the gear change; further problems arose when both rear shock absorbers failed. Later, when the windscreen became dislodged, it was carried on the back seat of the vehicle for the remainder of the race.

When he checked the lap records W.O. became aware that the official timekeeper had missed one of the Bentley's laps, showing the car to be slower than it actually was. Luckily, W.O. had instructed Hillstead to keep an accurate record using stop watches and writing the lap times in a book. W.O. made an official complaint, and when the correct timings were displayed on the scoreboard they showed the Bentley to be maintaining a hold on the leading car, a straight-eight Chenard-Walcker which had been tipped to win the event. Clement put the Bentley into the lead when the Chenard-Walcker caught fire and was substantially damaged, and Duff, having subsequently taken over the driving, crossed the finish line at 4pm to win at 53.78mph, some 1,290 miles having been covered in the 24 hours.

An incident during the race was to cause W.O. much anguish. Duff had returned to the pit to change wheels, some one and a half hours of the race remaining. The front wheels had been easy to remove, but not so the rears. At first it was thought the problem lay with that malady known as 'swollen hubs', but further investigation showed signs of sabotage, there being evidence of swarf and the filing of hub splines. It was inconceivable to W.O. that any of the competing teams could have stooped so low as to purposely damage another's car, but the evidence was there nonetheless. Following discovery of the damage a day and night watch was maintained on the cars.

After the race there were ecstatic scenes in the Bentley camp, but at the celebration dinner that followed in the evening W.O. slipped into one of his silent and depressive moods. While his companions were in the highest of spirits, W.O. trawled over the events of the day in his mind. The thought that anyone could sabotage the car troubled him deeply. Bentley Motors and its success meant everything to W.O. and when his ambitions were thwarted, whether racing, in an engineering capacity or in the boardroom, he became taciturn and unresponsive. The ever-ebullient Bertie Kensington Moir, sensing W.O.'s blackening mood, took command of the situation and ordered a bottle of the most expensive champagne to toast the company's success. Plans for an evening of merriment remained in place until W.O. dourly announced that he was leaving to drive back to Dieppe.

W.O., accompanied by Witchell, Hillstead and Kensington Moir, made an early departure, all plans for an evening's high spirits having been firmly abandoned. Witchell and Hillstead undertook to do the driving, while W.O. installed himself on the rear seat and slept. He had a knack for knowing exactly where he was when travelling while asleep, and should the wrong direction or road be taken he would awaken immediately with an appropriate remark or chastisement. This happened when Witchell was driving towards Rouen and became hopelessly lost after giving a farmer a lift to his home, which, he had assured Witchell, was on the main route to the city. The fact that Witchell had been hoodwinked remained the matter of much leg-pulling for months afterwards.

The Bentley victory at Le Mans was covered to good effect by the motoring press and a number of sales resulted from the publicity. All good publicity was welcome, especially since, as Hillstead records in *Those Bentley Days*, sales were not as good as had been anticipated, and it was often hard work to convince agents to order another chassis or two. He makes the point, too, that on occasions he would visit W.O. at Pelham Crescent on his way home to discuss any pertinent matters, and would never leave without a very generous measure of whisky. One sale in particular was especially significant: that of a car to the millionaire racing driver Woolf Barnato.

W.O.'s dour moods were often brought on by the constant worries of cash flow problems, keeping the company afloat, and the state of his marriage to Audrey. H.M. did all he could to keep an even keel under trying conditions, but at times the future of Bentley Motors looked extremely bleak. One such occasion arose in the middle of 1924. H.M. had made it clear that unless an injection of funds was forthcoming by the end of the week, there would be no money for the wages, and the company would cease trading. Hillstead was despatched to various sympathetic agents to encourage them to advance some money, and H.M. went to Blackpool to meet George Porter. George obviously did a magnificent job and H.M. returned to Hanover Court in a much relieved state of mind. Exactly how H.M. had managed to collect the necessary capital remains unexplained, but at least a number of suppliers relaxed their demands for payment. For the time being, at least, the company was saved from going under.

W.O. decided to take 'The Sun' to Lyon to watch the French (and European) Grand Prix that was scheduled for 3 August. He was again accompanied by Witchell, Hillstead and Kensington Moir, while a fourth passenger, Michaelis, who worked for Hoopers the coachbuilders, made up the party of five. For the journey W.O. had decided to fit the new type of Dunlop balloon tyres which were intended to run at low pressure (16lbs) and thus provide more comfort. They were not entirely satisfactory when used with such a heavy car as the experimental Bentley with its full complement of passengers and driven at high speeds, and by the time Lyon was reached all of the tyres had burst, including the spares, each lasting little more than 100 miles. At risk of being stranded, W.O. telegraphed Dunlop and arranged for them to put some tyres on the next Imperial Airways flight to Tours.

The experimental Bentley had been the subject of much curiosity at Le Mans. There was no indication that the car was a Bentley, and certainly no one in W.O.'s party was going to say otherwise. In order to prevent further questioning and inquisitiveness, W.O. had shrouded the front of the car with a large dust sheet. At Lyon the car again attracted attention, and still no one was left any the wiser.

An incident on the journey home was to cause a change in Bentley history. When approaching the junction of two Routes Nationales, W.O. was aware of another car travelling at speed on the adjacent road and heading towards the crossroads ahead. The other car was a large and impressive machine and it appeared that it would reach the convergence at the same time as the Bentley. The experimental Bentley was of just as much interest to the crew of the other car as theirs was to W.O. It was only when the cars were almost side by side that W.O. recognised the other as the prototype Rolls-Royce New Phantom, which had taken to the road at much the same time as the prototype Bentley. The Rolls-Royce test drivers recognised the car as a Bentley, and in all probability recognised W.O., who was at the wheel.

Until that moment the Bentley had been cruising at a steady 65mph. The situation now was too good an opportunity to miss, and W.O. increased the speed of the car to around 80mph. The driver of the Phantom did likewise, and the two cars battled for supremacy for several miles, side by side along the straight and deserted poplar-lined road. The Rolls eventually drew back after the cap of one of the drivers was blown away, leaving W.O. to proceed at a more stately pace and to conserve the wear on the remaining balloon tyres.

The incident in France meant that W.O. decided to increase the capacity of the six-cylinder engine from 4½ to 6½-litres. Anticipating that Rolls-Royce would be raising the performance of the Phantom, he therefore considered that substantially increasing the size of the Bentley engine would command a lead over the rival car. Thus began a rivalry between the two companies that lasted until 1931. In later years W.O. enthusiastically remarked that both the 6½-litre and the short chassis Speed Six were faster than Rolls-Royce's Continental Phantom.

The news of the 1924 Le Mans victory brought the bacteriologist Dr J. Dudley Benjafield into the Bentley showroom. An eminent Harley Street physician, Dr Benjafield specialised in the effects of dental infections on certain diseases, but he was also a highly competent sports car driver. Even so, for some reason he purchased a long wheelbase chassis, to which he fitted a heavy and cumbersome body which did little for the 3-litre's performance.

On an occasion when Benjafield was visiting the Bentley service station he mentioned the car's unhurried performance to Bertie Kensington Moir, who promptly introduced him to Frank Clement's rather dirty red two-seater, which was parked in a corner. Somehow, Benjafield found himself at Brooklands the following afternoon, the two-seater ready to go and Kensington Moir at the wheel. Donning goggles he climbed in beside the driver and the car set off at frightening speed. Even for such an practised driver as Benjafield, the experience was beyond anything that he had ever known, and when he climbed from the machine he was trembling like a leaf and utterly terrified.

In spite of his alarming experience he nevertheless agreed to buy the car – he later admitted that he had never understood how he had been talked into the purchase – and with Kensington Moir's helpful tuition, aided by Bert Browning, he found himself competing at a Brooklands event, coming in a creditable fourth. Further successes followed, which gave Bentley Motors some welcome publicity, and with it several enquiries from racing enthusiasts. W.O. eventually asked 'Benjy' to join the Bentley racing team and share driving at the 1925 Le Mans event.

W.O. recalled Dudley Benjafield as 'tough, thickset and totally bald and wonderful fun.' A first-class driver, Benjafield's mechanical knowledge was nevertheless almost non-existent, and W.O. once wrote that he doubted whether he ever mastered which way the hub caps on a Bentley should be rotated! In spite of this Benjafield remained an essential member of the Bentley team, driving in the 1926, 1927, 1928 and 1929 Le Mans races.

Writing about his motor racing experiences Dudley Benjafield admitted that until he got to know W.O. better, he had been in awe of him. He said of W.O. (whom he often referred to as the 'Skipper') that he was capable of putting the fear of God into someone by fixing them a strong stare of his dark brown eyes and telling them what he thought of them. To his discomfort, Benjafield felt the sharp edge of W.O.'s tongue when, on the journey to Le Mans in 1925, he accidentally allowed customs officials at Dieppe to rip apart a large brown-paper parcel containing a solid mass of cigarettes. The parcel belonged to W.O., who was furious with Benjafield for allowing it to be opened, and all the more annoyed because he had was forced to pay a huge fine that worked out in excess of five francs per cigarette! Benjafield remembered that W.O. and Bertie Kensington Moir were compulsive smokers, always with a cigarette alight. They only stopped smoking to eat and drink.

Benjafield's training for the 1925 Le Mans race began some six weeks before the event. Firstly he was fitted for the driving seat at the Cricklewood works, before undergoing serious exercise, which in this instance included a couple of hours digging Bertie Kensington Moir's garden three or four evenings a week! A week before the race the Bentley team departed for Newhaven complete with the two racing cars and a couple of tenders filled with all the tools and equipment that might be needed. The team were accommodated in two hotels, the Hôtel Moderne, where the mechanics stayed, and the Hôtel de Paris, the choice of W.O. and his drivers. The two establishments served the Bentley team extremely well throughout the company's Le Mans years.

Benjy had been nominated driver of one of the two cars, Duff and Clement the other. Bentley's victory the previous year had led W.O. to enter two vehicles, and another entry included two 3-litre Sunbeams driven by Henry Segrave and George Duller, and Jean Chassagne with Sammy Davis. This was the first year of the famous Le Mans start whereby cars were lined up at an angle and drivers ran across the road when the flag fell to raise the hood, start the engine and drive away.

The French believed that the Bentley team would win the race but it was not to be. First away was John Duff, who, with great alacrity, sprinted to his car and erected the hood in the fastest time, showing the other 48 drivers how it was done. Expecting to see Duff's Bentley as the first car round the course, the crowd was surprised to see Segrave's Sunbeam leading the field, closely followed by Kensington Moir, with Duff trailing in third position. At the end of five laps Moir was only 18 seconds behind Segrave, and after two hours wrestled the lead from the Sunbeam. Moir's lead was short lived as he lost the cap on his oil overflow pipe and had to retire to the pits while another was improvised from the cork of a bottle of Vichy mineral water.

Moir's luck failed to hold out when at Pontlieue his car ran out of petrol. His hard driving with the hood up had upset the fuel calculations during practice, and he was forced to retire 15 miles before the permitted refuelling time. Duff experienced a fractured petrol feed while negotiating the far leg of the circuit at about the same time as Moir retired. Leaving his car he ran across country through a dense pine forest to the Bentley pit to demand some petrol. Contemporary race reports say that he acquired the necessary replacement fuel line before dashing off again into the closing light of the evening. According to W.O. what had happened was that Duff had grabbed a can of fuel contrary to his instructions and run back to the car. When he got there he found it surrounded by officials and it took some devious action on his behalf to surreptitiously pour sufficient petrol into the autovac to start the engine and get to the pit, where the fuel line was replaced. Refuelling during a race wasn't allowed, but Duff managed to do it nevertheless. It took him an hour and a half to carry out the repair, after which Clement took up the chase to catch the Sunbeam. Disaster struck when, at five in the morning, having caught up and passed the rival car, Clement's Bentley caught fire when a carburettor float chamber broke.

The race was not a happy one for W.O.. The atmosphere in the pit following the retirement of both Bentleys was almost unbearable, and the team sensed that their return to Cricklewood would be met with some disparaging comments from those shareholders who were opposed to the costs involved with racing.

News of the 6½-litre Bentley was published in the middle of June 1925. *The Autocar* assured its readers that the 3-litre was to remain in production, and that the new chassis could easily accommodate the heavy and luxurious type of enclosed coachwork that so many customers preferred without compromising performance.

Writing about the 6½-litre W.O. recalled that the cylinder block and valve gear were similar to that on the 3-litre, but to make the engine quieter the cam-shaft was driven using triple connecting rods coupling two sets of small three-throw eccentrics, the drive being taken from the rear of the crankshaft. This represented a throwback to W.O.'s railway days. To improve the general running of the engine it was secured to the chassis using rubber mountings, which W.O. claimed were neatly camouflaged because the company was reluctant to admit to such a feature. He believed that gaining silent running with flexibility and reliability in this manner was a first for any manufacturer.

The 6½-litre chassis was available in three wheelbases, 11ft, 12ft and 12ft 6in. (However, an 11ft 6in and a 12ft 8½in chassis were made to special order). When the Speed Six model appeared in October 1928 it was fitted with a tuned version of the engine with twin SU carburettors. In total there were 363 6½-litre cars built, and a further 182 Speed Sixes.

In 1926 W.O. agreed to participate in three major sporting events. In the spring W.O. decided it would be profitable to participate in endurance racing at Montlhéry near Paris. John Duff, with Dudley Benjafield as co-driver, had already attempted the 24-hour record at the circuit the previous summer and had done extremely well by snatching the 1,000-mile record from Renault at 97.7mph. Then, just before the opening of the London Motor Show, Duff tried again, this time taking Woolf Barnato with him. They took the 24-hour record from Renault at a speed of 95.02mph, which meant that the car had covered 2,280.9 miles without the bonnet having been opened. The Bentley lapped Montlhéry at 96.6mph, Duff and Barnato changing over driving every three hours.

It was late March when the Bentley team, headed by W.O., arrived at the Paris Autodrome. Woolf Barnato was there, as were Dudley Benjafield, George Duller, Kensington Moir and Clement. The car was a 3-litre with a 9ft chassis fitted with a lightweight body by Gordon England. Motor racing historian William Boddy refers to the event, explaining that the Bentley's attack on the 24-hour record was delayed by a body defect and then by rain, and then thwarted after 16 hours because of a broken engine valve spring and a fractured valve stem. During the first hour of the attempt the car had averaged 103.47mph.

W.O. enjoyed himself enormously on that trip. With Barnato, Kensington Moir and Benjafield around there could be nothing but fun, although they all worked hard on the track and were strictly professional. The Bentley Boys stayed at the Carlton Hotel on the Champs Elysées, and after a sumptuous dinner one evening decided that the social highlights of Paris were too good an opportunity to miss.

W.O. and Kensington Moir decided not to go with the others, preferring instead to relax at the hotel, no doubt enjoying a few good whiskies. The others were not so disciplined, and one found himself at a house of ill-repute without any money to pay for favours. W.O. was woken from his slumbers at some unearthly hour by a representative from the British Embassy asking him to go to the establishment and bail him out to the sum of £26. W.O. took Bertie Kensington Moir along with him, gained the release of the fellow, who was the worse for wear through alcohol, only to lose him when he hopped out of a taxi when it stopped at traffic lights. This time it was the gendarmerie who picked him up, and W.O. was forced to bail him out a second time!

W.O. returned to the course in June, the car under the charge of Barnato, Duller and Clement. A near-tragedy stopped the attempt after 16½ hours, but not before the Bentley had raised the 12-hour record to 100.92mph. Duller was driving when he went into a skid and spun the car several times before the engine stalled. He managed to get to the pit, where he hoped for a change of driver, but no one was there except for one of the mechanics, Wally Hassan. Thinking that he could take over from Duller, to keep the record attempt going until another driver could be found, Hassan jumped into the car and was away.

Driving such a car as a short-chassis Bentley on wet and greasy concrete at speeds of around 100mph calls for skills that young Wally did not have, and before he had completed a third of a lap he was out of control. The car hit the barrier, somersaulted twice and came to rest upside down in a ditch, Hassan trapped beneath. It was a miracle that he was not killed, and had he not ducked down into the cockpit he would have been decapitated by the car's streamlining as it sheared from its fixings. First on the scene were Wally Saunders and a Frenchman, and between them they managed to extricate the driver, believing him to be dead.

Wally Hassan was taken in the company's little Morris to a doctor in a nearby village, who could do little to help. W.O. turned up in his 6½-litre shortly afterwards, and with Wally laid out on the back seat he drove him with the others to the American Hospital in Paris, which was some 25 kilometres away. He was kept there for three weeks and nursed to a full recovery.

Wally, lying in his hospital bed, feared the worst, believing that W.O. would fire him for being so impetuous. That was not in W.O.'s nature, and later that day, or the next morning, he went to see the patient. He told him he wasn't angry with him, and that he had done a very plucky thing.

It was during the endurance testing that W.O. was taken ill with congestion of the lungs. He, too, was taken to hospital where, he recalls, a nun performed a sinister operation on him, inserting a dozen or so tiny glass flasks into his chest, filling them with a spirit and then igniting them. During the operation Bertie Kensington Moir suddenly arrived on the scene, and the expression of horror on his face was such that W.O. began laughing helplessly. Needless to say the unconventional remedy helped W.O. make a quick recovery.

The two other events were the Le Mans 24-Hour race and the Georges Boillot Cup that was held at the Boulogne Circuit on 3 September. The Bentley team consisted of three 3-litre cars, two of which were Speed models, one driven by Sammy Davis and Dudley Benjafield, the other by Frank Clement and George Duller. In addition to being an ardent racing driver, George was also keen on horses and was an experienced jockey. The Davis/Benjafield car carried the number 7 and was known afterwards as 'Old Number 7'. Clement and Duller's car carried number 8. Clive Gallop returned to the Bentley scene to drive the third car, his co-driver being T. 'Scrap' Thistlethwayte.

As in 1925, the 1926 race did not bring W.O. the success that he so badly wanted. W.O. had personally supervised the day-to-day preparation of the cars, talking to the drivers, listening intently to their comments and making sure that everything that could be done to ensure success was done. A week before the start of the race the team left for Newhaven, and the cars were in as near perfect condition as could be achieved in the time available. W.O. had been able to acquire the garage facilities at the Hôtel Moderne which had previously been occupied by Sunbeam, who were not competing, and which had also been used for Ferenc Szisz's famous Renault and by James Murphy when he won the French Grand Prix in 1921 driving a Duesenberg. Some 13 hours after the drivers had arrived at Le Mans with their cars, the team's tender, a somewhat dilapidated-looking French lorry that was completely overloaded, turned up having been driven by Nobby Clark and L.V. Head.

W.O.'s insistence on thorough practising meant that even the most insignificant detail was checked, and if not exactly perfect was remedied. Everybody in the team, from W.O. to the errand boy, worked strenuously before the race, causing Sammy Davis to remark that 'practice here was worth yards of theory.'

The Bentleys were the only British entry, and their fate was sealed when Duller and Clement's car failed with a broken valve. Next to go was the Gallop and Thistlethwayte car with a broken rocker arm, after which all hopes for a victory rested with Davis and Benjafield. With 20 minutes to go before the race end Sammy Davis was in third position and closing in on the second car, a Lorraine-Dietrich. Even if he couldn't win W.O. hoped for a placing. As he tried to pass the Lorraine to get into second place on the run down to the Mulsanne Corner – if he didn't pass before reaching there he would have to wait until the grandstand for another opportunity – he realised it was going to be difficult to reduce speed sufficiently to take the corner. He felt the brakes holding the car's speed, but on the damp road surface the car began to slide. Checking the slide was to no avail and the car slid round at such an angle that taking the escape road was out of the question. He attempted to leave the corner by the road, crashing headlong through a palisade only to finish up in a sandbank having missed a tree by inches. Extricating himself from the sand proved impossible and Sammy was taken back to the pits in the official car.

W.O. was distraught at being out of the race. There was fury on his face as Sammy walked towards him, obviously in a distressed state and trying to apologise for making a fool of himself and damaging the car. Recalling the incident, Sammy felt deeply ashamed at letting the team down, W.O. in particular. All the more hurtful was the fact that W.O. knew that he had been responsible for Bentley's failure. There was nothing else for Sammy to do but to take a long walk on his own: his feelings can only be imagined, and later he was to admit that at the time he wished he were dead!

That night at the Hôtel de Paris there was a blanket of gloom over the Bentley camp. Sammy Davis decided not to show his face. W.O. tried not to show his feelings but everyone could see he was almost broken. To make matters worse, Bertie Kensington Moir tried to compensate for the depressive atmosphere and thus became more boisterous than usual.

Dudley Benjafield bought 'Old Number 7' after the ill-fated race and entered it for the Georges Boillot Cup at the Boulogne Circuit with Bertie Kensington Moir as co-driver. After the first six laps the car's brakes faded due to rod stretch, and after being adjusted Benjafield made up for some of the lost time. The race was a 350-mile handicap event, and towards the end Benjafield, totally exhausted and forgetting about his fading brakes, went into the Baincthun bends at around 90mph, only to discover his brakes were virtually useless. Unable to clear the corner he crashed into a tree and was severely injured. Fortunately Benjafield recovered from his crash: the car was repaired, and both continued racing.

Back at Cricklewood W.O. faced some difficult decisions. There were those within the works that believed Bentley's racing days were over.

The recent defeats were persuading W.O. to consider withdrawing from racing completely, a judgement that was largely influenced by Bentley Motors' troublesome financial position.

CHAPTER 7

Woolf Barnato and More About the Bentley Boys

THE financial problems experienced by Bentley Motors were among the many difficult issues that W.O. faced between 1924 and 1925. While the company sold more cars in 1924 than any in other year, and a seemingly healthy manufacturing profit proved encouraging, the true picture was far less satisfactory.

Bentley's racing activities had been partly responsible for draining the company's resources, as had the development of the 6½-litre. According to Donald Bastow, who some years ago discussed the model's origins with Harry Varley, the 6½-litre was conceived between 1922 and 1923. Recalling the period in question in his book *Those Bentley Days*, Arthur Hillstead commented that at times it seemed almost impossible for the company to continue in existence. That it did so was only through the extreme efforts of some of the directors, and the friendly and understanding attitude that was shown by the company's suppliers. By the time the 6½-litre was shown at Olympia in the autumn of 1925 the company's financial standing was in a critical state. Trading figures for 1924 indicated a manufacturing profit of £13,529, which was undermined by development and other costs which amounted to almost £42,000. The details of this amount were unexplained and remain a mystery as they were listed under 'indirect expenditure'.

There was absolutely no doubt that the company's racing successes, which brought publicity and hence increased interest in the marque, were instrumental in producing increased sales. However, these advances were not always as profitable as might be imagined. Increasing numbers of orders called for more extensive production facilities at Cricklewood and the hiring of additional personnel. Significant changes within the Bentley Motors organisation were ultimately made as a result, the service station being moved to Kingsbury in premises leased from Vanden Plas, the coachbuilders responsible for many of Bentley's bodies. Bertie Kensington Moir was moved from service to the experimental department, where he helped perfect the 6½-litre. Sometime later the racing shop moved away from Cricklewood to adjacent premises in Kingsbury, also leased from Vanden Plas, which were known to everyone as 'Down the Alley'. One of the reasons for relocating the racing shop was that W.O. was concerned that the department should be self-contained to prevent unauthorized personnel and visitors from wandering in and out at will. He was emphatic that Bentley's racing programme, along with vehicle preparation and competition strategies, should be kept confidential.

There is every reason to believe that W.O., backed by other directors, was convinced that the frugality that had been necessary in the formative days of the company was at last beginning to pay off, and ahead lay a more secure and profitable era. As it transpired, however, the company's financial problems were increasing, and to such an extent that the liquidator was never far away.

For all its financial constraints, some of the company's expenditure was certainly questionable: the fact is that few were inclined to query some of the figures. Delve into some of the reminiscences of those at the front line of the firm and it is clear that making economies was not always a priority. Hillstead, H.M. and W.O. always stayed at the best hotels and wined and dined in the most sophisticated manner, while huge sums of money were spent on the domestic arrangements for the firm's racing activities. The evidence is that even the racing mechanics enjoyed a fairly extravagant lifestyle while at Le Mans, and it was Frank Clement's job to settle all the accounts once the races were over. By the time the team had departed it was too late to properly check any expenses. Bentley Motors was not unique in this respect: motor racing was big business and attracted considerable wealth. To participate in the sport commanded a particular commitment, and Bentley customers and shareholders were keen to see the company appropriately represented.

As a company, Bentley exuded wealth. Apart from its racing interests the progressive development of existing and new models called for extensive testing, which meant that W.O. and others would be away from the works for long periods at a time. It has already been mentioned that W.O. seldom took holidays as such, but he did put vehicle testing opportunities to good use by embarking on lengthy Continental tours during which he stayed at some of the finest and most expensive establishments.

W.O. found solace in testing his cars on the Continent. Being away from the works he could indulge in a certain amount of relaxation that was otherwise impossible, even if he did discipline himself on occasions to cover hundreds of miles at a stretch. He liked nothing better than to drive through France, Belgium and Italy, often at high speeds in order to gauge a car's cooling efficiency, descending passes with a verve that tested braking capacity to the limit. When behind the wheel he was able to concentrate on any difficulties that arose during testing, and how they should be resolved. In that way he was able to engineer his cars to perfection. Later he once drove his 6½-litre, fitted with an 8-litre engine, from Cannes to Dieppe in a day, cruising the 740 miles or so effortlessly and in comfort, averaging 85mph and reaching his destination before dusk. Driving the same distance today in a modern car would present a challenge, even when using France's fine autoroutes. Imagine what a feat it must have been in the late 1920s and early 1930s, despite the lack of traffic.

It is significant that W.O. often used Cannes as a base for his testing activities because he and his wife Audrey owned a small villa at Miramar, some 15 kilometres away. 'Le Balcon' was in an idyllic location overlooking the beach, but it is curious that Bentley never referred to it in his writings. Audrey spent a lot of time there, which gave rise to the speculation that the couple mostly lived their lives apart. The villa had access to a private seawater pool, which W.O. designed so that Audrey could swim in safety and isolation. The Bentleys also owned a small motorboat, which could be navigated into the shelter of the pool, and W.O. devised a hoist in order that the vessel could be lifted out of the water and dry-stored.

Testing was not restricted to the Continent. One of W.O.'s favourite proving runs was to drive from London to Carlisle and back in a day using the A6 trunk road, starting at nine in the morning and returning at 11 at night. The route provided all types of terrain from the quiet countryside of the northern home counties to the ruggedness of Lancashire, Westmorland and Cumberland, including the notorious climb over Shap.

In view of the company's fragile financial status it is difficult to conceive how, at the time, W.O., H.M. and other Bentley Motors directors agreed to the mortgaging of all the company's properties and its assets, to include tools and equipment, for the sum of £40,000. But that is exactly what happened. The mortgage, which gave the company a welcome injection of cash, was arranged in June 1923 through Druces and Atlee courtesy of Arthur Savill, who was one of the partners along with W.O.'s brother Hardy.

How W.O. was able to manage the Bentley racing team while overseeing development and testing of the 6½-litre is difficult to appreciate. Add to that his endeavours dealing with the daily routine of the works, and it becomes clear how he, and the Bentley name, emerged as legends in their lifetime, helping to perpetuate the marque's mysticism. W.O. undoubtedly suffered through pressure of work and although he was not given to extremes of temperament, it is recorded that at times he appeared ashen-faced and totally fatigued. He once said that managing a season's racing could take years off one's life.

By the end of 1925 the company's financial problems had reached a point where the uncertainty of the situation was seriously affecting morale among the workforce, as it became widely known within Bentley Motors that the company was facing bankruptcy. It was a day to day business to stave off receivership. For all that there was no skimping on quality, in materials or workmanship. Each member of staff, knowing that they had been hand picked for the job, was far too proud to let either W.O. or the company down. Of the many reminiscences and anecdotes that have been recorded about those days, the one thing that is most evident is that W.O. understood and appreciated each person's virtues: to let him down was akin to letting oneself down.

The situation had become so dire that on occasions there was insufficient money to meet the wages. That no one went without being paid was partly due to H.M. advancing money from his own private funds, and partly because Hubert Pike, the service director, put his own money into the company by buying a chassis each week for several weeks. Both Leslie Pennal and Arthur Saunders recalled that happening, the cost of a 6½-litre chassis being approximately equal to the wages bill for a week. They remembered the chassis being lined up within the works for later sale.

Without assistance from its suppliers the firm could certainly not have carried on. However much was owed, components were delivered to Cricklewood as normal, the chassis frames having been sent on a weekly basis from Scotland.

There is evidence that, in looking for a solution to the problem, W.O. sought the collaboration of a number of other motor manufacturers. Exactly whom he courted, apart from William Morris of Morris Motors, remains unrecorded. W.O. made an approach to Morris towards the end of 1925 and records indicate that tentative negotiations continued into the first few weeks of 1926. Morris's policy had been to keep clear of the City, the large merchant bankers and insurance institutions for finance, and in this W.O. recognised a particular astuteness.

W.O. wrote to Morris asking for an appointment, which was granted, so on a fine winter's day he took an experimental 6½-litre to Oxford. He found Morris in his office, a small house that was surrounded by the huge works. W.O. was given a tour of the Morris factory, which he referred to as vast compared to his own premises at Cricklewood. He then took Morris for a drive in the Bentley, and while Morris showed some enthusiasm for its appointment and performance, he could not be persuaded to make a commitment to back W.O. financially. A couple of days later W.O. received a courteous letter from Morris, who had decided that he didn't think he could successfully market a popular and inexpensive vehicle as well as an expensive luxury sports car.

In a surprise move, however, Morris paid £730,000 for the bankrupt firm of Wolseley Motors in 1927, and in 1938, as Viscount Nuffield, he purchased Riley Motors. In hindsight one wonders what might have happened had Morris accepted W.O.'s merger proposals: would the Bentley marque have followed some of the other famous names that comprised the British Motor Corporation into oblivion?

When Woolf Barnato bought his first Bentley he already knew much about the company and its cars. He had raced at Brooklands and had seen W.O. there with his Bentleys; he knew their capabilities and recognised in W.O. a fierce sense of determination which was very similar to his own. He also saw in him a brilliant engineer and racing team manager, but perhaps it is best not said what his perceptions of Bentley the businessman were.

With his 6ft frame and stocky muscular build, Barnato made for a distinctive figure that was emphasised by his mahogany complexion, dark wavy hair and brown eyes. His physique was remarkable, as was his stamina, and he excelled in everything he did. Before he began motor racing he had been a successful boxer at Cambridge, had played cricket for Surrey and was a noted wicket-keeper. He acquired a reputation for being an all-round athlete and was a match for any skier. He was also a country lover, enjoying nothing better than foxhunting and joining a shoot, and he was no mean golfer. He was also a man about town who belonged to the most prestigious clubs, kept company with celebrities of stage and screen, among others, and enjoyed a spectacularly lavish lifestyle.

Barnato's grandfather, Isaac Isaacs, was a Jewish man with a successful business trading clothes from his shop in London's East End. He had a daughter, Leah, and two sons, Harry and Barnett, the latter having adopted the name Barney before changing his family name to Barnato. Barney, when not helping his father with the family business, frequented the city's music halls, appearing on stage as a juggler; at the age of 21 he decided to go to South Africa to seek his fortune in the diamond trade. By the end of the 19th century Barnato, having challenged Cecil Rhodes to negotiate a £5 million merger, became a Life Governor of De Beers. He was chairman of several businesses and established for himself a fabulous wealth. On his return to Britain by ship from Cape Town in 1898 he mysteriously disappeared overboard off the coast of Africa. There was no evidence that his disappearance was suspicious, but a verdict of suicide was recorded. Whether in fact his death was suicide, murder or an accident remains debatable. Woolf Barnato was two years old when his father died, and he inherited the fortune.

Woolf was brought up by his mother, Fanny, whose maiden name was Bees. In addition to owning a luxury flat near Marble Arch, she had a large house in North Wales and a villa in Brighton. She sent her two sons to Charterhouse and Cambridge. Jack, the elder, joined the RNAS and was was among the first pilots to bomb Constantinople. He died in

1918 after contracting bronchial pneumonia. The younger son, Woolf, known as 'Babe' within the family, joined the army as a private and served for a year in the ranks before being promoted to captain.

Woolf Barnato had a flamboyant nature. He loved nothing more than having a wager, and he mostly won them. When his second wife (he was married three times) was about to give birth in her suite in London's Dorchester Hotel he arranged a sweepstake on the hour and date of the baby's arrival. When the news arrived that he had been presented with a son he danced for joy around the hotel foyer before buying drinks for all the hotel's 500 staff. For all that he disliked lending money, even small sums to friends, and was never happy until the debt was repaid.

Of all the sports he enjoyed, none could rival his love of fast racing cars. W.O. referred to him as a brilliant driver, and thought him the best at the time. Barnato was also a playboy, totally self-assured and boisterous, and was admired by women wherever he went. He gloried in the adulation, and with his huge wealth it was known for him to spend in the region of £800–£900 (which would relate to around £40,000 at today's values) each week on parties and racing. Then there was Ardenrun Hall near Lingfield, a stately mansion and just one of Barnato's homes. It was at his stud on the Ardenrun Estate that Barnato bred some of the finest racehorses. W.O. said of Barnato that he was a formidable man whether behind a glass of whisky, behind the wheel of a motor car, or behind the board room table. Babe Barnato had an aversion to offering anyone his cigarettes, and it was the intention of many to get their fingers inside the gold cigarette case that he kept in a specially-tailored deep pocket in all his suits. One of the few people to do so was Bertie Kensington Moir.

Barnato was only too aware of the difficulties that Bentley Motors were experiencing. He was sufficiently close to W.O. to appreciate that the company was running on an absolute knife edge, and his business knowledge and connections within the finance world would have revealed the extent of its difficulties.

W.O. and H.M. had talked endlessly about ways of finding the necessary capital to remain in business, for if a financier were not found, there was no alternative but to go into liquidation. There is evidence that had W.O. not approached Barnato, inviting him to invest in the company, then Barnato would have approached W.O. The essence of it was that Barnato loved Bentleys, and racing them was his passion.

Without the company, and more specifically without W.O., there would be no Bentleys to race.

According to Arthur Hillstead he first put the idea of approaching Barnato into H.M.'s head. This followed an announcement in the press that Barnato, already a multi-millionaire, had inherited a further £1½ million. Certainly Hillstead refers to H.M. suggesting that an approach be made to Barnato, and he also recalls taking an open 6½-litre to Ardenrun Hall to take Barnato for a trial run in the car. Over lunch Hillstead was quizzed about Bentley's sales and marketing operations, and there is every reason to believe that he left Ardenrun Hall with the notion that some assistance could be forthcoming for advertising and marketing. Hillstead's memoirs suggest that a meeting between W.O. and Barnato had already taken place, for when he reported back to Hanover Court, H.M. appeared not to be particularly enthusiastic. H.M. confided in Hillstead that there was a possibility that Barnato might take over the company's finances, and a reconstruction of the board of directors would probably ensue.

W.O. had first posed the matter of financing Bentley Motors at a meeting in Barnato's London apartment in Grosvenor Square, soon after the abortive negotiations with Morris. It was a very different Barnato that W.O. encountered here, far removed from the one he knew on the race track. He was cold and calculating, every bit the hard-nosed financier. Barnato was on top of the situation, and W.O. was to admit some years later that the meeting had been a difficult one. They talked figures and strategies, and the one thing that became very evident was that in return for providing the required capital Barnato would take control of the company.

Losing his status was a bitter pill for W.O. to swallow. He nevertheless accepted the situation, acknowledging there was little alternative, and treated the affair with his usual quiet stoicism. Barnato conducted the business arrangements through his advisers, John Kennedy Carruth and Ramsey Manners, and it was in early February 1926 that an Extraordinary General Meeting was held at Hanover Court to allow Bentley Motors to be wound up, and for a new company, Bentley Motors Limited, to be created. The liquidators were Clancy Horsfall McKnight and William Kay Forster. A month later the full extent of Barnato's proposals were published, the first shock being that the nominal value of the former company's shares was slashed from 20 shillings (£1) to just one shilling (5p), thus virtually wiping out most shareholders' investments.

Another shock was that Barnato's proposals were, in effect, a total takeover of Bentley Motors. There were further conditions which all but dissolved W.O.'s financial interests in the company: while he temporarily retained the title of managing director he was nevertheless committed to sign an agreement on 10 March which made him the new company's chief engineer, with a reduction in salary from £2,000 per annum to £1,000. A further indignation was that he was barred from involving himself in any design work with another motor manufacturer which could be interpreted as being in competition with Bentley Motors Ltd. As for the Hanover Court showroom and offices, Barnato considered them inadequate and arranged for new and more spacious premises at Pollen House in Cork Street to be acquired. The three-storey building (including a basement where directors' cars were parked) allowed for Barnato's advisers to be accommodated on the floor above the sales area.

Cork Street runs parallel to New Bond Street, and for some reason, at the time of Bentley's acquisition of Pollen House, was known by retailers as 'The Street of the Dead.' Pollen House, externally at least, has survived the vagaries of time and war, and apart from replacement showroom windows, appears much as it did in 1926.

For W.O., one of the most disheartening aspects of the arrangement was that there was no room in the new organisation for H.M. W.O.'s brother had previously tended the finances of Bentley Motors, but henceforward this would be work for Barnato's own advisers. W.O. also lost the services of Arthur Hillstead, who did not care much for Barnato's regime and decided that the special relationship he had enjoyed with the old company was lost forever. H.M. took over the lease of the Hanover Court showroom to establish himself as a Bentley dealership under the name H.M. Bentley & Partners Ltd. Hillstead, too, set up in business, with Geoffrey Cunliffe, son of the one-time Governor of the Bank of England. Although he specialised in various makes of motor car, Bentleys were always his favourite.

The resentment and bitterness on W.O.'s part is obvious. While he characteristically refers little to his feelings at the time, there are, nonetheless, some vital clues about his state of mind. He refers to Carruth and Manners as Barnato's 'cronies', and in later life recalls certain periods, Léonie's death, Barnato's takeover, and the acquisition of the firm in 1931 by Rolls-Royce, as particular low points.

When the financial structure of the new company was published it was revealed that the nominal capital was £175,000. This comprised 162,500 preference shares at £1 each and 250,000 ordinary shares at one shilling. Barnato's shareholding amounted to 109,400 £1 preference shares, along with 114,700 one shilling shares. H.M. Bentley held 6,300 preference and 3,150 ordinary shares, while W.O. had 6,000 and 3,000 respectively. The other shareholders were Hubert Pike with 17,700 preference and 8,850 ordinaries; Ebeneza Pike with 6,900 and 3,450; Noel van Raalte with 4,200 and 2,100; G.A. Peck with 500 and 250 and S.A. de la Rue with 7,800 and 3,900. Manners and Carruth each held 10,000 ordinaries.

Without Woolf Barnato's injection of cash Bentley Motors would certainly have gone into liquidation. This, however, was not apparent from statements that appeared in the finance pages of the newspapers regarding the change of company name, the millionaire's involvement being 'merely a step in the steady growth and increasing prosperity of the company'. This declaration hid the fact that Bentley Motors' creditors had been paid off in full, a figure that amounted to £75,000, equal in today's values to around £4 million.

W.O. retained his position as managing director in the new company for a little over a year, after which Barnato appointed the international sportsman and racing driver the Marquis of Casa Maury as joint managing director and a member of the board of directors. Casa Maury was a Cuban banker and one of Barnato's closest associates, and his appointment clearly compromised W.O.'s authority within the company. W.O. characteristically hid was must have been bitter disappointment by adopting his usual stoicism, and outwardly he appeared to accept the situation. As it transpired the Cuban was not very interested in the daily affairs of the company, and became more engrossed in its competitive profile and the design of racing cars. Here at least W.O. reigned supreme, for no one knew more about the cars and racing than he did, and Barnato knew it.

Barnato could not ignore W.O.'s abilities as an engineer, for without him there could be no development of new models. As racing manager W.O. was immovable, and although Barnato was company chairman, he never once overruled W.O. on a racing matter. Despite his status he regarded himself as one of the team drivers and did exactly as W.O. directed. This must have been difficult for Barnato, yet he remained assured of W.O.'s integrity and expertise.

For the company as a whole, Barnato's investment was its saviour, and all talk of abandoning racing was forgotten. In fact the emphasis on the racing programme enabled it to become a priority, especially with the move of the racing shop to Kingsbury. As it happened the location was highly significant, for the majority of racing bodies were built by Vanden Plas and having the coachbuilders virtually next door meant that it was easy to push a chassis into the adjacent works. For the first time, too, the company had a dedicated racing policy, with W.O. at the helm supported by a committee comprised of different company departmental managers. Not only was a racing agenda prepared well in advance of a season, a strict timetable of development was devised. Vehicles were ready in good time, and participated in some of the so-called minor events, which provided valuable practice and evaluation for the international meetings, such as the Le Mans 24-Hours. The team of racing mechanics was overhauled, and engineers of such calibre as Stan Ivermee, Jack Sopp, Puddephatt, Kemish and Prior were added to the crew. A point of interest is that between themselves the racing mechanics were known as the 'Bentley Boys', a term which was more widely, and retrospectively, used when referring to the Bentley racing drivers.

For the racing mechanics, although Barnato's money gave an added sense of security, the move to Kingsbury did not mean that their working conditions improved. On the contrary, the facilities were pretty meagre and they were not even equipped with effective heating in winter.

The 1927 racing season was the first under Barnato's regime, and the first event the company participated in was the Essex Six-Hour race at Brooklands on 7 May. W.O. had entered four cars, Dudley Benjafield's Old Number 7, which was driven by Benjafield and Barnato, and three others, which were driven by Leslie Callingham, Frank Clement and the Birkin brothers – Sir Henry (Tim) and Archie. This was Tim Birkin's first race since 1921, when he had driven a DFP, and his first driving for Bentley. The pause in his racing career was due to his marriage and a commitment to give up racing. Six years on Birkin was unable to keep his promise any longer. His brother was not a recognised racing driver, but was a very good one nonetheless, and had been commandeered by Tim for the occasion.

Sir Henry was of independent means, his wealth having come from Nottingham's lace industry. Often seen as an utterly ruthless driver, he was popular with his team mates even though he adopted a brutal and fearless attitude when behind the wheel. As long as he could win he had absolutely no compassion for the cars that he drove. He was in fact a brilliant and very competent driver, who took care never to unbalance his car through coarse use or control.

While acknowledging Birkin's driving abilities, W.O.,was somewhat critical of the treatment to which he subjected his vehicles, claiming that he knew of nobody who could tear up a piece of machinery so swiftly and completely. Tim Birkin's exploits were followed with great eagerness by the media, and his adventures were the topic of conversation of most schoolboys at the time. A hero he most certainly was, but for all that he was the first to admit to his short stature and unfortunate speech impediment.

Birkin was also a manic depressive. In 1933 he suffered serious burns when his forearm came into contact with his car's exhaust pipe, and a few weeks later he fell ill and was diagnosed with blood poisoning. Some reports claim that his death on 22 June 1933 was as a result of the burns, but this is not entirely true. The cause of death appears to have been malarial poisoning, recurring after Birkin contracted the disease in Palestine during World War One. At the inquest the coroner returned a verdict of accidental death, but since then there has been a certain amount of speculation surrounding the events that led to his death.

W.O. was gratified to see that by the end of the first hour of the race – which had a Le Mans type start and thus suited Bentley's drivers, for they excelled in getting away quicker than anyone else – Clement and Benjafield's cars were leading the field, with the twin-cam Sunbeams of Duller and Segrave in pursuit. Benjafield took the lead when Clement returned to the pits with misfiring problems. Shortly afterwards Barnato took over from his teammate, but his car was also misfiring. This gave Duller the lead with Birkin following, leaving Callingham to do what he could to support him. Then Callingham's car began to misfire and lost ground, and he was later forced to retire. The fact that Birkin's car kept going – he, too experienced mechanical problems when his gearbox became jammed in third – was due to his being the only Bentley that was not fitted with duralumin engine rockers. Birkin put up a tremendous show and would have finished in second place had not his spare wheel and carrier broken loose from their mounting and fallen off, thus allowing the Alvis driven by Sammy Davis to pass him as he spent precious minutes fixing it.

W.O. was also encouraged by the speed at which the refuelling of his cars was conducted. At his instigation petrol storage tanks had been installed on the roof of the Bentley pit, and using large bore hoses the time taken to refill a car by gravity was noticeably reduced. No doubt his arrangement provoked debate and disquiet among the track officials.

The following month W.O. took the Bentley team to Le Mans, which was staged over 18 and 19 June. After two successive defeats nothing was left to chance and he appointed a carefully considered group of drivers. There was Benjafield and Old Number 7, with Sammy Davis as co-driver, despite the latter's unfortunate performance the previous year. D'Erlanger and George Duller drove the other 3-litre, while Frank Clement and Leslie Callingham were in charge of a prototype four-cylinder 4½-litre car, W.O.'s new design.

The 4½-litre was devised by W.O. to be a modern alternative to the 3-litre, which was to remain in production, albeit in limited numbers, until 1929. It was to complement the 6½-litre, and shared some of that model's technology while offering greater flexibility than the 3-litre, especially when clothed in heavier coachwork. To suggest that the 4½-litre was something of a hybrid would be incorrect, but it did use the 3-litre's frame, transmission and brakes. It employed the crankcase of the later type of 3-litre models modified to accept the larger crank, and with the same bore and stroke as the 6½-litre car (100x140mm) it represented a shortened version of the 6-cylinder engine. In W.O.'s words the 4½-litre was 'the Big Six less a pair of cylinders'. Deliveries of the 4½-litre began in late 1927, the model having been shown at Olympia during the autumn. *The Autocar* referred to it as 'two cars in one', ideal for the sporting enthusiast keen to get the most out of the car on the open road as well as the owner who requires a more sedate and comfortable style of motoring. In retrospect the 4½-litre has proved to be the most popular of all Bentley models for those enthusiasts who use their cars for racing.

Clement and Callingham's 3-litre practice car was fitted with the first 4½-litre engine to be built at Cricklewood, and this was subsequently fitted to their Le Mans car, which thereafter became known as 'Old Mother Gun'. W.O. was quite aware that while the 3-litre possessed impressive performance, it was, nevertheless, experiencing some competition, especially from Vauxhall's 30/98, which displayed outstanding acceleration with a high maximum speed. For racing, therefore, the 4½-litre promised to give the Bentley team a much better chance of victory.

It wasn't just about having a new car for the 1927 Le Mans race. W.O. put in many hours perfecting the way the pit was operated and he insisted on a strict code of discipline for his drivers. He turned to innovative measures to ensure that the entire crew knew exactly what they were doing, and introduced the filming of pit procedures using a movie camera. Practice, practice, practice! That's what he instilled in everybody. Only by continually evaluating his team's efforts could he be sure that race drill was at its most efficient. Valuable seconds were saved by devising a novel way of replenishing the oil in the new 3 and 4½-litres, by fitting a quick-release external filler cap thus avoiding the time taken unstrapping and opening the bonnet. It was another of his innovations that saved refuelling times: 30 gallons of petrol could be rapidly drained into the petrol tank via a specially designed giant funnel, while other essential functions were completed. Through trial and error W.O. managed to reduce pit-stop times to under three minutes at best, time in which the pit crew not only refuelled and replenished oil and water but adjusted shock absorbers and changed wheels when necessary. A particular asset used for the first time was a W.O.-designed mechanism that allowed drivers to make adjustments to the brake cable from within the cockpit while the car was on the move. By compensating for cable slackness in this manner valuable time was saved by not having to return to the pits to have adjustments carried out.

With the cars garaged overnight at the Hôtel Moderne, practising for the race began at 4am each day. W.O. had decided on this early hour to avoid meeting traffic. Sammy Davis was not alone in finding the routine irksome and he recalled how breakfast was consumed in virtual silence. The drive up to the course dispelled all tiredness, and the roar from the cars' exhausts probably awakened the folk of Le Mans! At the end of the practice session the drivers and W.O. met up at the Café de l'Hippodrome for another hearty breakfast, by which time the atmosphere was more cordial and relaxed.

At the drop of the yellow flag at the start of the race the three Bentleys roared ahead of the field, the only casualty being Baron d'Erlanger's hood, which had become unfastened after barely 100 yards, thus causing him to stop and secure it. At the end of the first lap the 4½-litre with Clement at the wheel was in front, having completed the 10.7-mile course in 9 mins 35 secs; behind him in second place was Benjafield, and d'Erlanger was third. To the joy of the considerable British contingent, Clement, on his second lap, beat the existing lap record of 71.9mph, and at the end of the first hour the running order remained the same. After two hours Clement had completed 13 laps and covered 140.86 miles, the last lap having been taken at an average speed of 73.01mph. After 20 laps he refuelled and folded his hood, an operation which took 3 mins 23 secs. According to *The Motor* this was 'A really wonderful achievement when it is borne in mind that the whole of these operations had to be performed single-handed by a driver who had just come in from three hours at the wheel.' Callingham took over from Clement, and within 10 minutes the other two Bentleys were in the pit ready for driver changes.

W.O. must have been very satisfied with his team's effort, but nothing could have prepared him for what happened at White House Corner. Lap after lap the Bentley timekeeper recorded the team's performance, the regularity of the lap times creating some comfort. Then, just before 10pm, that routine was shattered as the distinctive roar of the Bentley exhausts was suddenly absent – the silence was mentally excruciating. As the timekeeper turned to see what was happening he found W.O. standing behind him, his face white with apprehension. No words were uttered; there was no need for any. A minute under such circumstances can seem an hour, but out of the silence there came the familiar sound of an engine, not of a car at speed but of one limping along. Where it was usual to see a car's headlamps blazing, there remained darkness, and only when the car reached the glare of the illuminated grandstand could the incredibly battered state of the vehicle, which had a twisted front wheel, be appreciated.

The famous White House crash had involved all three Bentleys. Callingham, going into the blind corner at between 85 and 90mph, came across a French Th. Schneider four-seater that had got into difficulties and crashed, injuring the driver and blocking part of the road. Swerving to miss the wreckage, the 4½-litre also crashed, rolling into and out of a ditch and coming to rest on its side, blocking another section of road. Callingham was thrown clear of the car and tried to warn the other drivers about the debris, but was too late. George Duller ploughed into the 4½-litre with such force that the front axle was pushed back into the car's sump, leaving the vehicle semi-upright. The Th. Schneider and the tangled mess of the two Bentleys was the scene that greeted Sammy Davis as he lunged into the bend, the only warning of impending danger being a scatter of earth and pieces of splintered wood on the road. Sammy did all he could to avoid a collision, but to no avail. There was a sickening crash as he met the wreckage, the lights of his car were extinguished and he realised with shock that the two cars piled in front of him were those of his teammates. Trembling as he eased himself from the cockpit, Sammy's thoughts were for Duller and Callingham, and only when he saw Duller running towards him, assuring him Callingham was still alive and out of his car, did he begin to relax.

But the race had to go on! When Davis realised that his car was still driveable he started the engine and pulled carefully away from the debris, heading towards the pits, leaving Duller to warn others of the danger. Even as he headed Old Number 7 in the direction of the pits he heard the thump and sound of grating metal as yet another car ploughed into the mangled wreckage.

The sight that awaited W.O. at the Bentley pit must have convinced him that this was another disastrous event for his team. Against his protestations Sammy Davis proceeded to bend the mudguard into some sort of shape, and with some desperation managed to get the headlamps working again. W.O. was concerned about the axle, which was slightly bent, as was the chassis frame. The front cross tube was bowed and the headlamp steady was twisted, but it was with some relief that when fitted the spare wheel ran fairly true. Davis was adamant that he was going to continue the race and set off as soon as he had secured the battery, which was dangling from the running board.

The steering and the brakes of Old Number 7 were in a dire state, and it was all that Davis could do to nurse the car along. Negotiating right-hand bends proved difficult because of insufficient illumination, the off-side headlamp having been completely wrecked. When Benjafield took over driving the car at midnight he was also determined that it should finish the race, although to be placed seemed almost impossible. In front of him was Robert Laly driving an Ariès, and all night he endeavoured to close the distance between the two cars. Sammy Davis took over the car again at 11am, by which time the Ariès's lead had been shortened to just four laps.

W.O. watched the performance of the Ariès and Old Number 7 intently. He was sure that the engine of the French car sounded ominous, and he concluded that if the car were made to go faster it might burst. By getting Old Number 7 to increase its speed, he would provoke Laly to do the same, with calamitous consequences. The Ariès did fail and lost ground by two laps as the driver wrestled with the engine by the side of the road. When Laly eventually got it going and returned to the pit, Jean Chassagne took over the driving.

The race continued and eventually the Ariès succumbed to complete engine failure. When he knew that the Bentley might make the finish after all, Benjafield stopped to secure the wobbling running board before drawing into the pit to allow his teammate Davis to drive the final laps. And what a finish it was! The crowd cheered and smothered Old Number 7 with flowers as it made its lap of honour, but of W.O. there was no sign.

In his usual fashion W.O. slipped quietly into the background when the glory was Bentley's. His inherent shyness and reserved character made him more comfortable away from the limelight, which is one reason why there are so few photographs of W.O. with his cars and their drivers.

A very distinguished visitor graced the subsequent celebratory dinner at the Savoy Hotel in London. Sir Edward Illiffe, chairing the event, announced that a lady was outside who really should be present for the occasion, and with that the banqueting room doors opened and in came Old Number 7 in her proud but dishevelled state, complete with engine running and her remaining headlamp ablaze. Getting the car up the steps of the Savoy and into the banqueting suite had called for a major operation. The car's axles were removed so that the chassis could be secured to a trolley, and once it had entered the hotel via a specially constructed ramp, they were refitted.

W.O. took the 4½-litre, now repaired, to Montlhéry for the Grand Prix de Paris on 9 August. The drivers were Clement and Duller, and from the start of the race the car took the lead. It was not an easy race though, as 18 hours into the event petrol leaking from the fuel tank on to the exhaust pipe caused the car to catch fire. While Clement was able to extinguish the flames quickly, a second fire during the following lap was more serious. The damage was not as extensive as had at first been thought, but ground was lost while repairs to the wiring were effected and the fuel tank sealed.

The 4½-litre was victorious; its first win. It was a hollow victory, however. The event organisers were bankrupt and there were insufficient funds even for a cup, let alone any prize money.

The 1928 season saw W.O. enter three 4½-litre cars for the Six Hours race at Brooklands, one of which had been the victim of the White House crash the previous year. Frank Clement and Woolf Barnato drove this car while the Birkin brothers and Dudley Benjafield and Bernard Rubin crewed the other two. There were two private entries, both 3-litres, one belonging to Humphrey Cook, the other to W.B. Scott. W.O. was delighted that Bentley took the team prize with his cars taking first, second and third places. Birkin covered 433.64 miles at 72.27mph in his 4½-litre to win, Rubin came second at 71.36mph, while Barnato and Clement were third at 70.35mph.

The same cars were entered for the Le Mans 24-Hours, the crews comprising Clement and Benjafield, Barnato and Rubin, and Chassagne and Tim Birkin. Bernard Rubin was an Australian who had been educated at Eton, and while he loved fast cars he shared Benjafield's lack of mechanical knowledge. He was introduced to W.O. through H.M. and Barnato, and his lifestyle, like that of Barnato and Birkin, was lavish to say the least.

First away from the start was Brisson and Bloch's Stutz, with Birkin in hot pursuit, followed by Clement and Barnato in fifth position. The three Bentleys were in the lead after the first lap and Clement took the lap record on the fourth at 76.2mph. Birkin punctured a tyre on lap 20, its remains wrapping themselves tightly around the brake drum. As the team had dispensed with carrying jacks on the cars in the interests of weight-saving, and in the belief that the tyres were designed to withstand punctures, he was forced to hack away the rubber with a knife. This proved extremely difficult, especially in the gruelling heat of the sun, and took him an hour or so to complete. Driving on a bare rim at speeds in excess of 60mph, and using the grass verge as much as possible, the wheel finally collapsed under the stress, causing the car to swerve into a ditch. Birkin ran the three miles to the pits, where he arrived in an exhausted state. His 47-year old co-driver, Jean Chassagne, picked up a couple of jacks, tucked one under each arm, and ran back to the stricken car to change the wheel before driving back to the pit. It was important that the damaged wheel was carried back to the pit in the vehicle in order to avoid disqualification. W.O. knew that despite his team's magnificent efforts the three hours that had been lost had virtually eliminated that car's chance of success.

Barnato, in third position, handed over to Rubin. Benjafield, who came into the pit with clouds of smoke coming from under the bonnet, handed over to Clement, who was able to trace the problem to a broken oil pipe to the camshaft and rectify it before setting off. The Barnato-Rubin car was now in second place. Problems continued to plague Clement's car; the chassis frame fractured as a result of the pounding sustained from negotiating a ridge across the road near to White House Corner, and he eventually retired from the race. For W.O. there was stark realisation that Barnato's car would probably suffer the same fate. It was agonising for him to watch Barnato taking lap after lap, quite oblivious to any impending trouble. Barnato even took the lead from the Stutz while Birkin and Chassagne made their way steadily up the field.

Barnato and Rubin's car appeared to be in a good position to take the race, but suddenly everything changed and W.O.'s worst fears were realised. One of the radiator trunnion bolts worked loose to allow the radiator to vibrate on the front chassis cross member and a water leak appeared. Although the engine was getting ever hotter due to this water loss, Barnato nevertheless carried on. To make matters worse, Stutz's team manager realised the Bentley was in trouble, and gave out a 'go faster' sign to his driver. Barnato responded, daring to take his vehicle beyond all acceptable limits, but his endeavours paid off and the car crossed the finish line in first place to huge applause from the crowds. With the car safely in the pit it was found that practically no water was left in the radiator. Birkin and Chassagne came a very creditable fifth, having broken the lap record by averaging 79.73mph on their final lap.

W.O. had arranged to compete in the Tourist Trophy race at the Ards Circuit in Belfast which was held on 23 August, but when it became evident that the handicap system employed for the race meant little chance of victory for the Bentley team, W.O. withdrew. His racing policy was quite clear: effective publicity was only gained when the team did well, and the company engaged in the sport for business gain. Tim

Birkin and Humphrey Cook decided to enter their cars privately, but it was Kaye Don driving a Lea-Francis who was the victor, the two Bentleys coming fifth and seventh respectively.

Woolf Barnato and Dudley Benjafield drove the first racing 6½-litre Speed Six, now affectionately referred to as 'Old Number 1', in the 1929 Double Twelve-Hour race at Brooklands on 10 and 11 May. Their teammates were Frank Clement and Humphrey Cook, the young and wealthy Sir Ronald Gunter with Sammy Davis, and Tim Birkin and N. Holder, all of whom were driving 4½-litres. The event was seen as an attempt to emulate the Le Mans 24-Hours, but the operating principles were quite different. Night driving was not permitted out of consideration for the local residents, something the Brooklands authorities took very seriously. After the first day's racing the cars were locked in a parc fermé so that no work could be undertaken on them, and they were kept under strict surveillance until the start of the race on the second day.

The Speed Six averaged 92mph for the first hour of the race, leading the field from the other Bentleys, which were averaging around 86mph. After four hours with Benjafield driving, the car was brought into the pit for a rear wheel change, and shortly after that he was back with an electrical fault. The problem lay with the dynamo drive, one of the couplings having failed. The dynamo was removed, Benjafield throwing it to the rear of the car before setting off again. Two hours later the race officials decided that Benjafield had disqualified himself because the rules of the race clearly stated that a car's electrical system had to be in proper working order.

W.O. was not in the least pleased at the car being retired, and to add insult to injury it was even suggested by the course management that the car continue running despite being disqualified, in the interest of gate receipts the following day! Understandably W.O. was furious. Referring to the incident years later he commented that Bentley Motors were committed to 'sales and nothing else', and that they were not in racing for spectator enjoyment. He acknowledged his attitude was hardly sporting, but it was, nevertheless, one that was hard-nosed and business related, something Woolf Barnato would have understood. Davis and Gunter went on to take second place.

In early May W.O. received a telephone call from the Hon. Mrs Victor Bruce, already a veteran of Montlhéry, Brooklands and the Monte Carlo Rally. She was the first woman to appear in court on a speeding charge, and in 1927 took her AC 200 miles inside the Arctic Circle. She wanted to attempt the world record for single-handed driving for 24 hours, and it was a Bentley that she wanted to achieve her goal.

W.O. agreed to an interview, and accordingly Mrs Bruce arrived at Cricklewood the following morning. He was in his office with Woolf Barnato, and briefly she told them that she wanted to borrow a car and take it to Montlhéry. W.O. was not entirely convinced that it was such a good idea, and told her so immediately, for there was only one vehicle available, a 4½-litre which was due to be shared between Tim Birkin and Earl Howe during the racing season. Mrs Bruce argued that by the time the car was required for Le Mans it would be nicely run-in. Still unconvinced, W.O. argued that should the car be damaged, then she would have to face not only him and Barnato, but also the two drivers and their mechanics. When she told him that she wanted the car to be capable of averaging 100mph, which meant driving at speeds of around 107mph, and that she did not intend to have a co-driver, a look of obvious distrust came over W.O.'s face. For all that, however, he recognised that his visitor would not be satisfied until he agreed to her request, and not only that, he saw in her a distinct determination which he admired.

W.O. finally agreed to help. He suggested that the car would need to be modified with a high-ratio rear axle and three carburettors. There was only a week available for practice, and Mrs Bruce left the works in the knowledge that she had to return the car in one piece and in good condition. When she offered to pay for the mechanics' time and the costs involved in getting the car to Montlhéry, W.O. merely smiled. He told her not to worry and said that the Bentley would be waiting for her at the track. Jack Sopp and Wally Saunders accompanied Mrs Bruce for the record attempt, which she took averaging 89.57mph over the 24 hours including all pit stops. News of her attempt became known, and among those waiting to congratulate her as she stepped from the car was Earl Howe, then President of the British Racing Drivers' Club. Over dinner that evening in Paris, she learnt that he was behind a proposal to confer her with honorary life membership of the BRDC.

For the Le Mans race a month later W.O. entered a team of five cars, the leader being the Speed Six driven by Barnato and Birkin and carrying No.1. The other four cars were all 4½-litres driven by Clement and Chassagne (No.8), Glen Kidston and Jack Dunfee (No.9),

Benjafield and d'Erlanger (No.10), and Earl Howe and Bernard Rubin driving the Montlhéry record-breaking car (No.11). W.O. had decided that there should be two pit teams, one under the direction of Nobby Clarke looking after the Speed Six and Nos 8 and 9, and Bertie Kensington Moir managing Nos 10 and 11. The cars under Bertie Moir's supervision were late entries because the cars that W.O. had intended to run were not ready.

This was Birkin's first Le Mans race and he was first away from the start, closely followed by Clement in No.8. Earl Howe was eliminated fairly early on because of magneto failure (which was nothing to do with the car's earlier record attempt), but this set-back was compensated by Birkin lapping at a fraction under 80mph. In fact he took the lap record for the race at 82.984mph in the 99th lap. Barnato took over No.1 after 20 laps, and thereafter the remaining cars returned to the pit for a change of drivers. The four Bentleys held the first four positions by 6pm, but their luck was not to last. W.O. became anxious when, during the darkness, the headlamps of both Nos 8 and 9 displayed intermittent faults, causing both lamps to flicker, and on occasions to fail completely. Some time was lost as the cars were forced to slow down, and the problems were traced to the their P100 lamp carriers working loose. Then No.10 was in trouble, firstly with another lighting problem whereby, due to a faulty connection, the lamps failed on right hand bends, and secondly because of a leaking water pump gland. Clement's car experienced further troubles when its ballast moved, causing the body to foul the brake rods. He lost ground while this was repaired.

To W.O.'s relief all four cars were back in the lead by daylight on Sunday, although they were not entirely free from problems. No.10's brakes were inoperative, the shoes having worn out, but Benjafield, who was driving, managed to carry on.

Just before the end of the race and with W.O. sure of his cars taking the first four places, the lead car was late in approaching the pit. Nor was there any sign of the other three. W.O.'s heart was in his mouth for he had not forgotten the traumas of the White House crash. To his relief the cars appeared, at reduced speed, the drivers enjoying their final lap before taking the chequered flag at exactly 4pm.

1929 was Bentley's most triumphant racing year. Not only did the team win at Le Mans for the fourth time, and the third time in succession, it competed in a number of other events with some success.

Two works' cars were entered for the Six Hours race at Brooklands on 29 June, with Woolf Barnato and Jack Dunfee taking first place in the Speed Six at 75.88mph, and Callingham and Cook in a 4½-litre came in third on handicap. Another works' team competed in the Irish Grand Prix in Dublin on 13 July. This time the Speed Six was driven by Glen Kidston and two 4½-litres were in the hands of Beris Harcourt-Wood and Cook. The Speed Six came in at second place with the two 4½s being placed fourth and fifth.

A month later W.O. went to Belfast, where he himself rode in the Tourist Trophy race at Ards. He entered the Speed Six, which was driven by Glen Kidston, and Old Number 7, its last race. Birkin was there with three supercharged 4½-litres, one driven by Harcourt-Wood, another by Bernard Rubin. Birkin himself drove the third car, W.O. having agreed to ride with him as mechanic.

The fact that W.O. even rode in the race raises a number of questions. His life insurance policy barred him from competing in a race, but it would appear that he arranged special cover for the event and paid the appropriate premium. It would be unfair to suggest that Tim Birkin had talked W.O. into riding as his mechanic: he had suggested such an idea at a dinner some time previously, and despite protestations from Bertie Kensington Moir – who was seriously worried for his safety – W.O. nevertheless agreed on the premise that it would give him a better understanding of what the mechanics and pit crews had to contend with: a brief reminder, perhaps, of his own racing days not so long ago.

The Ards circuit was a challenging course that comprised narrow roads through villages that were always packed with spectators at the most dangerous locations. The race itself proved to be a terrifying experience for W.O., since Birkin was at his most determined and drove in a wholly ruthless manner. W.O. said of him that he drove flat out, 'scorching round the corners in great slides'. It didn't get any better when W.O. saw Rubin's car upside-down on the summit of Mill Hill, and when he saw the Speed Six astride a ditch and bank, his spirits fell to an all-time low! At last, after five hours, he was consoled by a class win and second place in the speed category despite being placed 11th overall.

The final major event of the season was the 500 Mile at Brooklands on 12 October. The Speed Six had been re-bodied and was driven by Sammy Davis and Clive Dunfee, Jack's brother. Frank Clement and Jack Barclay drove one of three 4½-litres, the other two being crewed by Rose-Richards and Fiennes, and Jack Dunfee. This was another success for W.O., with Clement and Barclay taking first place, Davis and Clive Dunfee second, and Rose-Richards and Fiennes fifth. There had been some heart-stopping moments when Jack Barclay lost control on the members' banking at 110mph, and almost came to grief later a short time later when he narrowly missed going over the top of the banking. After this incident Jack Barclay was called into the pit where he faced W.O.'s wrath, and Frank Clement drove for the rest of the race.

In the true tradition of the Bentley Boys, Glen Kidston was something of a hero. W.O. said of him that he was a born adventurer with a powerful build. He came close to death when he was the sole survivor of a London–Paris airliner that was lost in fog and crashed into trees. On another occasion he survived when the submarine he was on became embedded on the seabed, although rescuers had given up all hope for him. He died in an aeroplane accident flying over South Africa when his heavily overloaded Tiger Moth broke up in bad weather.

Clive and Jack Dunfee were the sons of Colonel Vickers Dunfee CBE, the creator of the London City Police Reserve. Neither brother was a full-time racing professional, although Jack was highly skilled. Sadly Clive was killed at Brooklands in 1932 while driving Old Number 1 in the 500 Mile race. The car went over the banking.

It cannot really be said that W.O. himself was one of the 'Bentley Boys', for he was far too reserved to be included in the band of drivers that literally lived their lives to the full in lavish and flamboyant style. Several of them had apartments in an around Grosvenor Square, and the parties they threw, the money that was spent and the ladies with whom they were acquainted, are legendary.

Woolf Barnato was the biggest spender of all. Having invested further amounts of money in Bentley Motors Limited between 1926 and 1930 – £35,000 having been made available in July 1927 with a further £40,000 loan arranged through London Life, and another £25,000 in 1929 – he was renowned for his extravagant and wild parties at Ardenrun. His daughter, Diana Barnato Walker, recalls some of those occasions when the Bentley Boys, and their entourage of 'Bentley Girls', would arrive in high spirits. They would drive at high speed along the entrance drive and pull up in the Brooklands-style pits that he had constructed, where they met for champagne.

For W.O. there was the 1930 racing season to plan: deciding which cars would be raced and appointing a team of drivers. There was also urgent business to resolve regarding development of a new and more powerful Bentley, the 8-litre, which he thought would rival the Rolls-Royce Phantom models in terms of refinement and performance. Foremost in his thoughts, though, was a desire from some quarters of his racing team to progress an idea for supercharging the 4½-litre engine for racing purposes, a development he was completely opposed to on technical grounds.

CHAPTER 8

An Unwelcome Alliance

AN initial study of the 1929 Bentley Motors Limited Directors' Report made encouraging reading:

> The financial year now ended (31 March 1929) may be generally described as one of steady progress. The net profits as shown by the audited accounts amount to £28,467 19s 5d, after making ample allowance for depreciation and contingencies and after writing off the balance of the cost of converting to the 1928 specification all the first produced six and a half litre chassis.

The investments described at the end of the previous chapter permitted the construction of the company's own machine shop at Cricklewood, and the building of new general offices at the works, both projects being detailed in the same Directors' Report. As with previous loans the investments were secured against all the company's assets, including the new showroom and offices at Pollen House. As it happened the new machine shop arrived too late to provide the company any real manufacturing benefits, and the only components that were produced there were those for the ill-fated 4-litre, of which more later.

The evidence shows that all was not well within the company. Its finances were directly linked to the London Stock Exchange, and thus at the mercy of national trends. A good week's trading in stocks and shares usually resulted in more sales of cars than a bad week's trading, which often led to despair.

By the end of the summer there was evidence that the American economy had drastically cooled, leading to a national downturn in production output. The Wall Street Crash that followed had serious repercussions for Britain and the rest of the world, and for W.O. it heralded another turning point in his life. The fragile state of Bentley Motors' finances was about to suffer such devastation that recovery was always going to be difficult, impossible even.

W.O.'s racing programme for 1930 was dominated by problems with Tim Birkin and the 4½-litre. When Birkin entered his 4½-litre in the German Grand Prix at the Nürburgring in July 1928 he found himself completely outclassed by the supercharged 7-litre Mercedes and was placed eighth. When W.O. withdrew the Bentley team entry before the Ards race Birkin competed on his own and was placed fifth. He was again placed fifth when he competed in the Coupe Georges Boillot in September, following W.O.'s team withdrawal.

Birkin was convinced that future success lay with supercharging the 4½-litre, a view that was not supported by W.O., who had decided that the most productive route was to progress development of the 6½-litre into the Speed Six. Birkin was not to be persuaded otherwise and made it clear that he would not race another Bentley 4½-litre unless it was fitted with a supercharger. Birkin had the ear of Barnato, who on hearing his ideas about what supercharging might do for the marque and its racing success showed complete enthusiasm for the project. Here we have, therefore, yet another indication of W.O.'s diminishing authority within the company, even though he was joint managing director.

That W.O. was vehemently opposed to supercharging is apparent from his own notes, which he incorporated into his autobiography. In his opinion supercharging depraved the Bentley design and produced levels of performance that had never been envisaged. It compromised all the qualities that a Bentley was noted for, and induced speeds that would cause an engine ultimately to fail. In order to retain the Bentley refinement, W.O. was emphatic that the only way to allow greater speeds was to increase engine size.

Dudley Benjafield, however, puts the supercharging issue in a rather different context as far as W.O. is concerned. In his highly revered 'scrapbook' *The Bentleys At Le Mans*, which was published in 1948, he tells of his exploits racing his 3-litre. As much tuning of the car's engine as was possible had been carried out, and ultimately Bertie Kensington

Moir and Benjafield sought W.O.'s advice on how to derive more 'horses' from it. Referring to W.O.'s appraisal of the situation, Benjafield wrote: 'Having heard our story, the "Great Man" said there was only one thing left to do if more "horses" were to be extracted from the 3-litre and that was to supercharge.' It can be presumed that once he had considered all the aspects of supercharging, W.O. ultimately revised his opinion. Benjafield is adamant that he considered the 3-litre a far better candidate for supercharging than the 4½-litre.

Against W.O.'s advice, Birkin decided to proceed with supercharging the 4½-litre and invited Charles Amherst Villiers to assist with the project. Villiers had an engineering background, having been apprenticed to the Royal Aircraft Factory at Farnborough, where he worked in the experimental department. After the war he helped Raymond Mays tune and develop his cars, an exercise which led to him going to work for Bugatti at Molsheim. Villiers was also associated with Malcolm Campbell, working for him in connection with his *Bluebird* land speed record car, and he was acquainted with Humphrey Cook, who was a recognised authority on racing Bentleys. Villiers was recognised, too, for the supercharging work he carried out on Cook's 1922 TT Vauxhall with such outstanding success when campaigned by Raymond Mays in the late 1920s. In 1927 he was involved in supercharging a Rolls-Royce New Phantom belonging to captain J.F.C. Kruse, which he took to Brooklands. Subsequently a report appeared in *The Autocar* which Villiers thought was disparaging, and he replied to criticisms raised in the journal in no uncertain manner through Charles B. Lowe, the manager of Amherst Villiers & Co.

Following Birkin's approach, Villiers went to see W.O. at Cricklewood. If he had anticipated that W.O. might be receptive to supercharging the 4½-litre engine he was mistaken. He found W.O. to be difficult about the project as a whole and unwilling to co-operate. They argued about the design parameters that would be required to allow the supercharger to operate efficiently, and W.O. told Villiers that in any case it would not fit under the bonnet. When Villiers was given a set of blueprint drawings of the 4½-litre engine he was critical about the crankshaft design, claiming that it would need balance weights, something which W.O. considered abhorrent. Nor would W.O. agree to any royalty payment, as he considered that the car remained a Bentley, and the amount of publicity Villiers would receive would be quite sufficient recompense for his efforts. That the two were never going to agree was obvious.

Barnato, having been persuaded by Birkin to back his proposal, played a careful role. Supercharging the 4½-litre appealed to him, and he foresaw that at least part of the development cost could be privately funded. It was without W.O.'s approval, therefore, that Birkin, Villiers and Bentley Motors Ltd entered into an agreement that was dated 18 October 1928.

In essence the arrangement was that Villiers would design and build four suitable superchargers, together with all the necessary ancillary equipment. Bentley Motors Ltd would fit six or more superchargers to their cars (in addition to the initial four) and standardisation of the equipment would be assumed, in which case Villiers would receive royalty payments. Standardisation would only be confirmed following satisfactory demonstration, after which any patents on behalf of Villiers would remain in force until 30 May 1929. The agreement allowed for the Villiers name to appear on all the superchargers, except in cases where joint development was acknowledged, in which case the name Villiers-Bentley would appear. Following standardisation by Bentley, all drawings, patterns and tools would become the company's property.

Birkin and Villiers worked closely on the project, the former having a workshop at Feltham in Middlesex before leasing premises from Vanden Plas in Kingsbury. It had been his intention to relocate to Cricklewood near to the Bentley works, but he eventually decided to take premises at Welwyn Garden City. Villiers, as consulting engineer, was established in Sackville Street in an office that was part of Piccadilly House, and while he undertook all the necessary design work, it was at Birkin's workshop that the engineering was carried out.

The first supercharger was fitted on Bernard Rubin's 4½-litre. Thereafter Birkin purchased four chassis direct from Bentley Motors, with the intention of having the cars supercharged. Much has been said elsewhere about supercharging and the design of the 'Blower' Bentleys, and exactly what went on between Amherst Villiers and W.O. remains something of a mystery, mainly because the matter was treated with strict secrecy, and those people who did have information are now dead.

In order to develop and perfect the supercharged cars, Birkin enlisted the help of Clive Gallop and Bertie Kensington Moir, both of whom had been stalwarts of W.O.'s regime during the Bentley Motors era. Gallop went to Birkin's works in Welwyn as works manager, and it is at this point that the whole matter of supercharging appears to have come into question, especially as Villiers and Gallop differed greatly in their technical opinions. As it transpired changes to the design of Villiers's supercharger were found to be necessary, which gave rise to the difficulties that existed between him and Gallop. In fact Gallop, in later years, was moved to agree with W.O. about supercharging.

W.O. did not bury his head in the sand when it came to the subject of supercharging. As detailed in the previous chapter, W.O. had even agreed to ride with Birkin as mechanic in his blown 4½-litre in Ireland. It was that experience, which he refers to as absolutely terrifying, which convinced him that supercharging was not the route to follow.

In order to finance his supercharging operations and racing activities, Birkin needed the backing of a sympathetic sponsor, whom he found in the Hon. Dorothy Paget. She was the daughter of Lord Queensbury and was extremely wealthy in her own right. Born in 1905, Dorothy Paget remains something of an enigma: she funded horse racing and had very successful stables; she appears to have had an aversion to men and was inordinately overweight and in excess of 20 stone. Said to have been the richest unmarried woman in England, her interest in motor racing, and Bentleys in particular, stems from having watched the 500 Mile race at Brooklands. It was with Paget's money that Birkin was able to buy and modify the Bentley chassis at Welwyn.

In his determination to have a team of 'Blower' Bentleys in the 1930 Le Mans race, Birkin successfully persuaded Barnato to enter a team of four cars. To do so meant that Bentley Motors was obliged to build at least 50 examples of the model to qualify for the event, and accordingly the supercharged 4½-litre was introduced and shown at the 1929 London Motor Show, deliveries commencing in the following April.

To many enthusiasts of the marque the 4½-litre supercharged Bentley was the ultimate sports car, with its 103mph performance as tested by *The Motor*. The speed was academic, however; although Tim Birkin squeezed 135.33mph out of the car at Brooklands in 1930, a record which was raised to a staggering 137.99mph two years later, the Blower Bentley has always attracted a unique reputation for its image and sheer power.

For the 1930 Double Twelve Hour race at Brooklands the Bentley team comprised two Speed Sixes, to be driven by Barnato and Clement and Davis and Clive Dunfee. Dorothy Paget also entered three 4½-litre supercharged Bentleys, which were to be driven by Birkin and Chassagne, Kidston and Jack Dunfee, and d'Erlanger with Benjafield. Initially the performance of the Blowers looked promising, but it became clear that at least two of the cars were experiencing problems. All three Blowers ultimately retired, leaving the Bentley works' team of two 6½-litres to take first and second place.

For the Le Mans 24-Hours on 21–22 June, W.O. entered three Speed Sixes, Clement and Dick Watney driving No.2, Davis and Clive Dunfee No.3, and Barnato and Kidston in car No.4. Dorothy Paget also entered three cars but problems with fuel and the cars' compression ratio meant that only two ran, Jack Dunfee and Beris Harcourt-Wood's car being withdrawn at the last minute. The two that did run were those of Birkin with Chassagne and Benjafield with Ramponi.

The reason for Birkin's cars having been beset by problems lay with the type of fuel that was supplied by the French, which caused the engines to overheat. Shortly before the start of the race Birkin decided to raise the compression, by removing one of the compression plates from between the crankcase and the block. There was no animosity between W.O. and Birkin, and in fact W.O. ordered his mechanics to assist those working for Birkin.

In the lead-up to the race the French were philosophical about the result. Their opinion was that Bentley had had Le Mans almost to themselves for the past few years, and it seemed unlikely that this would change. Meanwhile in the British camp there was continued speculation about how to outwit the Germans. In their usual fashion the drivers and mechanics debated over long hours spent in the hotel restaurants and bars.

The race will forever be remembered as the great Bentley-Mercedes duel. Caracciola, with Werner as co-driver, led from the start, but was overtaken by Birkin in his Blower Bentley in the fourth lap. When Birkin's tyre burst immediately before the Mulsanne corner he carried on, but was forced to slow when the tyre finally collapsed at the Arnage S-bends. Limping to the pit he was obliged to stop and change the wheel while the other Bentleys maintained the chase. As the first day wore on Barnato and Kidston's Speed Six took the lead from the Mercedes, only for the Mercedes to regain it. So the combat continued, Bentley and Mercedes hunting each other until the Mercedes refused to start after a pit stop. W.O. had worked out the 'cat and mouse' race strategy, and

Barnato followed his instructions implicitly, which helped the team achieve victory. For the Germans the failure of the Mercedes was a catastrophe, since the rules of the race did not permit a car to be hand or push-started. There was camaraderie and rivalry between the two Bentley teams, the Speed Sixes vying for supremacy with the Blowers. For Birkin the consolation was that he raised the lap record to 89.696mph, with a stripped tyre tread, before retiring. In fact tyre and mechanical problems plagued the Blowers throughout the race.

From the beginning of the race it had been W.O.'s strategy to prove the stamina of his cars against the sheer might of the Mercedes. He believed that by making the Mercedes drivers use their superchargers as much as possible the Germans would be tested to the limit. W.O. was convinced that the supercharged Bentleys would not stay the course of the race, but he knew that Birkin's drivers could put extreme pressure on their rivals during the early stages. That would leave the works' team of Speed Sixes to maintain a position ready to harass the Germans later. Birkin was happy to go along with W.O.'s plan for a combined and carefully planned attack. Both of the supercharged Bentleys retired during the race, leaving the two Speed Sixes to drive to victory. Barnato and Kidston were first to cross the finish line, with Clement and Watney in pursuit.

The victory, the fifth in a row for Bentley, marked the end of the company's racing programme. In July an announcement was made that Bentley Motors was to retire from motorsport with immediate effect, and almost simultaneously another announcement, issued on Woolf Barnato's behalf by J.K. Carruth, declared his own retirement from motor racing. There were official reasons for both decisions, as well as those that were not revealed at the time.

W.O. had already entered a team for the Irish Grand Prix scheduled to take place in Dublin the following month, and this was withdrawn. So of course was Bentley's assumed entry for the 1931 Le Mans, which gave the organising body, the Automobile Club de l'Ouest, sufficient notice of the company's absence. Nor did their withdrawal from racing preclude, for the time being, Dorothy Paget from continuing racing with Birkin's 4½-litre supercharged cars as private entries. In fact Birkin continued to race until his untimely death, by which time Dorothy Paget had withdrawn her support from his racing enterprise. The 1930 Tourist Trophy at Belfast was the last event she sponsored. Without having the capital or the sponsorship to proceed on his own, Tim had to drive mainly for foreign teams, including Maserati and Alfa Romeo.

The official reasons for withdrawing from the racing scene were that Bentley had achieved as much experience as was necessary from competition, and that the company wished to concentrate on production cars. Barnato's retreat from motorsport was said to be in favour of leaving the field open to younger competitors, who were better equipped to perpetuate the prestige that he and others had brought to the sport. He also wished to concentrate on racing motor boats, although he abandoned this plan after one of his vessels sank while competing at the Welsh Harp.

The real reasons behind the façade were that Barnato had achieved all he had wanted racing Bentleys, at a huge cost, not all of which was reflected in Bentley Motors' accounts. To put it concisely, Barnato's enthusiasm had waned and his financial advisers were telling him to pull out because of a worsening economic climate. Then there was the whole matter of Bentley Motors itself: fewer customers were specifying the true sports machines that W.O. had originally envisaged and which were the marque's hallmark. Increasing numbers of customers were specifying luxury sports saloons, and the company felt obliged to accommodate such demand.

For W.O. the end of Bentley racing was yet another factor to add to his gloom. The economic situation had meant that fewer orders for cars were being received, and even those were becoming harder to win in the first place. Natural progression of development meant that increased performance coupled with refinement heralded the requirement for a car of larger capacity than the 6½-litre, hence the introduction of the 8-litre at the London Motor Show in the autumn of 1930.

The announcement of the new car must have caused some disquiet at Rolls-Royce, for not only was it at the time the largest car on the British market, but its chassis price was also £50 above that of the Phantom II. Rolls-Royce, therefore, even if the company refused to admit it, had a genuine rival. The extent of Rolls-Royce's concern about the 8-litre can be gauged from the fact that Jack Barclay, who was agent for both Bentley and Rolls-Royce, admitted that it was difficult to sell a Continental Phantom II against the Sports Bentley.

Ernest Hives and W.A. Robotham had previously evaluated a 6½-litre, which they decided was less than satisfactory. They reported then that 'Bentleys seem to be failing badly'. It was natural for Rolls-Royce to find fault with its competitor, just it did in 1928 when Barnato's own 4½-litre was tested by the Derby sales staff. The outcome of the test then was that Rolls-Royce claimed that the car could not be considered a rival to its own models.

Barnato had, in 1930, undertaken to race the *Flêche d'Or* train from Cannes to London, using a 6½-litre Speed Six that had been specially constructed for him. He was testing the car with its closed aerodynamic body when the idea of racing the *Flêche d'Or* occurred to him. With Dale Bourne, a golfing friend, as passenger, they arrived in London some three and three-quarter hours before the train's passengers arrived at Victoria Station aboard the *Golden Arrow*, the British extension of the *Flêche d'Or*. Barnato's feat was naturally seized on by the media, thus giving Bentley Motors huge publicity, which gave Rolls-Royce even more reason to be perturbed by their rival's achievement.

Barnato's race against steam power was a clever and romantic publicity stunt. A similar feat was attempted by Dudley Noble and Harold Pemberton, also in 1930, when they drove a works' Rover Light Six from St Raphaël to Calais, arriving at the northern French port 20 minutes ahead of the express. Without devaluing Barnato's efforts in any way, racing the *Flêche d'Or* was an accomplishment that bolstered Bentley's reputation considerably when it was most needed.

The car that Barnato had used to race the Blue Train was until recently thought to be chassis GJ 3811, which has survived, and not surprisingly has been revered by Bentley enthusiasts around the world. Through information supplied by Diana Barnato Walker it has been revealed that in fact it was a similar car that Barnato used.

Rolls-Royce was naturally very keen to get its hands on an 8-litre to see exactly how it performed. They were dismissive about it being a genuine 100mph car, and invited Rolls-Royce and Bentley agent Jack Barclay to take his demonstrator to Brooklands for a test run. Even with heavy coachwork the 8-litre's performance was such that Rolls-Royce had to accept Bentley's claim. There is some irony in the fact that the 8-litre's development was conducted by Thomas Barwell Barrington, who had been appointed chief designer following Frederick Burgess's death. Burgess had been ill for some time and he was greatly missed by W.O. Barrington had for a time worked for both Rolls-Royce and Napier, and he returned to the former company when it acquired Bentley. As chief designer working on aero engines in 1934 he was sent to America in connection with the Merlin engine, and he died there in 1941. In Bentley company history Barrington is something of an enigma, especially since W.O. never referred to him in any of his writings or notes, thus giving the impression thatthey did not particularly get on.

The 8-litre was W.O.'s favourite car, and his enjoyment testing his own vehicle has been mentioned elsewhere. W.O.'s own car was exceedingly fast, which was due in part to it being a modified 6½-litre. On the open road it was possible to achieve 110mph, a speed that was not attained on production models. In fact testing of the production 8-litre showed up some serious problems that were only addressed a short time before deliveries commenced. The source of the trouble was the lack of rigidity of certain types of heavy coachwork when fitted to the 6½-litre frame. Modifications were therefore incorporated when designing the 8-litre frame, but in some circumstances it proved to be too rigid. To his concern W.O. discovered that on occasions the front axle would begin to vibrate, the malady transferring to the frame in sympathy, the symptom being known as 'tramping'. This happened to W.O. one day at the wheel of a car he was testing. Approaching a bend at 80mph, he found himself in a very tricky situation when tramping set in, and all efforts to steer the car around the bend were in vain. This experience unnerved him and he later recorded that he had no idea how he had extricated himself from the predicament. After that further modifications were made to the fixing of the body scuttle to the dash structure, and only when W.O. had personally tested each vehicle until he was satisfied with its behaviour did he sanction its delivery.

W.O.'s view of the 1930 London Motor Show was that it was the precursor to misery. The economic situation affected all manufacturers, although it has to be said that the purveyors of luxury cars felt the pinch rather more than those offering popular and less expensive machines. The sales situation within Bentley Motors was dire, but that was not the image the company projected. The 8-litre really was the star of the show: a magnificent motor car in every respect, it gave the Bentley display the edge over its Derby rival. Together with the cars on the Bentley stand and those gracing separate coachbuilders' displays, there were no fewer than six 8-litre cars represented at Olympia.

The 8-litre was the best car that Bentley ever made – those are the words that W.O. used when reflecting on the 'Bentley era'. It had been his aim to produce a genuine 100mph motor car, and this is what the

Bentley flagship achieved. It was also Barnato's favourite car, and he owned at least two examples.

After the success of the 8-litre – 63 of these very expensive cars were sold in nine months – came bitter disappointment. The worsening finances of the company forced Barnato to take some unpalatable decisions, which involved a shake-up of the board of directors. Both Casa Maury and W.O. were removed as joint managing directors, and in their place Barnato appointed Jack Carruth. W.K. Forster was displaced as company secretary, Barnato appointing Robert Montgomerie (another of his 'cronies', according to W.O.) in his place. Another casualty was the firm's chief buyer, Peter Purves, who was succeeded by his deputy, Darren Few. Elsewhere W.O. is referred to as being highly complimentary about Purves, but the evidence suggests that something happened to make W.O. change his opinion. Winifred Leafe was W.O.'s secretary for a number of years, and her later marriage to Purves appears to have annoyed W.O.

Being replaced as joint managing director came as a huge shock to W.O. Although he retained his position as chief engineer, along with his place on the board of directors, there was, nevertheless, a suggestion of no confidence, and coming to terms with this was very difficult for him. When company directors decided that a new model of car be developed which moved away from some of the traditional Bentley values, it was another blow to W.O.'s self-confidence. The car that was planned would rival the Rolls-Royce 20/25hp and undersell it.

Everything possible had been done to encourage sales of cars. The sales team, now headed by Hugh Kevill-Davies, arranged for special 'Bentley Weeks' to be held throughout the country to support Bentley dealers. The arrangement was in effect a travelling showroom, which displayed Bentley models in differing coachwork styles.

It was the attitude of his fellow directors that particularly incensed W.O. As chief engineer he was told that the performance of the intended car really didn't matter, and that there was no room for engines that adhered to W.O. design principles. What was needed, they told him, was a straightforward six-cylinder engine with push-rod operated valves, something W.O. considered abhorrent. The directors, it seems, had already established the car's recipe: it would use the 8-litre chassis, as there were plenty available!

The car in which the directors put their faith was a 4-litre. While W.O. lobbied against its development, Barnato refused to back him, preferring instead to listen to his advisers. The 4-litre was, in W.O.'s estimation, a boardroom car, and it is understandable that whatever happened he was always going to be averse to it. His argument was that the type of engine that was proposed would lack the refinement and acceleration expected of a Bentley when fitted to the 8-litre chassis, which would be burdened with heavy and cumbersome coachwork. Bentley customers, he maintained, would avoid the car and it would not sell in the numbers envisaged.

W.O. claims to have declined to have anything to do with the 4-litre engine, but in late August 1929 he wrote to the well-known engineer Harry Ricardo, enlisting his support for jointly designing and developing a new engine. W.O. subsequently visited Ricardo at Shoreham in Sussex, where he was shown a scheme for an inlet over exhaust (IOE) intended for fitment to the six-cylinder engine then being developed at Cricklewood. In *Engines and Enterprise*, the biography of Sir Harry Ricardo, John Reynolds refers to two prototype six-cylinder engines running on the Bentley test-beds in June 1930.

Barrington was involved in the development of the 4-litre engine, and it is known that W.O. was not at all impressed with the test-bed results. One of the two engines on test was sent to Ricardos for examination following problems with the valve gear arrangement. The works' personnel who were involved with the 4-litre project had varying ideas about the engine's design. Wally Hassan believed it to be a fine unit although underpowered when fitted to the 8-litre chassis. He claims it was beautifully smooth and would have been perfect for use with the 4½-litre chassis. Frank Clement was adamant that it was a dreadful unit, a view also voiced by Wally Saunders, who recalled how difficult it had been to install it in the 8-litre chassis.

The 4-litre did find a few customers but Bentley enthusiasts in the main ignored it, and for many years they refused to accept it was a Bentley at all. With hindsight it can be appreciated that it might well have been a fine car, and had it worn a badge other than the winged B emblem it would undoubtedly have been more favourably received.

W.O.'s thoughts about developing the 4-litre, and smaller cars in general, are to be found in his book *The Cars in My Life*. He makes the point that the 6½-litre cost very little more to manufacture than the 3-litre, and that the 8-litre had a much higher profit margin than the smaller-engined models. He refers to Rolls-Royce's experience in developing an 18hp car of 2¾ litres and discovering that it was almost as expensive to build as the 20/25hp. The sole advantage, he maintains, is in the reduced weight of metal.

From his writings there would appear to be some regret on W.O.'s behalf that during the years of Bentley Motors he did not take a more active role in the day-to-day running of the company. He admits to keeping himself detached from the daily problems of theory and detail, and one can assume from this that he means more than just the technical aspects of the car. W.O. excelled in proving a car by thorough testing, both on the test-bed and the open road, and before the Barnato era he was largely dependent on H.M.'s expertise in business affairs.

Following W.O.'s displacement as joint managing director further cracks began to appear in the Bentley Motors management structure. Jack Carruth was obviously charged with looking after Barnato's financial interests, and this meant more alienation for W.O. Barnato realised that he could not continue carrying the company, especially in the light of the depressed economy, and began a campaign that would eventually see the demise of Bentley Motors in one form or another. An early indication of the route ahead lay with an overhaul of the sales team at Pollen House. The services of Hugh Kevill-Davies and Longman were dispensed with and Carruth appointed L.H. Johnson and K.C. Grey, both of whom were previously sales managers with Rolls-Royce. Johnson was the son of Claude Johnson, who effectively took over the day-to-day running of Rolls-Royce after Rolls's death and Royce's health problems. Two new directors were appointed on 17 January 1931 and Barnato hoped they would help improve the fortunes of the company. One was Sir Walrond Sinclair from Goodrich Rubber (Bentley were specifying Goodrich tyres exclusively), and the other was Richard (Dick) Witchell.

When it came to financial issues Barnato's hard-nosed attitude meant that there was little room for niceties, even when it came to personal issues between W.O. and himself. There is evidence that despite W.O.'s insistence that there was a good working relationship between himself and Barnato, it may not have been the case. Certainly Barnato appeared to have little concern for W.O. when he displaced him as joint managing director, and he showed no compunction in overruling him regarding the design of the 4-litre. In fact there is evidence that Barnato was working towards co-operation with Rolls-Royce well before Bentley Motors went into liquidation.

After World War Two Barnato revealed much about the final months of Bentley Motors. He intimated that because of perceived failings of company management it had been necessary for him to appoint joint managing directors when he took control. He even considered dispensing with W.O.'s services entirely. That he did not is arguably because his action would have caused a serious rift among fellow directors, and Barnato of all people recognised W.O.'s expertise as a racing manager. Barnato went on to suggest that had W.O.'s name been deleted from the list of directors, and were he to have been disassociated from the company, few people outside the firm would have been aware of his removal. There is, of course, the matter of W.O.'s contract with Bentley Motors Ltd, and breaching it could have cost the company dearly.

These are harsh words which Bentley devotees will find unpalatable. All the more insensitive are Barnato's comments that suggest that W.O.'s continued employment was inessential for the production of the Bentley car, and that the use of his name was not dependent on his continued association with the company.

What is certain is that following Casa Maury's appointment as joint managing director of Bentley Motors, W.O.'s own position became extremely fragile. The evidence suggests that policy differences between W.O. and his fellow directors were such that only special consideration made it possible for him to continue to serve on the board.

There are two subtle clues to the extent of the unrest between W.O. and Barnato. By 1930 it was clear to W.O. that the days of Bentley Motors were numbered, and it was a matter for speculation as to how long Barnato would, or could, support the company. W.O. refers to Barnato's continuing investment in his autobiography and mentions that he and Barnato never discussed the firm's liquidation after the event. The other clue is that Diana Barnato Walker refers to her father's relationship with W.O. by disclosing that they did not get on. Her comments are inconclusive because she does not relate them to a precise period, but it is presumed she refers to post-1928 and post-liquidation.

During the final year of Bentley Motors's existence Jack Carruth was effectively running the company. The financial situation was such that, in order to reduce its pecuniary problems, the company traded on a cash basis rather than credit to get the best discounts from suppliers. Consideration must also be given to W.O.'s personal life: not only was he depressed and demoralised in his business capacity, his marriage to Audrey, which was never really successful, was breaking down completely.

By the time the 4-litre was introduced on 14 May 1931 it was abundantly clear to W.O. that the company's situation was extremely fragile. There were enormous problems leading up to the car's launch at Pollen House, even to the extent that the brochures were not ready until the unveiling date, and even then they were delivered to Cork Street while the launch ceremony was actually taking place. There were more fundamental issues, however. Those who were involved in developing the 4-litre believed that the car was launched before it was anything like ready, which is one reason why the model had a bad reputation within the works. In fairness, the introduction of the car was not popular with the workforce, which had been with Bentley Motors since its establishment at Cricklewood. To them the car was not a true Bentley and therefore its success was undermined from the beginning.

There is also speculation that Bentley Motors wanted to keep certain aspects of the 4-litre's design secret. This can only be supposed because the cars' bonnets were sealed before chassis were despatched to coachbuilders. It has been asserted that this may have been done on W.O.'s personal instructions, but in reality it might have been for no more sinister reason than to keep engine details of the car confidential until the launch date. Although an overhead valve six-cylinder engine had been proposed, it was an overhead inlet and side exhaust affair that materialised. Ironically, the immediate post-World War Two Bentley, the Mark VI, employed a similar configuration, which was shared with the ensuing R-type and early S-type models. The evidence is that one of the road test personnel was sent to H.J. Mulliner to seal the bonnets of the cars that had been despatched there. Another explanation could be the fact that Bentley wanted to keep the information from Rolls-Royce, which was anxious to find out how the 4-litre might compete with the 20/25hp.

Woolf Barnato was in no doubt about the huge drain on his finances that Bentley Motors presented. Having given up motor racing the need to keep the company afloat had clearly diminished, and Carruth's prediction that the equivalent of around £1.75 million in today's values (£35-40,000 then) was needed to bolster funds meant that some harsh decisions were called for.

When it went on sale the demand for the 4-litre was not as strong as Bentley directors had anticipated. This was not entirely due to the car's design, nor to its chassis price of £1,225, although it could be argued that the latter was disadvantaged by the recession that had strangled the world economy. Bentley Motors was in such dire financial circumstances that on Friday 5 June Carruth took the decision to drastically cut back production at Cricklewood. In effect, the end of Bentley Motors had come.

Carruth would have had Barnato's approval before he contacted Arthur Sidgreaves, Rolls-Royce's managing director, on 9 June. By telephone he requested a meeting at Derby, but he did not divulge the nature of his intended business. He followed up this initial approach with a long and detailed letter the next day, in which he virtually admitted that Bentley Motors should be placed in receivership.

The content of Carruth's letter acknowledged the disappointing sales of the 4-litre, although he maintained that the model was of fine design – 98 percent perfect was his claim, despite the car's sluggish performance, which he confessed. Carruth went on to propose common sales and service policies; for Rolls-Royce to take over manufacturing two-thirds of those components Bentley were obliged to buy in from external suppliers, estimated to be worth about £200,000 annually; for Rolls-Royce to have a large say in the future of Bentley Motors, and for W.O. to co-operate with Rolls-Royce in a technical capacity. Carruth advised that there was a secured mortgage of £105,000 on the company, which was amply covered, and that Barnato was prepared (presumably financially) to go to some lengths to maintain the Bentley name. All in all, this was a declaration that Bentley Motors could no longer continue trading in its present form.

Following Carruth's letter, Arthur Sidgreaves replied on 18 June stating that while Rolls-Royce was interested in the proposal he required more detailed information to submit to his directors. Before Carruth's proposals could be further evaluated he advised that Rolls-Royce needed to know Bentley Motors' precise financial status, its sales of motor cars and its stock of unsold vehicles. In addition to complying with Sidgreaves's request Carruth divulged his company's trading position relating to suppliers' accounts, and the particulars of both W.O.'s and Barrington's contracts, along with those of the sales personnel.

Carruth received the news of Rolls-Royce's negative deliberations at the end of June. Rolls-Royce was now, of course, party to all of Bentley Motors' affairs, and having such knowledge directly affected the future of both companies.

On 15 June the monthly interest payable to London Life, in respect of loans taken out, became due for payment by the 30th of the month. There were insufficient funds available, and whereas Barnato would usually have covered such payments from his own resources he declined to do so on this occasion. While he had been perfectly happy to be associated with Bentley Motors when racing successes were making headline news, he was less inclined to continue the association now that its failure was under the spotlight. Bentley Motors' fate was sealed.

When the interest payable to London Life remained unsettled on 30 June Bentley Motors had no alternative but to notify them of inability to pay. Accordingly London Life called in the debt, which was the amount of two mortgages, one of £40,000 and the other of £25,000. Ten days later when they were unable to meet the wages bill of around £1,000, Bentley Motors had no alternative but to agree to the appointment of a receiver. The following morning the news was carried by *The Times* to the effect that the London Life Association had applied for receivership in respect of Bentley Motors' debts of £65,000, and that the company, which had been financed by Captain Woolf Barnato, no longer had that source of income.

From W.O.'s account of what happened during the period that Bentley Motors was put into receivership, it would appear that Barnato was in America, and had been there for some time dealing with personal and business affairs. He claims that Barnato was possibly prejudiced by adverse reports emerging from England, and his advisers probably warned him that unless he let the company go, his losses would be certain to increase.

Contemporary newspaper reports suggest otherwise: Barnato, it would appear, was in Britain at the time of the receiver's appointment and gave a full account of Bentley Motors' problems to the editor of *The Star* newspaper. Another newspaper, *The Daily Sketch*, noted that Barnato had given a dinner party at Ardenrun and that he would be going to America at the end of July for some months.

Patrick Raper Frere was appointed receiver. He was a skilled manager and W.O. refers to him with cordiality and respect. Frere was no stranger to the Bentley family, having had business and social connections with both H.M. and Hardy. His interests were strongly in favour of Bentley Motors, and W.O. quickly appreciated that had he been at the helm of the company rather than Carruth, it would have profited from his expertise. It was Frere's belief that the company should continue operating, albeit on a much reduced basis, and moreover that it was essential to maintain the service facility at Kingsbury. Between July and November 1931 Frere was responsible for selling three 8-litre cars and a single 4-litre in addition to overseeing the completion of several partially finished chassis.

It didn't take long for shockwaves from Bentley Motors' collapse to reach other manufacturers. For W.O., the failure of Bentley Motors meant much more than being out of a job, it signalled total financial disaster. He lost everything. In later years when he reviewed Barnato's losses, W.O. was scathing, suggesting that he could have recouped a similar amount through the sale of a single diamond.

Patrick Frere had rightly anticipated that a company held in as much esteem as Bentley Motors would find a suitable buyer. He was satisfied when an approach was made by Napier of Acton, one of the country's premier engineering concerns, which had originally been founded in the early 1800s. Montague Stanley Napier had produced his first car in around 1898. Napier was renowned for its quality, which rivalled that of Rolls-Royce, but the company ceased motor manufacturing in 1924 in order to concentrate on designing and building aero engines. Napier's series of 'Lion' engines will always remain associated with the Schneider Trophy races of the 1920s and early 1930s, and in particular with Segrave's and Campbell's record breaking attempts with *Golden Arrow* and *Bluebird*.

Following Montague Napier's death in January 1931 H.T. Vane became the firm's new chairman. The company, while completely solvent, was short of work owing to receding aero engine orders, and efforts were made to source a diversity of engineering contracts. One option was to manufacture tractor units – mechanical horses as they became known. Another was to return to car manufacturing, and Bentley Motors' demise could not have come at a more opportune time for Napier.

Along with the prospect of returning to building luxury motor cars, it was buying the assets of Bentley Motors that most appealed. Chiefly though, it was the services of W.O. that were considered to be of most importance, and it was by stages that negotiations with the receiver progressed to the point whereby an offer of £103,675 was made.

W.O. was gratified by the arrangement for he fully appreciated the engineering acumen of the Napier firm. He was assured that if their offer was accepted he would remain as chief designer and have a place on the board of directors. By the end of July negotiations with Napier were more or less complete, and the only hurdle remaining was to have the arrangement ratified in court. Frere was satisfied that the deal was to the advantage of both sides and he allowed W.O. to begin work with Napier on a secret basis before the court's authentication.

Napier's new car, the Napier-Bentley, was designed with a 6¼-litre six-cylinder engine with a single overhead camshaft and four valves per cylinder. There were other reasons for W.O. to feel satisfied: Napier was contemplating designing a new aero engine, which would require his serious involvement.

The news of Napier's intention to return to car building using W.O.'s expertise was never likely to have been kept a secret. On 14 August *The Autocar* carried a full account of W.O.'s and Napier's plans, and then at the end of September the announcement of the winding up of Bentley Motors was broadcast.

The court hearing, which was seen as nothing more than a formality to approve Napier's acquisition of Bentley Motors, was arranged for 17 November. Certainly W.O., Frere and H.T. Vane were confident about the outcome, and the evening before the hearing they all went to the theatre to celebrate.

But events the next day did not go according to plan. The proceedings in court had been progressing in an entirely straightforward and predictable manner when there was an interruption from counsel representing the British Equitable Central Trust, who had been instructed to offer a higher bid for the assets of Bentley Motors than that of Napier. Frere, together with Napier's counsel, was taken aback by this unexpected intrusion, and following a brief adjournment Napier's counsel increased their offer.

The judge, who thought that the proceedings had begun to resemble an auction, was having nothing to do with offers and counter-offers, and instructed counsel to return to court at 4.30pm with sealed tenders.

The result was that the British Equitable Central Trust's bid of £125,275 was substantially higher than the £104,775 tendered by Napier, the latter being an increase of £1,100 on the sum of £103,675 that was originally proposed.

In his autobiography W.O. refers to the difference between the two bids as being 'Very small, a matter of a few hundred pounds.' Obviously he was mistaken, £20,500 being no mean sum. The discrepancy may not be all it seems, however. The amount that BECT's counsel was about to offer has not been disclosed, and may well have been a relatively small advance on Napier's bid. When it came to presenting sealed tenders, BECT would have been unaware of the value of Napier's revised submission, and was therefore forced to submit a bid that was significantly higher than that which had originally been proposed.

Exactly who or what the British Equitable Central Trust were, W.O. had no idea. Nor, for that matter, did Patrick Frere or Napier. W.O. was obviously in a state of shock at the result of the hearing and it is known that he sought solace from his brothers H.M. and Hardy. To add to his misery the newspapers made much of the affair, and for a couple of days there remained no indication of the buyer's identity.

The first clue about the anonymous buyer came as a result of a conversation overheard at a cocktail party which W.O.'s wife had attended. A gentleman whom she discovered to be Arthur Sidgreaves was heard to say that his company had just bought the old Bentley firm.

W.O. mentions the particular incident in his autobiography, and this is of some interest in relation to his personal circumstances. At the time W.O. was still married to Audrey, although as we know she is never referred to by name in the autobiography. Nor did W.O. even mention his second marriage, other than in a single comment that it had not been a success. So it would seem likely that here he means Margaret, his third wife, although that does not entirely fit with what we know about his life at the time. Audrey and W.O. had been married for around 11 years by the time the company was bought, not seven as W.O. claims in his autobiography, and it is known that she regularly frequented cocktail parties and social events, mostly unaccompanied by her husband. It would have been reasonable to suppose that in the relatively tight-knit society of luxury motor car manufacturers, the identity of Audrey Bentley would have been known, and likewise she would have known Arthur Sidgreaves. Remarks made by Sidgreaves in Audrey's presence would have been indiscreet, which also suggests that it might have been Margaret, rather than Audrey, that attended the party.

The purchase of Bentley Motors by Rolls-Royce in what can only be described as unusual circumstances – 'contentious' is a word that has sometimes been used – raises a number of questions, none of which have ever been fully answered. That Rolls-Royce was initially interested in acquiring Bentley is fully established, and the company were certainly privy to Bentley Motors' exact trading and financial position. Obviously Rolls-Royce was against the purchase of a company that was on the brink of bankruptcy because of the risk of taking on any undefined liabilities, but once the receiver had produced a statement of account the situation was different. Rolls-Royce would also have known about Napier's interest in buying Bentley.

The matter was all the more complex because Rolls-Royce had everything to fear from a motor car that was designed by W.O. and built to Napier's extremely high standards. Napier's heritage, combined with the prestige of the Bentley name, would seriously challenge their market share in luxury automobiles. There is evidence that Woolf Barnato, Jack Carruth and Robert Montgomerie all had dealings with Rolls-Royce during the period that Bentley Motors was in receivership, and information may well have been passed to Derby, unwittingly or otherwise. There are reports, too, that Barnato purchased large numbers of Rolls-Royce shares before the liquidation of Bentley Motors. This cannot be substantiated because share records from the time have been lost. Donald Bastow, who worked for W.O. over a number of years, is sure that W.O. knew who had informed Rolls-Royce of Napier's final bid (he never disclosed the information), and that the British Equitable Central Trust, working on Rolls-Royce's behalf, was paid £2,500 to act as their agent.

Rolls-Royce had nevertheless acquired Bentley Motors Ltd, and a new company was formed: Bentley Motors (1931) Ltd. Woolf Barnato was invited to join the new board of directors in late February 1934, a position he accepted early the following month.

That there was resentment and bitterness on W.O.'s part regarding the chain of events leading to Bentley Motors' demise has to be acknowledged. Woolf Barnato's position has also to be understood, and with hindsight it needs to be appreciated that he was entirely dependent on the advice given to him by his advisers. It was their opinion that continuing to plough money into what they perceived as a low-volume business building luxury cars in a depressed market was not an option, and to do so would only lead to further and greater losses. Barnato did, nevertheless, have a very generous and charitable side to his character, which is shown by the fact that as a goodwill gesture he gave each of the staff one month's wages when the company went into receivership. It could be argued that Barnato foresaw the fact that Rolls-Royce offered the best solution for the future of the Bentley name, and by buying a large number of shares and being appointed a director, he helped secure the marque's protection.

W.O. met Arthur Sidgreaves three days after the court hearing. On the surface the atmosphere was cordial, but because of events prior to the hearing it can be presumed there was an element of deep distrust on both sides. Three weeks later W.O. went to see Sir Henry Royce, who had been given a baronetcy in the 1930 honours list. From W.O.'s account of the meeting it was decidedly icy, Royce believing Bentley to be a 'commercial man' rather than an engineer, and a brilliant one at that, equalling (no doubt some Bentley enthusiasts would prefer *surpassing*) Royce's own status.

Bentley retorted that both of them had been apprenticed to the Great Northern Railway, Royce being a boy in the running sheds at Peterborough some years before W.O. served at Doncaster as a premium apprentice. Obviously W.O.'s reply hit a raw nerve as far as Royce was concerned; he merely grunted and allowed the subject to pass without further comment. According to Alec Harvey-Bailey, who worked with Royce and knew him well, Sir Henry's health was failing at the time and this probably had an effect on his decision-making capabilities. Another view that has been expressed is that W.O. could easily have become the head of Rolls-Royce following Sir Henry Royce's death in 1933.

It is clear from information contained in Rolls-Royce files that Royce did not have a high opinion of W.O. He wrote of him to Arthur Sidgreaves in a disparaging manner, suggesting that Rolls-Royce had more to teach W.O. than W.O. could offer in way of expertise. The real reason for Royce not wanting W.O. in any design or experimental capacity was probably that he was afraid he might defect to Napier or another manufacturer, thus compromising Rolls-Royce's future projects.

However, Sir Henry Royce did offer W.O. a position within the company, but not in an engineering or design capacity. W.O. found this prospect unpalatable, and understandably declined, by which time he had received an offer from Napier to work for them at Acton. Rolls-Royce was then put in a difficult position: they did not particularly want W.O.'s services and yet they were concerned that his expertise with another firm would be harmful to them. Accordingly Sidgreaves advised W.O. that purchasing the assets of Bentley Motors meant that in effect they had purchased his services. W.O. then sought a buy-out which would release him from contractual agreements dating from Bentley Motors days, and all further Bentley royalties. When Rolls-Royce declined, Napier, on W.O.'s behalf, began legal proceedings in January 1932 in order to secure his services.

In early March the court could not give judgement owing to the manner in which the case had been presented. Napier had already spent a huge sum bringing the issue to court and decided it was impossible to continue the campaign.

W.O. had little choice other than to refer himself back to Sidgreaves and accept the job that Rolls-Royce had previously offered. The essence of the ensuing agreement was that a debt of £2,480 which W.O. owed Bentley Motors was written off and he was paid a further £1,210 in exchange for allowing Rolls-Royce the rights to use the Bentley name under the banner of Bentley Motors (1931) Ltd. He was then given a five-year contract to work for Rolls-Royce, the contract being renewable by both parties after that period.

W.O. was appointed assistant to Percy Northey and was based at Conduit Street, ironically yards away from where he had designed the 3-litre Bentley with Burgess and Varley. Northey, too, had racing experience: he had driven a 20hp Rolls-Royce in the 1905 and 1906 Isle of Man Tourist Trophy events. W.O.'s brief was to attend the morning sales conferences, which were always held at 10 o'clock, to answer technical questions and criticisms, and to supervise the availability and condition of demonstration cars.

After the uncertainties of the previous months his new job was in some respects a blessing, certainly in financial terms. It was hardly challenging for him though, and the breaking up of Bentley Motors and the works that went with it was utterly demoralising. The Kingsbury service department continued to operate under Hubert Pike and Nobby Clarke, so at least one vestige of the old company remained.

CHAPTER 9

New Horizons

THE most miserable moment for W.O. during the events surrounding Rolls-Royce's controversial acquisition of Bentley Motors came when Arthur Sidgreaves told him to surrender his 8-litre. Exactly what this was meant to achieve, other than to make W.O. feel subservient, is unclear. The car that he so enjoyed driving and which had been a constant source of pleasure to him had represented the zenith of his design work on Bentleys, and now even that was being taken away from him. It was with utter resentment and dejection that he drove to Jack Barclay's showroom at 12a George Street. There he deposited the car, complete with its impressive mileage, unique provenance and too many memories. He walked home in a state of despondency; for the first time in many years he was without a motor car.

If that were not enough to make W.O. wholly pessimistic he had to watch the Oxgate Lane works being systematically dismantled, so much history being cast aside. He walked into his office for the last time, looked around, and sat at his desk. When he could no longer bear being there and seeing the factory being demolished around him he sought out his reliable storekeeper Fred Conway. He had been appointed to oversee the closure of the factory and W.O. asked him whether he would mind clearing his office for him.

And would he make sure to burn his desk, for he was emotionally unable to do it himself.

Happily W.O.'s office was preserved and remained virtually intact for many years. Just before W.O. died in 1971 he made a nostalgic visit to the works accompanied by a large group of Bentley enthusiasts, some of whom had travelled huge distances to acknowledge the 40th anniversary of the closure of Oxgate Lane and the demise of Bentley Motors.

Some of the Bentley Motors personnel who remained at Oxgate Lane until the works had been completely emptied spoke of the callous way in which Rolls-Royce destroyed all that remained of the company. The machine shop, having only recently been installed, was cleared of all of its equipment. What was considered usable was taken to Derby, while the remaining apparatus was sold for scrap or broken up.

Following the collapse of Bentley Motors W.O. fell into a state of deep depression. He would take long walks through and around Hyde Park to enable him to think as clearly as possible, to come to terms with recent events and to get his life into some perspective. He was also glad of the exercise. He had much to brood about, and he began to avoid meeting people, especially anyone associated with Bentleys.

His marriage was in tatters and he was virtually penniless. He had lost everything and admitted to having only around a hundred pounds or so. He neither knew nor cared how long that was going to last. It seems that he sold his villa Le Balcon near Miramar on the Côte d'Azur, although the exact position regarding the ownership of the property remains unclear. There is little to indicate when he purchased the property, or whether in fact he had jointly owned it with Audrey.

Absolute despair was averted when W.O. received a telephone call from Billy Rootes, the well-known motor dealer and distributor and a respected Bentley agent. Rootes had heard of W.O.'s plight, probably through 'Bentley Boy' Dick Watney, who had taken up a senior position with the Rootes brothers, and who thought that W.O. might be the right person to put the new Hillman Minx through its paces. There was no question of Rootes, who later became Lord Rootes, being patronising: he was grateful for W.O.'s honest opinion as an engineer, and in return W.O. appreciated having cars to drive in addition to knowing that his friends had not deserted him.

He might have been worried that the car, much smaller than a Bentley and not nearly so powerful, would not survive his hearty driving, especially when heavily loaded and subjected to long journeys through France to the Mediterranean. He was satisfied that the car performed admirably, and was so impressed with it that he bought an example when one was offered to him on extremely favourable terms.

His acquaintance with the Minx was the precursor to him evaluating a number of vehicles, not least the prototype 'Rolls-Bentley' that was proposed soon after the establishment of Bentley Motors (1931) Ltd. Rolls-Royce had correctly anticipated that the new 'Derby Bentley' would attract an enthusiastic clientele who, recognising the marque's reputation, would further appreciate the Rolls-Royce connection. Rolls-Royce was resigned to the fact that those Bentley devotees with 'Cricklewood' or 'W.O.' cars would feel aggrieved about the emergence of the new model.

Through an oversight the Bentley name had never been registered as a trademark when Bentley Motors had first been established. Neither was the omission noticed when Bentley Motors Ltd came into being in 1926. This had nevertheless been spotted by Rolls-Royce's legal advisers, who immediately addressed the situation. The outcome was that W.O. had little alternative but to agree to a condition which prevented him lending his name to any aero engine or car design for a period of 10 years should he leave the company.

The course that led to the release of the prototype Derby Bentley was a convoluted affair which was based on a redundant Rolls-Royce proposal, which has already been mentioned, for a sporting version of the 20/25hp. Rolls-Royce's aborted 'economy' car project was known by the Peregrine code name, the 18hp engine being of a little under 2½ litres. Initial proposals had been to supercharge the engine in order to increase its performance, but this idea was eventually abandoned on technical grounds. In finding a solution to designing an all-new Bentley, which for some time was known as 'Bensport', Rolls-Royce evaluated three cars in particular, the Alvis Speed 20, Lagonda and the Alfa Romeo. Months were lost while Rolls-Royce directors and engineers deliberated and argued about the form the new Bentley should take, and ultimately the decision was taken to use a more powerful version of the 20/25hp engine (it featured a six-inlet port crossflow head and a modified camshaft) and mate it with a modified Peregrine chassis. What to call the Bentley? The 3½-litre.

Happily for W.O. he was left very much to his own devices to test the 3½-litre, although it never ceased to rankle with him that he had been left out of the design process. During testing W.O. encountered a number of problems and it was with his help and advice that Rolls-Royce engineers were able to effect various modifications.

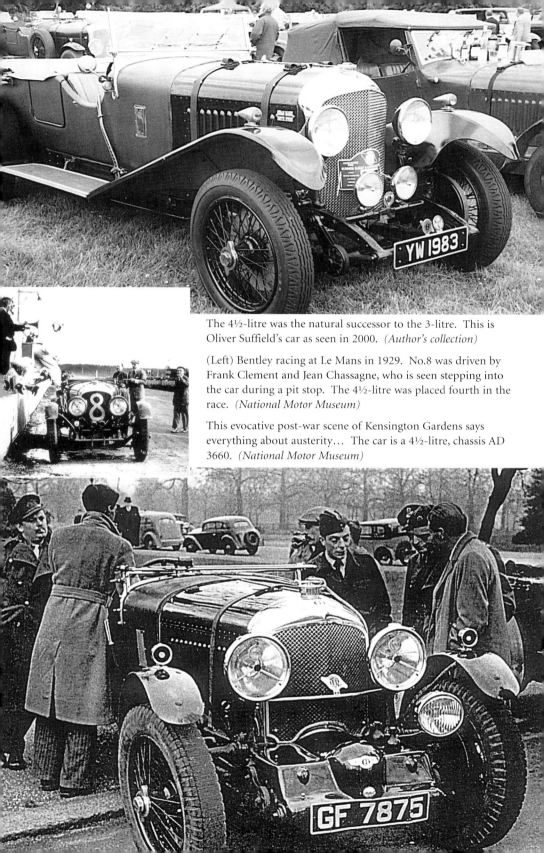

The 4½-litre was the natural successor to the 3-litre. This is Oliver Suffield's car as seen in 2000. *(Author's collection)*

(Left) Bentley racing at Le Mans in 1929. No.8 was driven by Frank Clement and Jean Chassagne, who is seen stepping into the car during a pit stop. The 4½-litre was placed fourth in the race. *(National Motor Museum)*

This evocative post-war scene of Kensington Gardens says everything about austerity… The car is a 4½-litre, chassis AD 3660. *(National Motor Museum)*

Supercharged 4½-litre. *(Rolls-Royce & Bentley Motor Cars Ltd)*

(Right) Bentley wheel fixing showing reverse thread. *(Author's collection)*

4½-litre supercharger. *(Author's collection)*

The 8-litre was the ultimate Cricklewood Bentley. This fine illustration succinctly depicts the car. *(National Motor Museum)*

The 8-litre was W.O.'s favourite car. This example is pictured amid regal surroundings. *(National Motor Museum)*

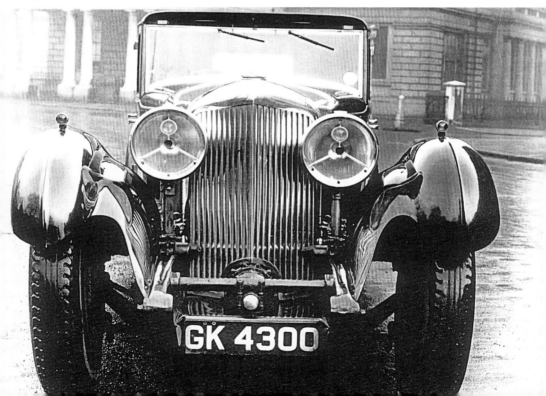

The sheer size of the 8-litre can be judged from this picture. *(Author's collection)*

Following Rolls-Royce's acquisition of Bentley in 1931 an all-new model, the 3½-litre, was introduced. The Cricklewood factory was closed and production of new models centred at Derby alongside Rolls-Royces. W.O. was disappointed that he was not involved in the car's development, although he was responsible for much of its testing. The car was available in a number of coachwork styles, including this sedanca coupé. *(Rolls-Royce & Bentley Motor Cars Ltd)*

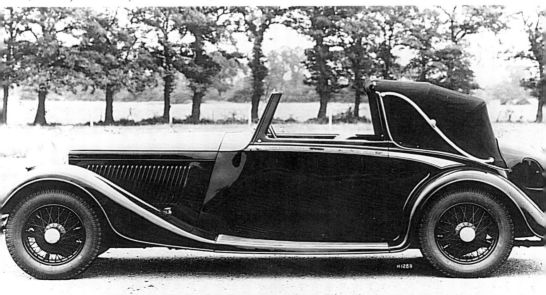

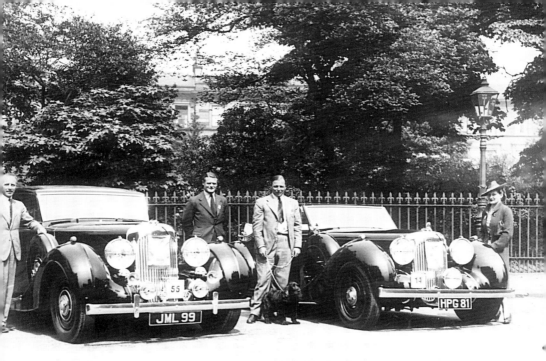

...O. left Rolls-Royce to work for Lagonda in 1935. He was responsible for developing the LG45 and the
...2. These two cars were entered in the 1938 Scottish Rally; Lord Waleran is seen adjacent to the drophead
...upé, and W.F. Watson is with the saloon. *(National Motor Museum)*

...O. was given the task of preparing two Lagonda V12s for the 1939 Le Mans race. One of them is seen
...re, at Brighton in 1946/7. Both Lagondas finished at Le Mans and were placed third and fourth.
...lational Motor Museum)

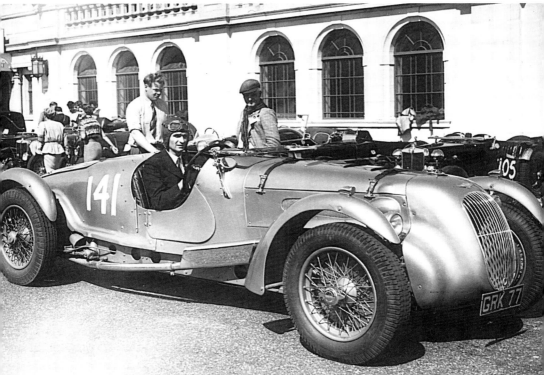

After World War Two production of Bentleys was transferred to Crewe. The Mk VI was the first post-war Bentley to enter production. *(Rolls-Royce & Bentley Motor Cars Ltd)*

(Right) Detail of the 'Flying B' Bentley radiator cap mascot. *(Author's collection)*

The Bentley S, the car that was introduced in 1955 having been styled by John Blatchley. In 1959 the model was fitted with a V8 engine which survives to this day in developed form when fitted to the Bentley Arnage Red Label models. *(Author's collection)*

Mans 1998, when Bentleys of all ages were invited to the circuit to honour the introduction of the ntley Arnage. *(Rolls-Royce & Bentley Motor Cars Ltd)*

O. in retirement with the 4½-litre and a DFP. *(National Motor Museum)*

.O. at the wheel of one of his creations, the 4½-litre. *(National Motor Museum)*

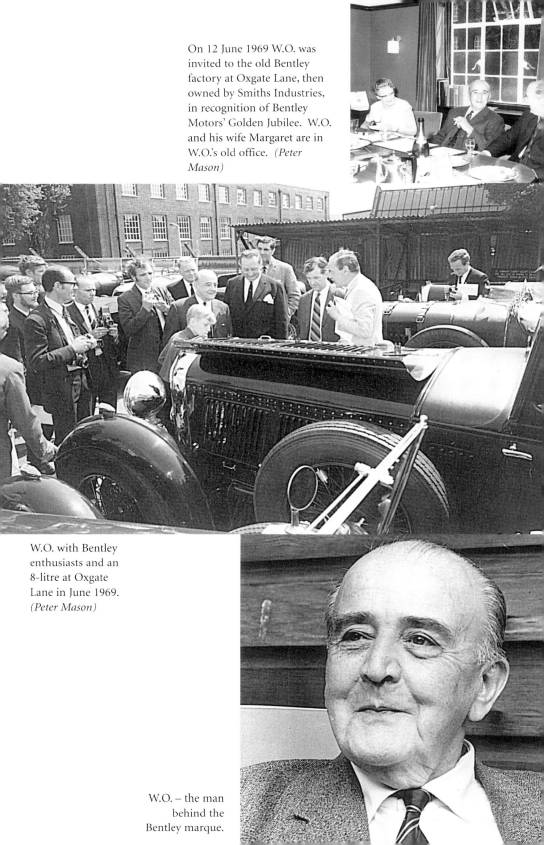

On 12 June 1969 W.O. was invited to the old Bentley factory at Oxgate Lane, then owned by Smiths Industries, in recognition of Bentley Motors' Golden Jubilee. W.O. and his wife Margaret are in W.O.'s old office. *(Peter Mason)*

W.O. with Bentley enthusiasts and an 8-litre at Oxgate Lane in June 1969. *(Peter Mason)*

W.O. – the man behind the Bentley marque.

The 3½-litre Bentley was announced to the press at the end of September 1933 with a judicious lunchtime launch at the Royal Hotel at Ascot. It was a grand occasion and one that finely promoted Bentley and Rolls-Royce's traditions of quality. It was W.O.'s responsibility, along with Percy Northey and sales manager Major Len Cox, to take invited motoring journalists on trial runs, using the occasion to put the demonstration cars to the test in the most spirited manner possible. It was a task that W.O. enjoyed immensely, and those guests driven by him were left in no doubt about the model's capabilities.

W.O. also enjoyed himself at the hotel proprietor's expense. He recognised him as the author of *An Innkeeper's Diary*, in which W.O. was described as 'A timid little man.' W.O. was gratified that the hotelier had not recognised him, and invited him to a demonstration run, the last of the day, in which he delighted in pushing the Bentley to its limit so that the hapless individual was almost sick with fear. Only when W.O. skidded to a halt outside the front entrance of the Royal did he tell the innkeeper who the timid little man was! There is no indication of the hotelier's response, but it is unlikely that he ever forgot the occasion.

When *The Autocar* published its first road test of the vehicle early in October the report was glowing: 'In effect, the new 3½-litre Bentley is a wonderful blend of a reasonably quiet car with all the attributes of a docile well-mannered touring vehicle, but possessed of a remarkable liveliness and the fierce acceleration associated with a high-spirited sporting car when occasion demands.' Naturally the finest coachwork from bespoke coachbuilders was available in the full Bentley tradition. A significant aspect of the new Bentley was that although it was built by Rolls-Royce at Derby alongside Rolls-Royce cars, the latter name never appeared on the car or any related publicity material. Derby Bentleys had their dedicated badging, even down to the B motif on the pedals and flooring material, and the car was marketed as 'The Silent Sportscar'. No mention was made of the Rolls-Royce name in the Bentley driver's handbook, nor in the warranty.

Within a month of the announcement of the new Bentley, W.O. was to experience another personal tragedy when his mother died on 23 October at the age of 80 from the effects of myocardial degeneration and pneumonia. She had been living at the Leinster Court Hotel in Leinster Gardens near Lancaster Gate since the death of her husband,

and in spite of her illness enjoyed as active a life as possible. H.M. registered her death and W.O.'s other brother Hardy, the family solicitor, administered her estate, her effects amounting to £199 9s 6d.

Deliveries of the 3½-litre began early in 1934, by which time W.O. was given leave to take an experimental model for extensive testing over some seven weeks. His brief was to take the car abroad, to go where he liked and to put the machine through its paces, even if he broke it. The vehicle assigned to him was 2-B-IV, registered RC 1238. The car had a chequered history, having been used for testing purposes the previous April and driven at Brooklands to see how it compared with the Speed 20 Alvis and the Talbot 95. Fitted with a green painted Park Ward Sports Saloon body, it was damaged by fire which partially destroyed the coachwork. Following mechanical repairs the car was sent to Park Ward for refurbishment, after which it was made available to the sales department at Conduit Street.

This was an opportunity not to be missed, especially since the testing programme doubled as a honeymoon. W.O. and Margaret Roberts Hutton married on 31 January 1934, the ceremony taking place at Kensington Register Office. H.M. and Lt Col W.J. Maule were the couple's witnesses. W.O. was 45 years old, and Margaret four years younger, and since their separation from their respective spouses they had been living at 86 Queens Gate, opposite the Natural History Museum. The marriage brought Margaret and W.O. true and lasting happiness, and the chance of several weeks away together could not have come at a better time. The divorce proceedings, Margaret from Charles Hutton and W.O. from Audrey, had been particularly difficult, especially with Margaret's former husband intent on securing relatively large sums of money from W.O. With the trauma of months of frustration and indecision now safely behind them, the future at last seemed promising.

W.O. saw to all the travel arrangements so that he and Margaret could leave for the Continent immediately after their wedding. He chose the familiar Newhaven to Dieppe route across the Channel, leaving the French port early the following morning to drive the 390 miles via Sens and Dijon to arrive at Pontarlier near the Swiss border at nightfall. It was a dreadful journey. Torrential rain slowed them down, and W.O. was conscious that the car shook and rattled excessively over the worst pavé surfaces. In his report at the end of the day he was critical of the car's weak frame and unsteady headlamps, and the fact that the windscreen wipers worked too slowly to clear the water. There were plus points, however. The sunroof proved to be watertight, and in the severe rain there was evidence of only the slightest leak from a corner of the windscreen.

Apart from the windscreen wipers failing on the second day due to a break in the wiper cable, the remainder of the first leg of the grand tour was completed without major incident. Their journey took them to Lausanne, Martigny, Brig and Gletch, where they stayed the night. On the third day they negotiated the Grimsel, Rurka, Oberalp, Schyn, Julier and Ofen passes. The rest of the tour took them to Lake Como via the Stelvio Pass, and on to Milan, Turin, Briançon, Galibier and Cannes.

The combination of fast long runs and negotiating some of Europe's steepest passes showed up two main deficiencies in the 3½-litre's design. Sustained high speeds were responsible for the radiator shutters remaining closed due to wind pressure, causing the water temperature to rise unchecked. Reducing speed for a while allowed the shutters to open and the water temperature to drop, but such a situation was quite unacceptable.

Brake fade was another problem, which W.O. discovered to his anguish while descending a series of hairpin bends. These defects were quickly reported to Rolls-Royce engineers, who immediately undertook to modify the brake design.

Soon after their return from Europe W.O. and Margaret moved from Queens Gate to a house in Addison Road, which was conveniently close to Shepherds Bush and Holland Park. While his duties were hardly challenging, W.O. enjoyed the following months at Conduit Street. He retained the use of 2-B-IV as a company vehicle and for private purposes, and even went on record to admit that 'taking all things into consideration, I would rather own this Bentley car than any car produced under that name.'

This would appear to be a very odd statement from the engineer who had sought perfection in designing the original Bentley motor car, the 8-litre firmly rivalling the Rolls-Royce Phantom. While he was prevented from contributing to the 3½-litre's design, W.O. was nevertheless kept informed about its development, and he had empathy with those Rolls-Royce engineers engaged on perfecting the model. It was a totally modern car, lighter and substantially quieter than the 3-litre. With its six-cylinder engine it possessed smooth and responsive performance, almost equal to that of the 4½-litre Bentley. The gearbox, with synchromesh on the upper ratios, was, in W.O.'s opinion, by far the best that Rolls-Royce had built.

W.O. was appointed technical adviser to the managing director of Rolls-Royce on Percy Northey's retirement. Although it was an elevated title W.O.'s new position was hardly demanding, his duties comprising checking thoroughly all the firm's official and demonstration cars as well as those in service with London agents. In addition to performing mundane tasks that required no more technical knowledge than to try out all the seats of a car to ensure they provided the requisite support and comfort, he was at least able to test a variety of motor vehicles other than Rolls-Royces. He made an acquaintance with the latest V16 Cadillac, a far cry from the model that he had teased Derby personnel with when visiting the factory on aero engine business.

Then there was the Railton Terraplane, a car with a formidable reputation and which W.O. was keen to put to the test at Brooklands. Lighter in weight than the Bentley 3½-litre, it had a 4,168cc engine and promised much in the way of performance, but W.O. found it disappointing. He managed to get his hands on a V12 Hispano-Suiza, which again failed to match his expectations, and he evaluated makes such as Lagonda and Alvis.

Gradually more and more time was spent testing both Bentley and Rolls-Royce models and undertaking long-distance Continental trials that could last up to six weeks at a time. There was no one better equipped than W.O. to conduct such extensive road testing, and often his findings were the result of subjecting a vehicle to near breaking point. His reports did not always make agreeable reading for certain senior Rolls-Royce managers who distrusted his loyalty to the firm. Rather than submit reports to them he decided to deal directly with those engineers at Derby that were responsible for development. When not testing cars abroad he took to visiting Derby on a weekly basis to discuss his opinions and findings with them. Not only did they appreciate W.O.'s technical acumen, he also made some good lasting friendships.

It was in 1935 that W.O. experienced a serious problem with his 3½-litre. He had been subjecting the vehicle to the most fierce braking when the nearside front wheel hit a brick that happened to be lying in the road on a sharp corner. The impact caused the tyre to burst, thus causing severe tramping to the extent that he was unable to steer the car properly. Nor did he have any braking reserve due to brake fade, the result being that the Bentley virtually demolished a Wolseley Hornet innocently approaching from the opposite direction.

Miraculously the driver of the Wolseley was unhurt. W.O.'s fate was somewhat more serious and resulted in the tip of his nose being nearly severed. He bore the scar for the rest of his life. He was issued with a summons for driving without due care and regard, which meant that he had to appear in court. Rolls-Royce directors were naturally concerned about the outcome of the hearing, not least the adverse publicity that it might attract. Although W.O. received a £10 fine it was obvious that the magistrate was not entirely happy. On his way out of court he took W.O. quietly to one side. Knowing full well that W.O. used the route of the accident to test his cars, he asked him exactly what had happened. W.O., it appears, innocently declined to comment. No more was said.

At the end of his five-year tenure with Rolls-Royce a new contract of employment for a further five-year period was drafted. Certainly W.O. could take heart from its more encompassing terms, which specified a significant salary increase. His service with Rolls-Royce had presented him with a number of difficulties, and he was aggrieved that he had been overlooked in his capacity as a designer and an engineer. He also sensed that his employment with the company was something of an embarrassment to Rolls-Royce directors, who really didn't know what to do with him. There was also the matter of a directorship on the board of the new company; much to his regret and disappointment such an appointment was never discussed.

W.O. remained in a quandary about what to do. He didn't particularly want to continue working for Rolls-Royce in what he considered to be a menial position, and yet he was bound by contract not to lend his name to any other design of vehicle. The dilemma was resolved for for him when Dick Watney called him with some news about the Lagonda company.

Lagonda had been associated with racing at Brooklands since 1909, although the company had been in existence since the late 1890s. Wilbur Gunn, an American engineer who was born in 1859, emigrated to Staines in England in his thirties and became known as a builder of steam yachts, said to be the fastest on the River Thames. He turned to building motorcycles in 1898, using the greenhouse in his garden as a workshop. A Lagonda motorcycle represented Great Britain in the Paris–Madrid International Cup races, and later the firm progressed to manufacturing forecars, which were motor tricycles capable of accommodating a passenger sitting in a specially constructed seat positioned between the two front wheels. Building motor cars ensued, firstly a 10hp machine and later one with a 16/18hp engine. It was an example of the latter which competed at Brooklands in 1909. Throughout the years Lagonda cars won recognition for their performance and quality, and like Bentley Motors it was a low-volume manufacturer. During the mid-1930s Lagonda experienced financial difficulties, and a receiver was appointed, but not before a Lagonda was victorious at Le Mans.

Dick Watney let it be known to W.O. that Alan Good, a barrister friend of his, was negotiating to buy Lagonda's assets with the intention of reprieving this famous firm and its motor cars. In doing so he required a designer, W.O. in particular. W.O. therefore delayed signing a new contract with Rolls-Royce until he was sure the deal between Good and the receiver was complete.

All this happened a few days before Lagonda's win at Le Mans. On the eve of the race W.O. had been required to accompany Arthur Sidgreaves on a matter of business and he anticipated that he would be expected to confirm or otherwise his new five-year contract. He was somewhat taken aback when Sidgreaves told him in confidence that Rolls-Royce was intending to put in an offer for Lagonda. Pry as he might, W.O. never discovered why Lagonda was of interest to Rolls-Royce.

As soon as Lagonda's victory at Le Mans was announced, W.O. contacted Dick Watney, telling him he would join the firm as long as the sale to Alan Good went through. When it did, and Rolls-Royce was unsuccessful in its bid, W.O. submitted his notice.

In taking over Lagonda, which was renamed LG Motors (Lagonda/Good), Alan Good as chairman appointed Dick Watney as managing director and W.O. as technical director. W.O.'s relief at being able to do what he knew best was profound, even if the working conditions at the Staines factory were austere and in some respects rather dilapidated. The drawing office was no more than a decrepit shed with a corrugated roof that leaked like a sieve. Working conditions were abysmal and had to remain that way until there was sufficient money to build new accommodation and extend the works. When complete, the factory occupied a prime site at The Causeway alongside the River Thames, opposite Staines Bridge.

An abundance of models, too profuse for a small manufacturer, was partly to blame for Lagonda having gone into liquidation. The firm had weathered the recession of the late 1920s but had failed to recover sufficiently to regain ground that had been lost. The first act of the new chairman was to axe all existing models except for the M45, a 4½-litre car that represented the best route towards an initial trading recovery. It was W.O.'s task to substantially modify the chassis and to improve it in time for the London Motor Show that autumn.

W.O. was commuting each day from Addison Road to Staines, which was not an easy journey. It seemed sensible, therefore, to move from London to be conveniently near to the factory, and he and Margaret purchased Millbrook House, an extensive country property near Poyle between Longford and Colnbrook. That part of south-east Buckinghamshire where it abuts with Middlesex was rural then, the surrounding rich arable farmlands yielding some of the finest crops and corn. Today the area is dominated by Heathrow Airport and accommodates much of the industry that is directly associated with it. Where once leafy lanes meandered through quiet countryside, there is now a plethora of industrial and business estates over which jets take off and land. Millbrook House, incidentally, was demolished in 1980 to make way for Millbrook Way Business Park, and the only remaining evidence of W.O.'s property is a pair of brick posts that supported entrance gates to the drive leading to his home.

W.O. worked wonders with the 4½-litre engine by refining it to make it quieter and smoother by modifying the combustion chambers and adding rubber insulation to the chassis mountings. Synchromesh gears and a right-hand gear change were all part of the package, as was softened suspension courtesy of longer road springs and the adoption of Luvax shock absorbers.

When it was shown at the Motor Show the LG45 also had a revised interior, which afforded greater luxury without compromising the overall sporting appeal. At around £1,000 it represented extremely good value.

The LG45 was designed in two model formats, a thoroughbred sporting saloon and a sports tourer. The flowing lines of the coachwork were the work of Frank Feeley, who became an intrinsic member of

W.O.'s design team. While these two models carried on the traditions of the Lagonda marque, W.O. worked hard to develop a new model, the V12. His brief was to have the new Lagonda ready within as short a time as possible, and a timescale like the four years it had taken Rolls-Royce to develop the Phantom III was just not acceptable. Alan Good and his financial backers agreed a period of between 18 months and two years in which to have the car ready. This was an adventurous proposition when it is considered that, unlike Rolls-Royce which had 16 designers working on the project, W.O. was assisted by a very small but select team of engineers, including Stan Ivermee from Bentley Motors days.

W.O. had the satisfaction of believing the V12 Lagonda to be the finest car he had yet designed. *The Autocar* in its road test of 11 March 1938 echoed these sentiments, although W.O. would secretly have liked to have been allowed another couple of years to further refine the car.

In his opinion the chassis frame was too heavy, and he would have liked to have been able to modify the steering to lighten it. He would also have preferred to further develop the engine so that maximum torque occurred at lower revs in order to achieve even better performance and driveability.

When it made its debut in 1937, the new car was shown to be equipped with a V12 4,480cc engine, producing 175bhp to give a maximum speed of around 105mph. *The Autocar's* road test boasted of exceptional performance coupled with superlative comfort, certainly sufficient for a rear-seat passenger to doze while the car was travelling at 100mph. Journalistic licence has to be taken into account, but nevertheless a reliable motoring writer recorded travelling at speeds in excess of 90mph over Salisbury Plain in total comfort.

Lord Howe and Stan Ivermee took a V12 and an LG45 to Brooklands in 1938 to carry out speed tests. During Bentley days such exercises were always found to be good for publicity and those for Lagonda proved equally useful. Stan Ivermee was able to achieve an impressive 96 miles in 60 minutes, but when Lord Howe took the wheel of the V12 he extracted 101½ miles from the car in the same time, and that included him stopping to change a wheel when a tyre became damaged due to the poor surface of the track. His best lap time indicated an astonishing speed in excess of 108mph.

W.O.'s biggest challenge came when Alan Good told him he wanted to enter the V12 for the 1939 Le Mans and improve on the earlier

Lagonda victory. Having only six months in which to prepare for the race W.O. was doubtful whether he could get two cars ready in time. Nor was he sure that Lagonda could profit sufficiently from the event, taking into consideration the huge effort and expense that went into the preparation. Nevertheless he bowed to Good's wishes and got on with the task, if somewhat reluctantly. Stan Ivermee was put in charge of preparations under W.O.'s watchful eye, and he was assisted by at least three other mechanics from Bentley days: Kemmish, Sopp and Taylor. Despite having reservations, W.O. was, of course, in his element, and to further his pride and satisfaction Margaret, unlike his ex-wife Audrey, took an active interest in the race.

The cars were only just prepared in time, although W.O. and his team had been working around the clock. During the final stages of preparation it seemed that Ivermee and his mechanics never stopped working. W.O. would often return to the works at The Causeway during the late evening to find a hive of activity. A week or so before the race the party left for Dieppe in a somewhat exhausted but nevertheless optimistic state. W.O., did, however, still have some doubts; there had only been time to test one of the cars at nearby Brooklands, and then for only a few hours. For the other car road testing comprised the run down from Staines to Newhaven.

Lagonda had chosen four drivers for the event, Charlie Brackenbury and Arthur Dobson in one car, the Lords Selsdon and Waleran in the other. The journey to Le Mans brought back many memories for W.O., mostly pleasant, a few otherwise. When the party arrived at the Sarthe Circuit W.O. was greeted with acclaim and enthusiasm from everybody, and he had the pleasure of introducing Margaret to his many friends. She enjoyed being involved in the event and put herself in charge of the thankless task of taking care of the domestic arrangements and seeing to the pit crew's welfare.

For the race W.O. had modified the overall design of the two V12s by fitting four carburettors and adopting lightweight and streamlined bodies. It was not his aim to pursue an outright win, but rather to allow his cars to finish by performing at a set speed of around 83mph, which was a little above that of the 1935 Le Mans winning car. The drivers were also ordered not to exceed 5,000rpm. That would provide W.O. with all the information he needed in order to take the production V12 to its next stage of development, which included the Rapide which was designed on a short chassis and would incorporate the four-carburettor arrangement of the Le Mans cars.

The mood at Le Mans was sombre. The talk of war, the onset of which seemed inevitable, cast a gloomy shadow. The course itself had changed since W.O.'s last visit in 1930. The road surface was perfectly even and had been widened, the corners and bends were eased and the trees cut away from the verges to give better visibility. The measures were largely responsible for narrowing lap times, the lap speed having been raised to 96mph, a notable increase from Tim Birkin's 89mph.

If the race lacked some of the excitement that had been evident in the Bentley era, W.O. was nevertheless completely satisfied with his team result, the Lagondas finishing third and fourth. All the more encouraging was that neither car experienced an involuntary stop, not even to change tyres or wheels. So there was no relief from the monotony for the pit crew, which was managed by Stan Ivermee.

With the race over, W.O. and Margaret took a well-earned holiday and drove to the Côte d'Azur in their Lagonda. It was while they were relaxing at the Hôtel San Christophe at Miramar, only yards from the villa which W.O. had once owned, that news of impending war emerged. The political situation in Europe had meant that Cannes and the Riviera were by then practically deserted by tourists, and W.O. and Margaret were among the few English people remaining there. Deciding it was no longer safe to be away from home owing to the imminent invasion of Poland by Germany, they packed immediately and left for Dieppe. On arriving at the port they were met with chaos, everybody trying to secure sailings. Although W.O. had already booked a passage it was clearly impossible to ship his car to England, and he had no alternative but to abandon it on the quayside along with hundreds of others. Hardly had the ship berthed at Newhaven than war was declared.

CHAPTER 10

Is There Such a Thing as Retirement?

L AGONDA, like all motor manufacturers, stopped car production at the beginning of World War Two in order to concentrate on the war effort. The emphasis on rebuilding Britain's military strength had begun in the mid-1930s when its depleted state was the cause of serious concern, a situation which had led to the establishment of shadow factories around the country. The shadow factory scheme was seen as a way of providing aero engines and various other components, and was mainly administered by motor manufacturers serving under government contracts.

In place of luxury motor cars the Staines factory produced a variety of armaments, including anti-aircraft rockets and components for aircraft including aero engines and tanks. Also built at The Causeway were flame throwers, gun carriages, diesel engines and generators. The Lagonda factory was heavily and effectively camouflaged and remained untargeted by the Luftwaffe, unlike the Vickers works only a few miles away which was devastated by enemy bombing on 4 September 1940.

W.O. foresaw that his engineering expertise might be useful to the Admiralty in respect of aero engine design and offered his services accordingly. He was disappointed when his approach was initially declined. Instead he busied himself contributing to the war effort by helping to manufacture components in quantity and quality at The Causeway. The Admiralty did call upon his services when Malta's Valletta harbour came under attack by the Italians, who bombarded the port using hydroplanes, which were akin to explosive motor boats. Launched from parent submarines, the craft were steered at high speed to the boom defence system that was intended to protect shipping within the harbour. When the hydroplanes 'skipped' over the defence boom the pilots would bale out.

The Admiralty was interested in building similar craft and called on W.O. for assistance. The project they had in mind was a lightweight vessel that could be dropped at low level from Sunderland flying boats, which Vospers at Southampton had the task of designing. Noted for its performance and weight-saving characteristics, it was the W.O.-designed Lagonda V12 engine that was considered the ideal means of propulsion, and W.O. and Dick Watney were asked to visit the Admiralty at Bath for consultations. Vospers and Lagonda were given three months in which to perfect their designs, which required an almost impossibly tight schedule.

When one of the Italian Alfa Romeo-powered weapons went astray and landed on the shore having failed to explode, the Admiralty was able to examine it in detail and was astonished to discover it to be extremely similar to that conceived by Vospers. Despite the intense activity in preparing the design and putting it into production, the project ultimately failed to materialise.

Back at Millbrook Margaret and W.O. found themselves regular hosts to the nearby balloon squadron. Officers were entertained at dinner parties, and in the warmer months personnel were invited to use the tennis court in the garden. When she wasn't catering for the officers, Margaret spent much of her time serving with the WVS.

Towards the end of the war W.O. began to give some thought to the sort of car that would be required when manufacturing resumed. Obviously there was a need for relatively inexpensive mass-produced machines, and he accepted that these were not in Lagonda's league as far as manufacturing facilities were concerned. He shared Alan Good's enthusiasm for continuing with the V12, but unlike Good he questioned whether a market would exist for such a vehicle. Good thought that there would be, but W.O. wasn't entirely convinced, and anyway the tooling equipment had been lost in the transition to building for the war effort.

The type of car most likely to succeed post-war was, in W.O.'s, opinion, one of 2½ litres, aimed at the quality rather than the luxury market. In devising the new model he studied the most significant developments in the motor industry and proposed incorporating some of the most appropriate of them into his new car. There were several designs of car that interested him but the one that was most significant was the front-wheel drive Citroën Traction Avant, a 12hp example of which he had driven many thousands of miles before the war. Assembled by Citroën at its nearby Slough factory, the Traction Avant had made its controversial debut in 1934 when it was hailed as the most modern and revolutionary car of its time. With its monocoque chassis, front-wheel drive, torsion bar suspension, wet-liner engine, hydraulic brakes and rack and pinion steering it presented a radical progression of ideas, especially since these features were packaged together for the first time for mass-production.

His experience with the Citroën showed the car to have exemplary road holding and driving characteristics. It had a phenomenal amount of room within the passenger cabin and the 'mustard-spoon' gear selector protruding through the dashboard proved to be delightful in operation despite its odd appearance. W.O. was not so happy about the gearbox: it was positioned ahead of the engine, which meant that actuation was controlled by a series of long levers, and it would be rather vulnerable in the event of an accident. Few other cars of similar power and dimensions possessed the Citroën's capacity for covering long-distances at high average speeds and in such comfort, and after W.O.'s use of it was at an end he passed it on to Stan Ivermee, who continued driving it over many more thousands of miles.

W.O. considered that front-wheel drive was ideal for a small economy car. He must have known what Citroën were doing in France with their Deux Chevaux project!. The recipe, he thought, would be all the better and more realistic using aero engine practice, so he devised, on paper at least, an idea for a five-cylinder radial engine driving the front wheels. His ideas were for an air-cooled ultra-lightweight unit with an aluminium head and a shrouded fan directing cooling air onto the cylinders. He envisaged using inclined valves that were pushrod operated, the cam gear reflecting his Bentley BR1/BR2 practice. By using hemispherical combustion chambers and aluminium pistons he could keep the weight factor as low as possible, the flywheel being the heaviest item. Such an engine could easily develop 15hp, and as long as it was adequately mounted to be as flexible as possible, it had great potential.

W.O. also considered an air-cooled flat-six horizontally opposed engine. His intention was to mate it with Citroën-type transmission

layout and torsion bar suspension. Nothing came of this idea, nor from
a proposal for a small car having a radial engine. Citroën, in fact, was
working along similar lines with a flat-six air-cooled engine when
devising a successor for its Traction Avant during the early post-war
years. When its replacement, the revolutionary DS, did make its debut,
it featured a conventional water-cooled in-line four-cylinder unit.

The car that did emerge from W.O.'s drawing board was to be the last
that he designed on a commercial basis. This was the 2,580cc six-
cylinder with an in-line engine incorporating twin overhead camshafts.
It gratified him, therefore, to know that it remained in production for
10 years, longer than any other attributed to him. The announcement of
the model was to have a profound effect on both W.O. and Lagonda, for
the Lagonda-Bentley, as it was to have been known, became the subject
of a most unpleasant legal dispute that ended in court action. Rolls-
Royce viewed the 2½-litre Lagonda-Bentley as an infringement of the
agreement negotiated with W.O. some 14 years earlier.

The suggestion of an infringement came as some surprise to W.O.,
who fully believed that he was only restricted from using the Bentley
name for a period of 10 years. Alan Good was adamant that W.O. had
a case for challenging Rolls-Royce and was about to enter a conflict
with Rolls-Royce's lawyers. Good was known for having an aggressive
temperament which W.O. thought would only complicate matters, and
he therefore proposed that he should first approach Ernest Hives (who
was elevated to the peerage in 1950), whom he had known and had
much respect for since his meeting with him at Derby during World War
One. As he had expected he found Hives, who was unaware of the 10-
year agreement, to be most accommodating.

Hives agreed with W.O. that according to the wording of the contract
W.O. was free to use the Bentley name since more than a decade had
elapsed since its establishment. Rolls-Royce's legal advisers took a
different position, however. In their view the argument centred around
the name being a trademark, which in a court of law might be difficult
to contest. The answer, it seemed, was for W.O. to surrender all further
claims to the Bentley name for a generous financial consideration. W.O.
had no reason not to accept Hives's offer and reported so to Alan Good
on his return to Staines.

Good was furious and insisted that Rolls-Royce no longer had any
claim to Bentley's name. He began legal action and issued an injunction

against them. W.O. was in a difficult position because he knew that in reality neither he nor Good had any genuine claim on Rolls-Royce, and he was forced to admit this in court. At the hearing in 1945 the judge predictably ruled in favour of Rolls-Royce, and Lagonda was left with damages of £10,000 to pay. In addition to the adverse publicity that Lagonda had suffered there was also the matter of disposing of the catalogues and advertising material that had been published, and the time and expense of devising replacements.

After the war the shortage of raw materials was so acute that the Ministry of Supply issued licences for consignments of steel to those manufacturers who could demonstrate an ability to produce the majority of their output for export sales in order to earn badly needed foreign currencies. A small company in comparison to Austin, Morris or Ford, Lagonda's steel quota was miserly, sufficient for no more than a hundred bodies. Alan Good had intended using Briggs of Dagenham to supply body panels, but obviously with such a small production run they declined to be involved. Furthermore there was no assurance that additional quotas would be forthcoming, which made Lagonda's future position bleak to say the least.

The few prototype Lagondas that had been built would have to suffice for the time being while Alan Good reviewed the company's position. Lying dormant was a superbly designed chassis with all-independent suspension, coil springs at the front and torsion bars at the rear. It also had rack and pinion steering, and provision for three engine sizes, of four, six and eight-cylinder configurations. What made the matter all the more frustrating was that Lagonda had advance orders for the car and could have sold it in substantial numbers.

There really was no alternative but to offer the company for sale, but even finding a suitable buyer proved to be difficult. When Good submitted his resignation in 1947 W.O. took his design to Jaguar, which was highly complimentary about it but lacked the commitment to proceed any further. Then there was Rootes, which considered the engine for their Humber models, and Lord Nuffield, who also showed interest.

Lagonda's plight and the fact that it was going into receivership became known to David Brown through Anthony Scatchard, a friend in Bradford who was a Lagonda agent. It was Scatchard who first suggested that buying Lagonda might be a useful proposition for the industrialist whose tractor business and Merritt-Brown caterpillar transmission systems had brought him fame and fortune before and after the war. Brown, who was knighted in 1968, was a Lagonda owner and enthusiast and it is believed he purchased one of the last models to leave the Staines factory before the war stopped production in 1939.

David Brown was known to the receiver, who let it be known that Armstrong-Siddeley, Jaguar and Rootes were all interested in buying Lagonda, which explains their negative discussions with W.O. The highest bid at the time was £250,000, but as soon as the Labour government's plans for nationalisation were unveiled, all three bids were withdrawn. It emerged that when Alan Good offered Lagonda for sale without the factory premises – these were acquired by Petter – a new offer for the Lagonda name, the assets of the firm and its goodwill was made to the value of £50,000 by an unknown bidder. When David Brown, who had just acquired Aston Martin nearby at Feltham, offered a further £2,500 to acquire Lagonda, the deal was settled following a meeting with W.O., who gave him a thorough demonstration of the car. Thus Aston Martin and Lagonda were merged in 1948.

The Lagonda names lives on. David Brown put the Lagonda into production at Feltham following extensive Continental testing by Percy Kemish. Whereas W.O. had preferred the French Cotal gearbox with its electromagnetic and clutchless operation while the car was in motion, British drivers were less impressed with the system, which persuaded Brown to install a conventional David Brown gearbox. Writing in *The Motor* in January 1950, Laurence Pomeroy, the magazine's technical editor, said of the car that in his opinion it was the most comfortable and stable in which he had ridden.

When the David Brown Organisation bought the Tickford coachbuilding firm in 1955 a version of the Lagonda was produced with a larger, wider body and a 3-litre engine. A year later production at Feltham was transferred to Newport Pagnell in Buckinghamshire. The last Lagondas which were to have Bentley input were made in 1958 and it was not until the motor show of 1961 that an all-new Lagonda was shown.

W.O. did not transfer to David Brown's Lagonda organisation. Instead he established himself as an independent consultant. Not for the first time he found himself without a car. New vehicles were extremely difficult to come by as production was mainly reserved for export, but he did manage to acquire a Standard Eight, which in comparison to the cars he was used to driving was very small and under powered.

Nevertheless, this 1946 example, similar to the pre-war design, proved to be invaluable and stood up well to the W.O. treatment of fully laden long hauls through France to the Mediterranean.

Among a number of commissions that came his way was one for a design for a forthcoming Armstrong-Siddeley. Based around a twin-camshaft six-cylinder 3-litre engine, the profile of the car emerged as being similar to the 2½-litre Lagonda. While W.O. was keen on the idea, which incorporated independent all-round suspension, it was nevertheless somewhat advanced for its time and ultimately Armstrong-Siddeley, which was also initially set on it, decided on a more conventional design, which became the Sapphire. The Sapphire is another of those superbly engineered cars that has helped perpetuate the Bentley name and design.

More radical by far was a flat-four aluminium engine which W.O. was commissioned to design for an American client. The purpose of the lightweight engine had been to propel an aircraft, but W.O. derived much pleasure from having it fitted to a Morris Minor for testing purposes. It proved to be highly successful although he could not persuade Morris to develop something similar for their production car. The Minor, incidentally, was a hit with W.O., who admired the design so much that he ran a whole succession of them throughout his retirement.

When it had become evident that there was no alternative but for Lagonda to go into receivership Margaret and W.O. decided to sell Millbrook and move further into the countryside. The recent litigation had badly affected W.O.'s morale, and not for the first time in his life he experienced unhappiness. Margaret, however, offered him every support and was able to lift him out of his depression. The growth of Heathrow into London's leading airport had begun: expansion meant that it would in time engulf the surrounding villages. In 1945 they chose a charming cottage at Shamley Green near Guildford, W.O. having decided it was time for him to generally retire, although he did continue his consultancy work.

W.O. had been aware that, since the mid-1930s, there had been growing enthusiasm for what had become known as the 'W.O.' or 'Cricklewood' Bentleys. Such passion seemed at first rather odd, for in his opinion the Bentley was merely a motor car which sooner or later would be superseded by some other make, and anyway cars like his had no more than a certain lifespan. After all total production amounted to 3,061 cars (W.O.'s figures).

Instead of waning, the clamour for W.O. Bentleys not only remained but increased. Whether he wanted it or not, it soon became apparent that the Bentley movement was keen to have him on their side. So on many occasions the Bentley home hosted marque enthusiasts, from both Great Britain and around the world.

Retirement also meant that W.O. could reacquaint himself with the railway industry. He soon discovered his love of steam had not diminished and he was welcomed back to Doncaster as a celebrity. He liked nothing better than to be invited to take occasional trips on the footplate of steam locomotives, and when, in the mid-1950s, diesel traction began replacing steam, he enjoyed riding in the cab of an English Electric 'Deltic' Locomotive, which was among the most powerful in service anywhere.

When he published his autobiography in 1958, W.O. was surprised to receive a considerable amount of mail from people whose lives, for some reason or another, had been influenced by his engineering designs. He received communications from Old Cliftonians and those who had been apprenticed to the Great Northern at Doncaster. One-time owners of DFPs got in touch, and then there were the engineers, pilots and ground crews that had been at the mercy of the Bentley modified Clerget aero engines, and, of course, the Bentley rotaries.

When their Shamley Green cottage became too much for them to look after, W.O. and Margaret moved to Little Garden Cottage, a bungalow they had built to W.O.'s design on adjacent land. Their homes at Millbrook and Shamley Green gave W.O. immense and lasting pleasure, and he had time to spend indulging some of the passions of his youth, such as gardening and music.

The interest shown in him and his cars was a source of much contentment for him. The sound of the burbling exhaust of many a vintage Bentley became a familiar aspect of life at Little Garden Cottage. W.O. and Margaret were often hosts to gatherings of Bentley enthusiasts and he liked nothing better than to appreciate the camaraderie that surrounded 'his cars'.

Little, however, could surpass the nostalgia and emotion he experienced when he returned to Cricklewood with Margaret on 12 June 1969, as principal guest to commemorate the Golden Jubilee of Bentley Motors' establishment in January 1919. The event had been instigated by Smiths Industries, custodians of the Oxgate Lane works, and the Bentley Drivers' Club, and it attracted Bentley devotees to Cricklewood from around the world. Never before had so many 'W.O.' Bentleys been seen at the factory. W.O. was taken to his old office, where he greeted marque enthusiasts who were invited to add their signature to an official Golden Jubilee book.

Following a tour of the old factory site, a buffet luncheon and speeches, W.O. unveiled a Jubilee Plaque. Never one to indulge in public speaking, he was more comfortable examining the cars present, some of which had travelled considerable distances. There was obvious delight on his face at seeing so many of his creations.

Years of pleasurable retirement were inevitably combined with sadness. Hardy died at Castle Keep, his country home at Kingsgate in Kent, on 7 June 1958, and H.M., to whom he had always been very close, died on 31 May 1967 at Rose Acre, a retirement nursing home at Compton near Guildford.

W.O. died in a nursing home at Woking in Surrey in the evening of 13 August 1971, at the age of 82. Margaret survived him by 18 years, in which time she perpetuated W.O.'s memory by attending Bentley enthusiasts' meetings. She died in 1989 at the age of nearly 98. A memorial service was held at Guildford Cathedral on 13 September, exactly one month after W.O.'s death and three days before his 83rd birthday. It was a celebration of a life, a good life, and to use W.O.'s words, 'A life worthwhile'.

CHAPTER 11

The Return of the Bentley Marque

FOLLOWING the acquisition of Bentley Motors by Rolls-Royce, W.O. had kept a keen interest in those cars bearing his name. The 3½-litre proved to be highly successful, as did its successor the 4½-litre, which was announced in 1936. The larger engine was introduced firstly as an option but was made standard almost immediately in the interests of improved performance and because of the preference by customers for heavier coachwork.

Shortly before the onset of World War Two, Rolls-Royce, under the banner of Bentley Motors (1931) Ltd, sought to develop an all-new high-performance Continental Tourer in much the same style as the 6½ and 8-litre 'W.O.' models and the Rolls-Royce Continental Phantoms. Two prototypes were built, one having an aerodynamic four-door saloon body by Vanvooren of Paris, the other being a two-door fastback featuring svelte streamlined coachwork by Pourtout, also of Paris.

The first car was badly damaged while undergoing testing in France; the chassis was returned to Derby for repair while the coachwork remained in France to be refurbished there. Sadly body and chassis were never reunited; when the repaired body was despatched to England it was detained at Dieppe and was damaged in enemy action.

The other prototype was built to the design of Georges Paulin for André Embiricos, the Greek racing driver. Paulin was a noted stylist and he had been responsible for the Peugeots that were entered for the 1937 Le Mans race. When it was subjected to intense testing the Embiricos

Bentley performed superbly, and in trials conducted at Brooklands with George Eyston at the wheel in 1939 it achieved 114 miles in the hour.

After the war the Continental theme was resumed with a design being approved for an exclusive high-performance tourer. This was a brave move at a time of austerity for when it was introduced it was both the fastest and most expensive production car in the British catalogue. Now known as the R-type Continental, the car was devised by H. Ivan Evernden with John Blatchley's assistance and has become a design icon. The car's impressive performance with its lightweight and aerodynamic coachwork heralded a series of Continental Bentleys that offered the ultimate in style and comfort.

Production of Bentley and Rolls-Royce cars was transferred to Crewe to what was previously a shadow factory. Merlin and Griffin aero engines had been constructed there, and the decline of orders following the armistice meant that it was more practical to use the premises for car production while Derby concentrated on aero technology. When motor manufacturing resumed it was the Bentley marque that spearheaded production of luxury vehicles. A policy of rationalisation instigated pre-war by Roy Robotham and Ernest Hives had been adopted which meant that Bentley and Rolls-Royce cars used mainly identical components, even down to the bodies that were supplied by Pressed Steel at Cowley. The bulk of cars that were delivered featured Standard Steel coachwork, although bespoke coachwork by preferred coachbuilders remained available for customer specification. Bentley badges and radiators were deemed to be less ostentatious than those of Rolls-Royce in the age of austerity, and therefore were accepted rather more readily.

The first model to be delivered from Crewe was the Bentley Mk VI, which had a 4¼-litre overhead inlet valve and side exhaust valve engine. Beautifully styled and engineered, these cars featured every luxury. They remained in production until June 1952 when the R-type, a restyled version of the Mk VI, was announced.

On Ivan Evernden's retirement John Blatchley was appointed chief stylist at Crewe. A brilliant designer who was appointed head of coachbuilder Gurney Nutting's design department at the age of 24, he was responsible for the modified styling of the R-type models. The first all-new vehicle to benefit from his design expertise was the S-Series Bentley, which was introduced in 1955. Four years later the S2 appeared with a V8 engine replacing the six-cylinder unit. The same engine was used to propel the S3 in 1963 with its revised styling, the last of the 'traditional' Bentleys.

When John Blatchley unveiled his T-Series Bentley in 1965 he showed it to be a radical car. In demonstrating modern technology the model supported a design that incorporated unitary construction with front and rear sub-frames, and a unique system of hydraulic self-levelling that had been developed by Citroën. For Bentley and Rolls-Royce (the Silver Shadow was introduced at the same time) this was a massive step forward, and the car was enthusiastically acclaimed by customers and the media alike.

Unitary construction by building chassis and body as a single unit resulted in the new Bentley being of relatively compact dimensions, while affording passengers all the space and comfort they had come to expect from the marque. Although the method of suspension was traditional enough with coil springs, hydraulic self-levelling afforded a delightfully smooth and compliant ride.

In addition to the four-door saloon Blatchley designed the Two-Door coupé and convertible models, which following Rolls-Royce's collapse in 1971 were renamed Corniche and Continental. Unlike the saloon, which had bodies supplied by Pressed Steel, the variants mostly had Mulliner Park Ward coachwork.

A sad state of affairs led to a decline in Bentley orders during the 1970s. There was virtually no difference between the Rolls-Royce and Bentley models save for the badging and radiator grilles, and even the price was the same to within a few pounds. Most customers selected the Rolls-Royce model, choosing the prestige of the RR monogram adorning the famous radiator shape along with the Spirit of Ecstasy, leaving Bentleys to be specified by an apparently dwindling band of marque devotees.

The Bentley T was superseded in 1980 by the Bentley Mulsanne, which was styled by Fritz Feller, John Blatchley's successor. The Rolls-Royce equivalent was the Silver Spirit, which outsold the Bentley by a huge margin. There was even a risk that the Bentley name would fall into obscurity. Thankfully company directors at Crewe had the Bentley marque at heart, for when a high performance version of the Mulsanne was announced in 1982 there began a Bentley revival. The Mulsanne Turbo demonstrated terrific power when it was taken to Le Mans for its debut, surging in speed from a standing start to 100mph in under 18 seconds. W.O. would have been impressed by the Bentley Turbo's top speed of 140mph.

By 1998, when a new generation of Rolls-Royce and Bentley motor cars was proclaimed, the tables had turned for Bentley. Substantially more Bentleys were being sold than Rolls-Royce cars. When the Arnage, which was styled by Graham Hull, was announced, it too made its debut at Le Mans. The new model caused fierce debate, partly because the engine was designed and built by BMW, but also because there were rumours that Rolls-Royce and Bentley Motor Cars Ltd were to be sold.

Customers that bought the Arnage remained unhappy with the car's engine, which was of different design to that fitted to the Rolls-Royce Silver Seraph. In comparison with the Silver Seraph's 5,379cc V12 engine many considered the 4.4-litre unit to be underpowered and lacking the performance of the venerable but superb V8 that had first been seen in 1959. To address the many criticisms the Arnage Red Label was introduced, featuring the hugely respected 6.75-litre V8.

The sale of Rolls-Royce and Bentley Motor Cars Ltd caused something of a furore. There were several bids to buy the company but ultimately it was a tussle between BMW and Volkswagen. Volkswagen bought the company along with the Bentley name and the Crewe factory. BMW, however, bought the rights to use the Rolls-Royce name and established a separate factory at Goodwood in Sussex. Since Volkswagen purchased Bentley it has invested heavily in the company. There has been a return to racing at Le Mans, and in 2002 a new Continental GT model was announced. A new mid-size car is due sometime in 2003 or 2004.

Wouldn't W.O. be amused to know that Bentley is back!

Bibliography

Bentley, W.O. *W.O. The Autobiography*. Hutchinson, 1958.

Bentley, W.O. *The Cars In My Life*. Hutchinson, 1961

Hillstead, A.F.C. *Those Bentley Days*. Faber &Faber, 1952

Hillstead, A.F.C. *Fifty Years With Motor Cars*. Faber & Faber, 1960

Dudley Benjafield, J. *The Bentleys At Le Mans*. Motor Racing Publications, 1948

Berthon, Darrell *A Racing History Of The Bentley*. The Bodley Head, 1956

Birkin, Sir Henry *Full Throttle*. Foulis 1932

Davis, S.C.H. *Motor Racing*. Iliffe & Sons, 1932

Davis, S.C.H. *Memories Of Men And Motor Cars*. Seeley, Service & Co Ltd., 1965

Nagle, Elizabeth *The Other Bentley Boys*. Harrap, 1964

Frostick, Michael *From Cricklewood To Crewe*. Osprey, 1980

Ellman-Brown, Michael *Bentley – The Silent Sportscar, 1931-1941*. Dalton Watson, 1989

Bastow, Donald *W.O.Bentley – Engineer*. Haynes, 1978

Hay, Michael *Bentley Factory Cars 1919-1931*. Osprey, 1993

Green, Johnnie *Bentley – Fifty Years Of The Marque*. Dalton Watson, 1969

Fletcher, Rivers *Bentley Past & Present*. Gentry Books, 1982

Houlding, Timothy *The Legends And The Thunder – Number 1*. Timothy Houlding, 1982

Davis, Vaughan *The Aero Engines Of W.O.Bentley M.B.E.*

Boddy, W. *The History Of Brooklands Motor Course 1906-1940*. Grenville Publishing Company Limited, 1957/1979

Wilson, C.H. & W.J. Reader *Men & Machines*. Weidenfeld and Nicholson, 1958

Venables, David *Napier – The first to wear the green*. Haynes, 1998

Gunston, Bill OBE *Fedden – The Life Of Sir Henry Fedden*. R-RHT, 1998

Jackson, Stanley *The Great Barnato*. Heinemann, 1970

Barnato Walker, Diana *Spreading My Wings*. Patrick Stephens Ltd., 1994

Stanford, John *The Sports Car*. Batsford, 1957

Setright, L.J.K. *The Designers*. Weidenfeld and Nicholson, 1976

Hough, Richard & L.J.K. Setright *A History Of The World's Motorcycles*. George Allen&Unwin, 1966

Ixion (Basil H. Davies) *Motor Cycle Reminiscences*. Illife & Sons, 1920

Bramson, Alan *Pure Luck*. Patrick Stephens Ltd., 1990

Amherst Villiers Superchargers Amherst Villiers Publicity Document

Kelly, Robert *T.T.Pioneers*. The Manx Experience, 1966

Hull, Peter & Norman Johnson *Alvis – The Vintage Years*. Alvis Register, 1996

Davey, Arnold *A Century of Lagonda*. The Lagonda Club

Newspapers and periodicals:
The Daily Telegraph
The Times
The Autocar
The Motor
Motor Sport
The Motor owner
Speed
The Automobile
Motor Cycling
Motorcycle

Index

ACU Quarterly Trials 49
Adlington 155-6
Aerolite Piston Company 102-3, 114
Air Ministry 113, 134
Airco 129
Aircraft Inspection Department 100
Alcock, Captain John 91
Alfa Romeo 206, 224
Aluminium Piston Company 102-3
Alvis 186, 224, 226, 228
Aquila Italiana 81
Ards Circuit 192, 196, 200
Argyll 106
Ariel 33, 37
Ariès 190
Armitage 94
Armstrong-Siddeley 240-1
Arrol-Johnston 72, 76, 106
Aslin, Petty Officer 94-5, 97
Asquith, Herbert 70
Aston Clinton 70, 73-4, 78, 85
Aston Martin 145, 155, 240
Atlee, Lord 114-15, 127, 177
Austin 239
Autocar 7, 52, 73, 79, 117, 133-4, 136, 138, 168, 186, 201, 217, 225, 232
Automobile Club de France 146
Baddeley 42
Balcon, Le 176, 223
BARC 50, 82
Barclay, Jack 196-7, 206-7, 222
Barnato, Captain Woolf 9, 145, 164, 169, 174-5, 177-81, 183, 185, 187, 189, 191, 193-7, 205, 213, 215, 219
Barrington, Thomas Barwell 207-8, 210, 214

Barry, Colonel Wolfe 115
Bastow, Donald 100, 174, 219
Bell-Quadrant 43
Bellinger, L.W. 43
Benjafield Dr J. Dudley 166-7, 169, 171-3, 184-6, 188-93, 195, 200-1, 204
Bennett, C.E. 50
Bensport 224
Bentley, Alfred 12, 14, 61, 109, 122
Bentley, Alfred Hardy 12, 64-5, 114, 123, 127, 226, 243
Bentley, Arthur 76-8
Bentley Arnage 204, 247
Bentley, Audrey 218
Bentley, Emily Maud 10, 12, 122
Bentley, Horace Milner (H.M.) 12-13, 16, 21-3, 37, 39-43, 58-68, 72-8, 80-1, 84-6, 89, 103-4, 106-8, 114-17, 123, 129-34, 175, 177, 180-3, 226, 243-7
Bentley, Leonard Holt 12-13, 59, 89
Bentley, Margaret 218-19, 226-7, 231, 233-4, 236, 241-3
Bentley, Peter 10
Bentley, William Waterhouse 12
Bentley Boys 86, 150-1, 153, 155, 157, 159, 161, 163, 165, 167, 169, 171, 173-5, 177, 179, 181, 183-5, 187, 189, 191, 193, 195, 197, 223
Bentley Mk VI 245
Bentley Mulsanne 246
Bentley Rotary 98-9, 101, 112, 133, 237
Bentley Turbo 246
Bessant, Jack 151, 156
Bianchi, Cecil 86

Bidlake, F.T. 41

Birkin, Tim 184-185, 191-6, 200-5, 234

Birtles 114

Blatchley, John 245-6

Bluebird 201, 216

BMW 247

Boddy, William 79, 169

Boileau, E.M.P. 52

Bonham-Carter, S.S. 20

Boston, Charles 128-9

Bourne, Dale 207

Bowen, H.H. 50

Brackenbury, Charlie 233

Brazil, John P. 24

Breeden, Carl 128

Briggs, Commander Wilfred 90, 93-4, 96, 99, 104, 111-12

Briggs Motor Bodies 239

Brisson 191

British Aluminium 103

British Motor Corporation 178

British Racing Drivers' Club (BRDC) 194

BRM 145

Brooklands 9, 46, 48-50, 75-6, 78-85, 95, 117-18, 134, 137, 142, 145-7, 150, 155-6, 166, 178, 184, 191, 193, 196-7, 201, 203, 207, 226, 228-30, 232-3, 245

Brooklands Automobile Racing Club 82

Brooklands Motor Cycle Racing Club 50

Brown, David 239-40

Brown, Lieutenant Arthur Whitten 91

Browne, Eugenia Marion Caulfeild 70

Browne, Eyles Irwin Caulfeild 70

Brownell, Frank 20

Browning, Bert 150-2, 166

Bruce, Mrs Victor 193-4

Brune, F. Prideaux 129

BSA 37

Buchanan 91

Buchet 59-60, 65

Bugatti 106, 144, 152, 201

Burbank, Mary 10

Burgess, Frederick Tasker 86-7, 97, 105-6, 110-11, 117-19, 135, 142, 147, 160, 207, 221

Cadillac 91-2, 228

Callingham, Leslie 184-6, 188-9, 196

Campbell, Malcolm 145-6, 151, 201, 216

Caracciola 204

Carruth, Jack 181-3, 209, 211-12, 219

Chapuis-Dornier 63

Chassagne, Jean 153, 167, 190-2, 194, 204

Chenard-Walckers 72, 81, 106, 157-8, 163

Citroën 237-8, 246

Clarke, Nobby 96, 118-120, 122, 139-140, 151, 171, 195, 221

Clement, Frank C. 24, 59, 86-7, 133, 142-6, 151-4, 156-61, 163, 166-72, 175, 184-6, 188, 190-7, 203-5, 210

Clerget 93-94, 96, 98-100, 242

Clément-Bayard 59

Clifton College 13, 17, 21

Coatalen, Louis 86, 92-3

Cobb, John 155

Colborn 54

Conway, Fred 144, 222

Cook, Humphrey 146, 191, 193, 201

Cooper, Ernest Herbert 124

Coquille, Emile 156

Corbett, Frank 130

Corbin 80-1, 84, 102